For Rose McTernan
who has helped

Bernard Shaw and Alfred Douglas

BERNARD SHAW
and
ALFRED DOUGLAS

A CORRESPONDENCE

Edited by Mary Hyde

John Murray

First Published in Great Britain 1982
by John Murray (Publishers) Ltd
50 Albemarle Street, London W1X 4BD

Printed in the USA

0 7195 3947 1

CONTENTS

Illustrations   ix

Introduction   xi

The Letters   I

Postscript and Acknowledgments   197

Appendices

    I   Earlier Letters   207

   II   *De Profundis*   211

 III   Letter to Frank Harris   215

 IV   Raymond Douglas   217

Index   221

ILLUSTRATIONS

Wilde and Douglas, Oxford, 1893   xii

Shaw in his mid-fifties. From the collection of
Dan H. Laurence   xxxviii

Douglas at the time of the Café Royal meeting   5

Shaw at 4 Whitehall Court. From the collection of
the Bettmann Archive   9

Harris's biography of Wilde (1918 edition) with
Douglas's marginal notes and Shaw's editorial
corrections   26

Pencil drawing by Walter Spindler of Douglas, used as
the frontispiece in his *Poems*, 1896. From the original
drawing in the collection of Edward Colman   29

Shaw at Ayot St Lawrence. Photograph by Charles
Bolles Rogers. From the collection of Charles Berst   31

Olive Eleanor Custance Douglas. From the collection
of Edward Colman   47

Childe Alfred to St Christopher, 15 July 1938   66

St Christopher to Childe Alfred, 19 July 1938   71

Douglas at eight, a pastel by Henry Graves. From the
collection of Edward Colman   85

Douglas at sixty-two. Photograph by E. Pannell   88

The bust of Shaw by Lady Kennet. From the
Russell-Cotes Art Gallery and Museum, Bournemouth   100

Shaw at work in his garden shelter. From the
collection of Dan H. Laurence   104

The five framed photographs of Shaw. From the
collection of Edward Colman   112

Douglas at 1 St Ann's Court, Hove. From the
collection of Edward Colman   141

Frank Harris. From the collection of the Bettmann
Archive   150

Shaw and his chauffeur sawing logs, Shaw splitting
logs with an axe. Photographs by Publishers' Photo
Service. From the collection of Dan H. Laurence   172

"Mrs Bernard Shaw, 1857–1943". This photograph,
taken by Shaw in the mid-thirties, he made into a
postcard and sent to friends after Charlotte's death.
From the collection of Edward Colman   178

Douglas's last picture: at Old Monk's Farm with
Sheila, Easter-time, 1944. Taken by Edward Colman.
From the Colman collection   198

Raymond Douglas in the 1920s. From the Douglas
collection at the University of South Florida in Tampa   219

INTRODUCTION

On a Monday in March 1895 Frank Harris had Bernard Shaw for lunch at the Café Royal in London. Shaw had recently been appointed drama critic of the *Saturday Review*, of which Harris was editor. Around three o'clock Oscar Wilde came to meet Harris, by arrangement. Shaw greeted him cordially; he was on good terms with Wilde, two years his senior, and he had a high regard for all his plays, except *The Importance of Being Earnest*, which he disliked intensely. This play and Wilde's *An Ideal Husband* were currently running in London.

Wilde was preoccupied and nervous and Shaw, sensing that Harris had some serious personal matter to discuss with him, rose from the table. Wilde pressed him to stay, and began at once to plead with Harris to give evidence in the imminent trial, his libel suit against the Marquess of Queensberry. Specifically, he asked Harris to testify that *The Picture of Dorian Gray* was not an immoral book. At this moment Queensberry's son, Lord Alfred Douglas, came in, not asked by Harris though half expected. Douglas was a slim young man with blue eyes and golden hair, aristocratic bearing, and striking good looks. Every motion was impatient. He was never still for a moment.

Harris was talking about Queensberry (the putative originator of the rules of boxing). The Marquess had left a card some days before at the Albemarle, one of Wilde's clubs, with a message accusing Wilde of posing as a 'somdomite', the word mis-spelled in anger. Now, he was proclaiming to everyone that his third son, Alfred, or Bosie, as he was called, had become the thrall of an Irish so-called wit and playwright and ageing aesthete (Wilde was forty, Douglas twenty-four). Bosie, his father said, had better forget his pretensions to poetry and soft luxuries and prepare himself for the Bar or some other respectable profession. He had come down from Oxford without a degree and was frittering away his life.

Wilde and Douglas, Oxford, 1893

Bosie had no intention of listening to this advice. His father, he said, was an inhuman brute, an atheist and lecher, who had harassed his wife for years and by turns neglected and ill-treated his four sons and daughter. His father was despicable and mad. His stated desire to save his son was hypocrisy; the real object was to persecute his divorced wife and to destroy his son. The entire Queensberry family sided with Bosie against the Marquess.

Wilde had found Queensberry's card some ten days after its delivery at the Albemarle Club. That night he had discussed the grave accusation at length with Robert Ross, a young art critic as devoted to him as Douglas was, the son of an Attorney General and grandson of the first Prime Minister of Upper Canada. Next morning Ross had taken Wilde to the office of C. O. Humphreys, the solicitor, and there the determination was made to prosecute Queensberry for libel. Douglas was told after the event, but he whole-heartedly agreed with the decision; he had been telling Wilde for two years that the only way to stop his father's attacks was to prosecute him. Sir Edward Clarke, an eminent leader at the Bar and Solicitor General under the recent Government, accepted Wilde's brief as counsel. The trial was scheduled for 3 April at the Old Bailey.

Now, at the Café Royal, Harris begged Wilde not to take action. If he did, Harris said, he would lose his case, for Queensberry was known to have positive evidence against him, incidents of indecent familiarity with a number of dubious characters. Harris urged Wilde to take his wife and two small sons and go to France, beyond the reach of the law. He told him to write a letter to *The Times* saying that he had been insulted by Queensberry and had sought a legal remedy but had come to realize that no jury would give a verdict against a father, however mistaken he might be. Wilde was a maker of beautiful things, Harris said, and Queensberry's only joy was in fighting. Wilde must refuse to fight.

As Shaw reported years later (2 February 1949) to another Marquess of Queensberry, Douglas's nephew Francis:

I took hardly any part in the conversation. Wilde came to ask Harris to testify at the trial that *Dorian Gray* was a masterpiece of literature and morality. Harris most earnestly urged him to put all that out of his head: that he had no notion of the terrible evidence of the hotel servants that would be brought against him, and that Clarke would throw up his brief: in short, exactly what happened. Oscar, he said, must leave the country instantly. Alfred then said that this showed what Oscar's friends were worth, and got up and marched Oscar out. He clearly dominated Oscar and was determined that the case should proceed, believing that Clarke could and would put him in the box, where he could expose his father and win the case. Wilde had no such confidence, but could not bring himself to run away.

No one present forgot the scene in the Café Royal. Douglas wrote to Harris long after the meeting:

> All I know is that if I had gone into the box I would have won the case for Wilde. . . . At the very worst, even if he had lost the case, there would have been no subsequent criminal prosecution of Wilde. All the sympathy and all the feeling would have been on our side instead of on Queensberry's. This is what I knew and what I was thinking when I met you and Shaw at the Café Royal. I had screwed Oscar up to the 'sticking place'. . . . When, therefore, you and Shaw gave your advice, based on a one-sided knowledge of the facts, I resented it, and I was terribly afraid that Oscar would weaken and throw up the sponge. . . . I did not dare tell you our case for fear that I might not convince you and that you and Shaw might, even after hearing it, argue Wilde out of the state of mind I had got him into. My one object was to get him out of the café as soon as possible. Hence my rudeness.[1]

2

The history of Wilde's first trial, and of the two trials resulting from it, is well known, but because they are continually discussed in the letters a brief outline of events is warranted.

The first trial, Wilde's prosecution for criminal libel against the Marquess of Queensberry, began on 3 April 1895 before Mr Justice Collins, at the Old Bailey; Wilde was represented by Sir Edward Clarke, Queens-

---

1 *The Autobiography of Lord Alfred Douglas* (2d ed), London, Martin Secker, 1931, p. 97.

berry by Edward Carson, an Ulsterman who had been with Wilde at Trinity College, Dublin, and now appeared in his first important case in an English court.

Queensberry's defence was justification; thus, in court he had to prove the truth of his accusation, that Wilde had 'posed' as a sodomite (the word *posing* he had used on legal advice). Queensberry's case was based on three types of evidence: Wilde's allegedly prurient writings, in particular 'Phrases and Philosophies for the Use of the Young' and *Dorian Gray*; two compromising letters from Wilde to Douglas, secured from a blackmailer; and Wilde's outright acts of indecency. In cross-examination on the first two subjects Wilde held his own, but the third was devastating.

Queensberry's agents had been able to collect testimony over the previous six months from hotel servants and male prostitutes concerning intimacies at the Savoy and elsewhere. Wilde's partners had been willing youths, grooms, valets, unemployed drifters, most of them provided by Alfred Taylor, a man in his thirties, of reputable background and education. Taylor, having gone through an inheritance, now supported himself by running a club for homosexuals in Fitzroy Street, Bloomsbury. The activities carried on in Taylor's perfumed rooms were well known to the police.

Revelations of Wilde's secret life came as a shattering surprise to Clarke, for Wilde had told him under oath that there was no truth in the libel, and on this assurance Clarke had taken the case.

After Wilde's cross-examination by Carson and re-examination by Clarke, Douglas expected to be put in the box, but Clarke did not call him. Instead, he surprised the court by announcing that the case for the prosecution was closed, just as Harris and Shaw had predicted. Clarke's reasoning was clear. He allowed Queensberry's libellous accusation of 'posing' as a sodomite to stand, because he feared that pursuit of the case to the end might result in Wilde's being arrested in open court.

The jury never left the box. After conferring for a few minutes, the foreman returned a verdict for Queensberry of not guilty. There was prolonged cheering from the onlookers, and Mr Justice Collins ordered Wilde to pay the Marquess's costs, a debt that in time was to bring deep humiliation.

More than thirty years later, in his correspondence with Shaw, Douglas was still ruminating over this trial and the two that followed it. Though he had written to Clarke on 26 May 1895, thanking him for his 'noble and generous and superb efforts', he changed his opinion afterwards and insisted that Clarke had lost the case because he had broken his promise to put him in the witness-box.

3

The first trial was over by noon of 5 April, and Wilde left the Old Bailey with Douglas and Ross, who had both been in the court-room throughout the trial. They begged Wilde to leave for France at once; Reginald Turner and other friends urged him likewise throughout the early afternoon, all realizing that the Director of Public Prosecutions was by then applying for a warrant to arrest Wilde. With some kindness, the Chief Magistrate delayed issuing this until after the last boat train left for France at five o'clock, but an hour and a half later officers came to the Cadogan Hotel, and Wilde was still there.

They took him to Bow Street Police Station, where he spent the night, and next morning he was charged with offences under Section XI of the Criminal Law Amendment Act of 1885, which made homosexual acts between males a criminal offence, even if committed in private. Bail was refused and Wilde was taken to Holloway Prison to await trial. As soon as Sir Edward Clarke heard of the arrest he wrote to Humphreys, offering to be defence counsel again (without fee) if Wilde so desired, which offer was gratefully accepted. The trial was set for 26 April.

Wilde's friends, with the exception of the homosexuals, who knew him for one of their own, were surprised and shocked by the exposé. Most of them stayed away, and many of the coterie of discreet homosexuals thought it wise to go abroad for the time being. Ross went to Rouen at the urging of his mother in exchange for her promise to contribute to the expenses of Wilde's defence. Douglas remained in London, visiting Holloway Prison almost daily, and Wilde responded to his loyalty with letters of romantic devotion. On the eve of the trial, Clarke insisted that Douglas leave England because his presence was prejudicial to the chances for acquittal. Wilde could only agree. Douglas, still hoping to testify, refused at first to go. In the end, however, Clarke's judgement prevailed. Douglas went to Calais and telegraphed Ross to join him there, which Ross did.

Two days before this trial began, there was a forced auction of Wilde's possessions in his Chelsea house, 16 Tite Street. His wife and sons were now homeless and she sought the protection of her relations. Wilde's plays were taken off the stage. All income ceased.

The trial of the Crown against Wilde and Taylor took place at the Old Bailey, from 26 April to 1 May 1895, before Mr Justice Charles. Charles Gill and Horace Avory were counsel for the Crown; Clarke again represented Wilde, and J. P. Grain represented Taylor. It was unfortunate for Wilde that he could not be tried separately from Taylor, whose character added to the prejudice against him.

Wilde was questioned on matters dealt with in the Queensberry trial, and youthful accomplices and blackmailers gave evidence of their association with him. Landladies and a tenant in a house where one of the boys lodged also gave evidence. At the end of the case Mr Justice Charles summed up the charges, and the jury withdrew to consider the verdict. Three hours later the foreman returned to say that the members of the jury could not reach a verdict. The case must be tried again.

4

With some difficulty Clarke managed to arrange for bail. The amount was fixed at five thousand pounds, half to be furnished by Wilde and half by two other sureties: Douglas's brother Percy, Lord Douglas of Hawick; and Stewart Headlam, a compassionate clergyman. For most of the period of his bail and throughout the third trial, Wilde stayed at the house of his friends Ernest and Ada Leverson, who treated him with great kindness. Wilde kept in touch with Douglas by letter.

The third trial took place again at the Old Bailey, 20–25 May, this time before Mr Justice Wills. Wilde continued to be represented by Sir Edward Clarke, without fee. The Crown was now represented by Sir Frank Lockwood, the Solicitor General, a choice which made it clear that the Government was determined to secure a conviction.

On one point Clarke was successful; he was able to obtain the judge's consent to try Wilde separately from Taylor; but Clarke failed in his second petition, to have Wilde's case heard first. Having to follow was damaging, because the testimony against Taylor was sordid and the jury had already found him guilty.

When Wilde's turn came, the familiar testimony was repeated by the youths and hotel witnesses. Wilde's two compromising letters to Douglas were again read aloud. The foreman of the jury asked Mr Justice Wills if a warrant had ever been issued for Lord Alfred Douglas, for if the letters were evidence of guilt, any guilt would apply as much to Lord Alfred as to the defendant. Mr Justice Wills answered testily that no such warrant had ever been contemplated. In his charge to the jury he made the further point that he was anxious to say nothing that might seriously damage the career of a young man on the threshold of life.

The jury rose to deliberate and returned in about three hours with a verdict of guilty. Taylor was brought back to the dock and both men were sentenced together. 'It is the worst case I have ever tried', said Mr Justice Wills, and in passing the severest sentence possible for the crime, two years' imprisonment with hard labour, he said, 'In my judgement it is totally inadequate for such a case as this'.[1]

5

Wilde served the first few weeks of his sentence at Pentonville Prison; then, on 4 July 1895, he was transferred to Wandsworth, on the south side of the Thames.

It was not long before articles appeared which treated his case in a sympathetic light. In June, W. T. Stead, editor of the *Review of Reviews*, published an account explaining Wilde's behaviour on psychological and medical grounds. Stead at once received a letter from Douglas, now in Paris, a passionate defence of homosexual conduct, which Stead did not see fit to print. Douglas wrote a similar letter to Henry Labouchere, editor of *Truth*, which likewise was not published, though it was later produced as damaging evidence in Douglas's libel suit against Arthur Ransome in 1913.

Douglas carried his writing campaign to great lengths, even addressing a petition to Queen Victoria, begging the Sovereign to exercise

[1] *The Trials of Oscar Wilde*, H. Montgomery Hyde, London, William Hodge, 1952, p. 339.

royal clemency. In France he appealed to leading writers, but although many expressed sympathy, they felt Douglas's defence was immature and sensational. They did not wish to be involved.

In opposition to his son's pleas for mercy, the Marquess of Queensberry took his final revenge in June. He petitioned, as a creditor, for the legal costs awarded in Wilde's libel suit, and this petition precipitated bankruptcy proceedings. An examination of Wilde's accounts showed that his liabilities, with Queensberry's costs of about seven hundred pounds and other debts, were over thirty-five hundred pounds. Ross, who had returned to England in July, and other friends were able to raise almost half the amount but could not muster the required figure. Members of the Queensberry family who at the time of the trial had promised to pay the expenses of the prosecution had not done so and made no offer now to help.

Shaw, though he did not contribute to the fund for Wilde, made an attempt to obtain clemency. He spent a railway journey on his way to a trade-union congress drafting a petition for Wilde's release, but this came to nothing in the end, for not enough signatures could be procured.

In August Douglas was still deep in his writing campaign, working on an article requested by the *Mercure de France*, an eloquent and poetic argument in support of Wilde. It included three beautiful but compromising letters from Wilde, one written the night before the final session of the libel trial, one while Wilde was on bail between the second and third trials, and one written while Taylor was being tried.[1] Robert Sherard, who lived in Paris, a devoted friend of Wilde though not a member of the coterie, cautioned Douglas—without success—against using the letters.

Shortly after this, Sherard visited Wilde in prison and, during their twenty minutes together, told Wilde of Douglas's proposed article. Wilde was horrified to hear that Douglas intended to publish his intimate letters and begged Sherard to stop him. When Sherard returned to Paris he was able to persuade the *Mercure de France* to omit the letters, but Douglas refused to publish the article without them. Thus it was never published, though typescripts survive.

[1] *The Letters of Oscar Wilde*, ed. Rupert Hart-Davis, London, Rupert Hart-Davis, 1962, pp. 393–394, 396–398.

Douglas wrote to Ada Leverson from Sorrento on 13 September 1895, saying that he could not understand the 'mystery about Oscar'. He had asked the Governor of Wandsworth Prison for permission to write to Wilde. (The number of letters a prisoner could receive was strictly limited; as with visits, one was allowed only every three months.) The Governor had replied that Wilde preferred not to hear from him. Ross also informed Douglas that Wilde wanted neither to hear from nor to see him. Douglas feared 'some secret influence was at work'. Sherard would not write to him, and Ross would not come to see him in Italy.

On 24 September Wilde was taken to Bankruptcy Court, handcuffed between two warders. His public examination, however, did not take place on this day, because Wilde's counsel asked the Registrar for an adjournment, saying that if more time were given he was hopeful all debts could be paid in full. Because there was no creditor present to object, the Registrar adjourned the public examination until November. Unfortunately, further solicitation from friends met with little success and on 12 November, when Wilde was again taken to the Court, he was declared a bankrupt.

On 20 November Wilde was transferred from Wandsworth to Reading Gaol. There, the harsh prison routine continued. He had already suffered greatly, both physically and mentally, but now had to undergo personal sorrow as well. His mother, to whom he was devoted, died on 3 February 1896. His wife arrived from Genoa on 19 February to break the news to him.

If Douglas had been in England he would have realized how much the events of the past year had changed Wilde and Wilde's feelings for him. But abroad and out of touch, he was aware only of his own attitude, which had not changed at all. He was still pursuing his crusade of justification, preparing an article for the *Revue Blanche* in an attempt to lift the Wilde scandal out of the police court and the Old Bailey into the higher air of romance and tragedy. Again Sherard tried to stop publication, but the article appeared in June 1896. Soon afterwards, Sherard and others learned that Douglas was planning to bring out a volume of his own poems, dedicated to Wilde.

When this news reached Reading Gaol, the prisoner told Ross to forbid the dedication; the 'proposal is revolting and grotesque'. Ross was to ask Douglas to return Wilde's letters and was to seal them up and destroy them if Wilde should die before he could do this himself. He was to retrieve all the presents. Douglas must not be allowed to keep anything that Wilde had ever given him. 'He has ruined my life—that should content him'.[1]

The weeks dragged on; in September another attempt was made to have Wilde's sentence shortened. More Adey, a close friend of Ross, had a petition printed to send to the Home Secretary. Like the earlier one, it had been drafted by Bernard Shaw, but again the petition was not sent, this time because a letter came from the Home Office saying that on no grounds would any mitigation of the sentence be considered.

In January 1897 Wilde began the long letter to Douglas accusing him of his downfall. His bitterness increased in February, when he received word that his sons Cyril and Vyvyan had been taken from him. The Chancery Court had appointed as joint guardians the boys' mother, Constance Wilde, and Adrian Hope, a connexion of hers, a man of fine character. The loss of his sons was a crushing blow. For three months Wilde continued to write his letter to Douglas, the devastating attack which came to be known as *De Profundis*.

6

After serving his full two-year term, Wilde was released early on the morning of 19 May 1897. He was met by More Adey and Stewart Headlam and he carried with him the manuscript of *De Profundis*, eighty folio pages. He had not been allowed to post his long letter to Douglas from prison, but he was permitted to take it away with him.

Late on the day of his release Wilde left England, never to return. He took the night boat from Newhaven to Dieppe, accompanied by Adey, and next morning they were met by Ross and Turner. After the four had spent a few days in Dieppe, Adey and Turner returned to London. Ross stayed on a little longer to help Wilde settle into a small hotel in nearby Berneval. When he too went home he carried with him the manuscript of *De Profundis*. Wilde had designated Ross as his literary executor while in prison, and had now given instructions for the handling of this manuscript (see Appendix II).

[1] *Letters of Oscar Wilde*, pp. 400–401.

At the simple, bourgeois Hôtel de la Plage Wilde was bored and lonely, but the management was friendly and he made a brave effort to begin a new life. He hoped that his wife would come with Cyril and Vyvyan to visit him. Constance, though not well (she was suffering from spinal trouble), agreed to see him later but refused to consider a meeting with the boys. She had changed their surname and her own to Holland, a family name. Constance's letters made him miserable. He tried to work and began *The Ballad of Reading Gaol*, but most days he felt too depressed to write. The only times his spirits rose were when some of his young friends paid him visits of two or three days. Then he would entertain them with food and drink and talk, his wit sharp as ever. And he would enjoy whatever affection they gave him.

Douglas wrote, saying that he did not understand why Wilde had turned against him and never wanted to see him again: he had 'done nothing but "stick to him through thick and thin" to [his] own great loss and detriment and to the exasperation of [his] father and "society" in general who condemned [him] for not abandoning him'.[1] Douglas said he did not think he deserved such unkindness and was longing to see him.

Within a few weeks Wilde was writing Douglas letters in the old adoring strain, and on 4 September Wilde went to Rouen to meet him. They walked about the city all day, hand in hand. Douglas offered to take Wilde to Italy. He would lease a villa in Naples, what Wilde had dreamed of in his letter from Holloway Prison, 'a little house where we could live together, oh! life would be sweeter than it has ever been'.[2]

Wilde agreed to all Douglas offered, then tried to explain his decision to Ross. 'I must love and be loved, whatever price I pay for it. I could have lived all my life with you, but you have other claims on you. . . .'.[3]

Ross was incensed by Wilde's return to Douglas and refused further financial aid. Constance was furious. By late September she had sent Cyril and Vyvyan off to school and was waiting for Wilde to visit her at Nervi, near Genoa. She could not understand why he did not come, and when she learned that he was in Naples with Douglas, she forbade

[1] *Oscar Wilde, a Summing-Up*, Lord Alfred Douglas, London, Duckworth, 1940, p. 133.
[2] *Letters of Oscar Wilde*, p. 393.
[3] *Letters of Oscar Wilde*, p. 644.

him to live there or anywhere under the same roof with Douglas; she stopped his allowance. Lady Queensberry, distressed by the renewal of the friendship, also threatened to cut off any money to her son. All friends disapproved, no money was forthcoming, and very little sympathy. One of the few kind gestures towards Wilde this autumn was Bernard Shaw's courageous suggestion that he be named for membership in the proposed British Academy of Letters.[1]

For more than two months Wilde and Douglas lived in the Villa Giudice at Posillipo, near Naples, and during this time Wilde completed *The Ballad of Reading Gaol* and Douglas wrote a number of his finest sonnets. But the venture of sharing their lives was doomed to failure. Wilde's infatuation was based on Douglas's personal beauty and, as the latter said, 'I was no longer quite so attractive in appearance as when he first met me'.[2] They had no money and their being together stirred general disapproval. 'I hated it', Douglas wrote to his mother in December from Rome, just after he had left Wilde. 'I was miserable, I wanted to go away. But I couldn't. I was tied by honour. . . . The only thing that happened was that I felt and saw that he didn't really wish me to stay and that it would really be a relief to him if I went away. . . . Now I am free'.[3] Douglas asked his mother to send two hundred pounds to pay bills and advance rent so that Wilde could stay on in the villa. Lady Queensberry complied, sending the money through More Adey.

Douglas returned to Paris and settled in a flat on the Avenue Kléber. Wilde soon followed, staying first at the Hôtel de Nice and then at the Hôtel d'Alsace. Though they never shared the same house again they saw each other frequently, talked, dined and made excursions—both still enjoying the boulevard boys.

In February 1898 the *Ballad*, Wilde's last book, was published by Leonard Smithers, but although it had a surprisingly active sale it realized little money either for him or for the author. One of the presentation copies of the book was sent to Shaw.

April found Wilde still in Paris, and in this month came the shocking

---

[1] *Bernard Shaw Collected Letters*, ed. Dan H. Laurence, New York, Dodd, Mead, 1965, p. 821.

[2] *Autobiography*, p. 138.

[3] *Without Apology*, Lord Alfred Douglas, London, Martin Secker, 1938, pp. 303, 305.

news of Constance's death, after an operation on her spine. She was only forty-one. Ross travelled from London to give Wilde sympathy.

In December 1898 Wilde accepted an invitation from Frank Harris to be his guest for three months on the Riviera, where Harris was trying to launch a hotel. Harris was an inconsiderate host, not arriving himself until February, and when he did he showed Wilde off as a raconteur and exhausted him with questions for two weeks, then departed again, leaving Wilde to his own devices. In Nice Wilde formed a friendship with Harold Mellor, a neurotic, well-to-do Lancashire man in his thirties, with whom he journeyed on to Switzerland, an unhappy time.

In January 1900 the Marquess of Queensberry died and Douglas inherited some fifteen thousand pounds, of which eight thousand were paid him at once. With this money Douglas settled himself at Chantilly and established a racing stable. Such selfish extravagance seemed unfair to Wilde, who was now desperate for money, and he told Douglas it was only right that he should guarantee him a yearly allowance; angry argument ensued. Harris's intrusion into the situation, his talk with Douglas on the subject at Chantilly, and his fly-by-night scheme for Douglas to invest two thousand pounds in his hotel venture—for the benefit of Wilde—are discussed at length in Douglas's letters to Shaw.

In June 1900 Ross offered Douglas a half share in all future royalties if he would pay off Wilde's remaining debt, which had now been reduced to eight hundred pounds, and so discharge his bankruptcy. Douglas refused, to his lasting regret. 'His chief hatred of me', Ross wrote years later to Wilde's son, Vyvyan Holland, 'was due to the fact that he had ignored my belief in the commercial possibilities of the estate and refused my sporting offer'.[1]

Throughout this last year of his life, Wilde was desperately short of money. He wrote cadging letters to friends in every quarter; a number sent money, but he never revealed the generosity of one to another, for fear it might prevent further contributions.

He was drinking heavily and was no longer able to write, but he still talked as well as, if not better than, ever. To a few listeners, he tried to sell the scenario of a play he had sketched out six years before in a letter to the actor-manager George Alexander.[2] Wilde received payment from

[1] Robert Ross to Vyvyan Holland, 9 June 1918 (Hyde).
[2] *Letters of Oscar Wilde*, pp. 360–362.

half a dozen persons, among them Frank Harris, who was as unaware of the subterfuge as all the others; but Harris took positive action which the others did not. He extracted a promise from Wilde to write a first act, and when Wilde did nothing he wrote the play himself and sold it to Mrs Patrick Campbell. The play, which came to be called *Mr and Mrs Daventry*, is discussed in this correspondence, and the whole pitiful episode prompted Shaw to call Wilde 'an unproductive drunkard and swindler'.[1]

Mr and Mrs Daventry opened successfully in London at the Royalty Theatre on 25 October 1900, adding anger and humiliation to the pain of suffering, for Wilde was ill. On 10 October he had had an operation, which it was hoped would repair the injury to his middle ear, the result of a fall in prison.

On 17 October Ross came to Paris to be with him and stayed almost a month, during which time Ross wrote to Douglas in Scotland, saying that the doctor thought Wilde very ill. On 13 November Ross left Paris to join his mother, as promised, in the south of France. Wilde tearfully entreated him not to leave, but there seemed no cause for alarm. After a week, however, Wilde's ear became abscessed and meningitis set in. Douglas's criticism that Ross had not given him ample warning of the seriousness of Wilde's condition until too late was hardly fair, for Ross himself was not informed.

By the time he returned to Paris on 28 November Wilde was barely conscious. Ross's first concern was to find a priest to administer the sacraments of Baptism and Extreme Unction, to carry out Wilde's wish of being received into the Roman Catholic church. There was much to be done in a very short while, but Ross did cable Douglas in Scotland.

Wilde died on 30 November, and on 2 December Douglas arrived in Paris. The funeral was the next morning, 3 December. Douglas was chief mourner, and it was he who paid the funeral expenses. Wilde was still a bankrupt when he died.

Among the matters Ross and Douglas discussed in Paris after Wilde's death was the question of what to do with his papers. Ross said he had looked through them and found nothing of importance. What did

---

[1] *Oscar Wilde: His Life and Confessions*, Frank Harris, 2 vols. (2d ed), New York, privately printed, 1918, II:31.

Douglas wish to have done with them? Douglas told Ross to do what he thought best. For a number of years Douglas thought nothing more about the matter, but the time was to come when his letters to Wilde, which were still among the papers, would be used against him in court.

7

I dreamed of him last night, I saw his face
All radiant and unshadowed of distress,
And as of old, in music measureless,
I heard his golden voice and marked him trace
Under the common thing the hidden grace,
And conjure wonder out of emptiness,
Till mean things put on beauty like a dress
And all the world was an enchanted place.

And then methought outside a fast locked gate
I mourned the loss of unrecorded words,
Forgotten tales and mysteries half said,
Wonders that might have been articulate,
And voiceless thoughts like murdered singing birds.
And so I woke and knew that he was dead.[1]

Douglas wrote this sonnet about Wilde the year after his death and continued to grieve for the extraordinary man who had been the centre of his world for almost a decade. But devoted as he was to Wilde's memory, he realized it was time to reconstruct his own life. This was not easy, for he was now thirty and had no employment and doubtful qualifications for any. His skills were in poetry and in sports, shooting, riding and racing. But these were pastimes only and his present circumstances forced him to face facts: his inheritance from his father was rapidly diminishing and he could no longer afford his racing stable. He must live less expensively. Early in 1901 he came to London and took rooms in Duke Street.

During the next few months two friends assumed great importance in his life. The first was George Montagu, heir to the Earl of Sandwich:

[1] *The Collected Poems of Lord Alfred Douglas*, London, Martin Secker, 1919, p. 88.

they had known each other at Winchester and now became inseparable, until Montagu's family advised him to sever the connexion because any association with the Wilde scandal would hurt his chances of election to Parliament.

The other friendship began with a letter, an appreciation of his poetry, sent to Douglas by another poet, Olive Custance, daughter of Eleanor and Frederic Custance of Weston Hall, Norwich. Colonel Custance (who claimed descent from the family of Francis Bacon) had recently retired from the Grenadier Guards, after distinguished service in the South African War. He would have been happier with a son than a daughter, and to have Olive, his only child, a precocious versifier was an embarrassment. From the age of thirteen she had been happiest when reading Shelley and Byron and writing verse; in her twenties, her talents had been recognized far beyond the confines of Weston Hall. John Lane had published *Opals*, her first volume of verse, in 1897, the proof sheets corrected by John Gray and Ernest Dowson.

When she wrote her letter to Douglas they were hardly children: he was thirty-one and she was twenty-seven, yet they seemed like children, pretty, playful and totally impractical. They were attracted to each other at once. 'Prince' and 'Princess', they called each other. She said in a poem:

> And this sweet Prince who never will grow old,
> This boy with great blue eyes and hair like gold,
> Will lead you, little Princess, by the hand
> Through all the gardens of his fairyland!

When the Custances became aware of the friendship, they forbade Olive to see Douglas. From then on the two met clandestinely in London, at various museums and also at the Carfax Gallery, run by Robert Ross and More Adey, both of whom took an interest in the intrigue. There was also a visit to Paris, where a relation of Olive's provided a certain amount of chaperonage. The 'Prince' and his 'Princess' (sometimes he called her his 'Page') realized that without family approval and support their love was hopeless, but somehow this fact only made the situation more romantic for them both.

In October 1901 Douglas sailed for America, the purpose of his journey, understood by Olive, being to secure his future by marriage. He visited Boston, New York and Washington, and though he gave no names, he reported in his *Autobiography* that he had a choice of at least three eligible heiresses, perhaps one in each city.

In Washington, however, at the Metropolitan Club, where he had been given visiting privileges, Douglas was spoken to insultingly because of the Wilde scandal. He was greatly offended, and matters were made worse when the *New York Herald* and other papers reported the story. Douglas went to New York, sent the *Herald* his own account of the incident and also an uncomplimentary sonnet on America. He sailed back to England in January 1902.

When he arrived in London he found a letter from Olive, saying that she was engaged to George Montagu. Her parents were delighted, and so was their close friend, King Edward VII, from whom they had received a letter of congratulation. Douglas insisted upon a meeting with Olive, and at this she confessed that she was marrying Montagu only because Douglas would not marry her. Douglas vowed he no longer thought of an American heiress and that it was Olive alone he wished to marry. They abandoned caution and had a runaway marriage at St George's, Hanover Square, at nine o'clock on the morning of 4 March 1902. Douglas's mother did not come to the service but the night before gave him a diamond ring for the bride, and promised an allowance.

Douglas's sister, Lady Edith Fox-Pitt, accompanied him to the ceremony and acted as a witness. There were very few persons in the church; Robert Ross was one of them. The only notice the Custances received of the wedding was a telegram, sent by the newlyweds from Victoria Station as they made their way to Paris for their honeymoon.

The Custances were enraged by the marriage, but it was a *fait accompli* and they had to make the best of it. The bride and groom visited Weston Hall, and Custance, one of the greatest fishermen in Norfolk, made Douglas an expert in yet another sport. For a brief time Douglas and Olive had a house in Chelsea, and there, on 17 November 1902, their only child was born, Raymond Wilfrid Sholto Douglas. 'Everything was different after Raymond was born', Olive wrote plaintively to Douglas in later years.

The difference was the necessary assumption of responsibility. Outwardly, however, all seemed well for a time. Douglas leased an attractive old house, Lake Farm, near Salisbury, and he and Olive led a quiet country life, with plenty of sport and agreeable neighbours, who accepted them despite the stigma of the Wilde disgrace. Olive brought out a second volume of verse, *Rainbows*, in 1902 and a third, *The Inn of Dreams*, was to come in 1910. Both Olive and Douglas were publishing poems in the *Academy*, a literary magazine of high standing.

Robert Ross was also a contributor to this magazine and in 1907, when Douglas wrote to him saying that he was bored in the country, hard up and desperate for something to do, Ross, who knew the *Academy* could be bought, made the suggestion that Douglas's cousin Pamela Wyndham Tennant and her husband, Edward Tennant, a brother of Margot Asquith, buy the journal and make Douglas the editor. Douglas greeted this idea with enthusiasm and his cousins were receptive. After talks with Ross, Tennant paid two thousand pounds for the magazine and promised three hundred pounds a year to the editor. Douglas took his responsibility very seriously, moving his household to Hampstead and leasing an office in Lincoln's Inn Fields. He set to work to make the *Academy* an outstanding journal.

8

Among the magazine's contributors was Bernard Shaw, now well established as a playwright. *Candida, John Bull's Other Island* and *Caesar and Cleopatra* had been successful in London; *Man and Superman, Candida* and *You Never Can Tell* had gone well in America. And *Mrs Warren's Profession* had had valuable publicity in New York though little viewing: the censor had forced it to close on opening night, the whole cast being duly arrested. *Arms and the Man* had been produced in Germany, *The Devil's Disciple* in Russia, Hungary and Poland, and *You Never Can Tell* in Sweden.

Shaw was not only producing plays, he was publishing them as well. Grant Richards brought out three volumes of his plays, and when John Murray turned down *Man and Superman* for fear it would offend conventional opinion, Shaw induced the Constable firm to take him 'on commission'; thus that highly productive connexion began. Shaw was successful even farther afield: for six years he was a council member for the London borough of St Pancras; he also continued to lecture for the Fabian Society and to write Fabian tracts. And he made frequent and caustic comment on world events in the press.

Much had happened in Shaw's private life as well. In 1896 he had met Charlotte Payne-Townshend, a distant relation of the Townshend in whose Dublin estate office he had been a clerk when a boy. Charlotte, as a new member of the Fabian Society, was introduced to Shaw by his close friends, Sidney and Beatrice Webb. Charlotte was forceful, intelligent and attractive, a family rebel, a 'green-eyed Irish millionairess'. At the time of their meeting, Shaw was romantically entangled with several other ladies, but Miss Payne-Townshend was something totally new in his experience, possessing qualities of mind he had not found before. There was no nonsense about her; she was even-tempered, forthright and practical; and she had genuine interest in his work. He enjoyed her company and realized how much he missed her whenever her insatiable desire for travel took her from London. She was abroad when Shaw became ill, overworked to the point of exhaustion; he had neglected a slight foot injury until such grave complications resulted that two operations were necessary. When Charlotte heard of the seriousness of the situation, she hurried home and went at once to Mrs Shaw's flat in Fitzroy Square. She was appalled by the discomfort and disorder in which Shaw and his mother were living. Charlotte told him that he was going to the country with her to have proper care. In response to this order, Shaw expressed scruples not found in his plays: he insisted that if he came to the country with her they must be married. She accepted the condition and made other conditions herself; one, that the marriage never be consummated.

Shaw's marriage, in its own way, was as unusual as Douglas's. On 1 June 1898 Shaw hobbled on crutches to the Registry Office in Henrietta Street, and there, in the presence of two witnesses, the ceremony took place. The bride was forty-one, the groom forty-two. He wrote the press report of the wedding himself, a typically Shavian account, to which the bride made no objection. Charlotte had the rare ability of observing life objectively, with a sense of humour.

From the early days of their acquaintance she had helped Shaw with his work, learning to type in order to be an efficient secretary. She was also an excellent critic, knowledgeable, outspoken and demanding. Beyond this, she was a firm general manager and, unlike Olive, not in the least competitive as a writer.

Shaw moved into Charlotte's London flat at the Adelphi Terrace, the grand old Adam building, by now considerably run down. They had the two upper floors at number 10, which Charlotte had taken a few years before to help Sidney and Beatrice Webb establish the London School of Economics on the floors below. The place was completely satisfactory to the Shaws as a London base but they soon wished to have a country house as well. They leased several different properties until 1906, when they rented the ugly, unpretentious red-brick house in Ayot St Lawrence, originally built as a rectory.

9

When Douglas became editor of the *Academy* in 1907 he held Shaw in high regard. He noted that the comedies were delightful, that Shaw was a brilliant and amusing writer as well as a profound thinker and averred that his pronouncements on social questions should be listened to with respect. In writing to Olive (25 June 1907) Douglas enclosed a pleasant letter from Shaw, congratulating him on the rising circulation of the *Academy*. There were a few other friendly letters exchanged between the two at this time.

Then suddenly, the *Academy* of 23 May 1908 carried a scathing review of *Getting Married*, Shaw's first 'conversation' play. The notice described it as an indecent piece that should never have been passed by the censor. Shaw wrote a letter of protest to the editor of the *Academy*. Douglas sent a rough reply, and Shaw a rejoinder. In all, five angry letters were exchanged (see Appendix I). After this, silence prevailed between Shaw and Douglas for more than twenty years.

The *Getting Married* incident was one example, and there were many others, of the strong moral stands the *Academy* was beginning to take on politics and religion: articles attacking Asquith and Lloyd George, articles arguing for High Anglican practices. In all these controversies Douglas was supported, often led on, by his assistant editor, the vitriolic T. W. H. Crosland (whom Shaw referred to in his letters as 'Thersites' Crosland). The political views expressed in the *Academy* became more and more disturbing to Edward Tennant, not only because he was a brother-in-law to Asquith (now Prime Minister) but also because of his own position as M.P. for Salisbury. In the realm of religion the articles were hardly less embarrassing to the Tennants because of Douglas's personal message. Now a High Anglican, he felt remorse for his pagan youth and expressed disapproval of homosexual behaviour in as impassioned terms as he had once defended it. The Tennants begged Douglas to return the *Academy* to its original literary, noncontroversial form. He refused, and they withdrew their support. After failing to gain help from any other quarter, Douglas assumed ownership himself, raising money on a reversionary interest in his mother's property.

As the *Academy's* violently controversial policy continued, Douglas's relationship was strained, not only with the Tennants, but also with Ross, who differed from him on every important issue. In August 1908, when the Douglases and Ross were members of a house-party in the country, the subject of the *Academy* provoked an explosion at the dinner table, embarrassing and unpleasant for the host, Frank Lawson, Reggie Turner's half-brother, and all others present. Olive tried to effect a reconciliation after the incident; at her urging, Ross invited Douglas to lunch at his club. There was very little the two could discuss. *Academy* policies and practices were touchy subjects for Ross; so was the subject of Freddie Smith, the young office clerk, now secretary, who lived with him; and touchy subjects for Douglas were all Ross's successful Wilde projects: paying off the estate's bankruptcy (full payment plus four per cent interest, in 1906); being made the administrator of Wilde's literary properties in consequence; and now, with Methuen's help, publishing the first collected edition of Wilde's works. The two men parted amicably enough but made no effort to meet again. In December 1908, on the occasion of a testimonial dinner given to honour Ross and to celebrate the appearance of the Methuen volumes, Wilde's friends were present in force but Douglas was conspicuous by his absence.

In February 1909 Olive asked Ross to lunch with her alone because 'I am afraid you and Bosie are not friends just now [and] I am sorry' (24 February 1909). Ross had refused an invitation a few days earlier and he now wrote a letter to Olive (28 February) explaining why it was wiser that he and Douglas should not ever meet. He had no hostile feelings towards Douglas, he said, he had known him well and long, but he realized it was best to forgo further friendship. Douglas at once replied to Olive's letter, and in the strongest terms, saying that he had no desire to continue his friendship with Ross: 'My own views have changed and I do not care now to meet those who are engaged in active propaganda of every kind of wickedness from anarchy and socialism to sodomy'. This passage caused Ross to seek counsel. On the advice of his solicitor, Sir George Lewis, he took no action, but towards the end of the year he offered the manuscript of *De Profundis* to the British Museum. It was accepted under seal until 1960, a 'time bomb for Douglas', as Shaw said later.

10

By 1910 the losses of the *Academy* despite its increased circulation forced Douglas to sell the journal. This was a bitter blow. He was depressed by his failure and deeply dissatisfied with his own life. The religious convictions which he had expressed editorially became more and more important to him personally. High Anglicanism no longer satisfied him, and in 1911 he joined the Roman Catholic church. His mother and his sister, Edith, followed, and nine-year-old Raymond was also brought into the church. Colonel Custance resented what he believed to be Douglas's pressure upon Raymond, as indeed he resented almost all Douglas's decisions for the boy.

During this year Custance was able to persuade Olive to sign away the entail of her grandfather's property in exchange for a settlement on Raymond and an allowance for herself. This he guaranteed to give at specific intervals, but soon he refused payments unless concessions were made concerning Raymond. Douglas, pressing Olive's claims, wrote provocative letters to his father-in-law which finally forced Custance to bring a libel suit.

The year 1913 was terrible for Douglas: he was declared bankrupt in January on the petition of a money-lender; his father-in-law brought a custody suit for Raymond; and Douglas was himself suing a young man, Arthur Ransome, for libel over passages in the latter's book *Oscar Wilde, a Critical Study* (1912). Certain sentences accused an individual, not named but clearly Douglas, of being the cause of Wilde's downfall.

Ransome had written his book under the guidance of Ross, and Ross now provided expert legal defence for him. In the midst of Douglas's court battles, Olive, impulsive and distraught, returned to her father's house with Raymond, creating a disastrous situation for Douglas: in the Custance libel case Douglas had to tender an apology and withdraw his accusations; the Chancery Court awarded the larger portion of Raymond's holiday time to Custance; and Douglas lost his case against Ransome.

In this trial, incriminating letters from earlier Wilde lawsuits were re-read, and for the first time hitherto-unpublished portions of De Profundis were made public in court, the manuscript having been subpoenaed from the British Museum. Later the passages were freely quoted in the press, fixing Douglas in the public mind as Wilde's evil genius and destroyer. Douglas stated under oath that he had not received the De Profundis letter in August 1897 as claimed, nor at any time thereafter, and that until a copy had been produced for him shortly before the trial, he had not known the letter was addressed to him.

The exposure of De Profundis turned Douglas against Wilde's memory. In anger and bitterness, he answered his charges in Oscar Wilde and Myself (1914), an attack on Wilde and a vindication of his own behaviour, written with Crosland's help. Some years later, Douglas disclaimed much of the book, saying that two-thirds of it had been written by Crosland. 'I deeply regret that the book was ever published'.[1]

11

When the Great War broke out, Douglas, forty-four years old, sought a commission but was turned down; 1914 found him not in the army but back in a court of law, prosecuted for criminal libel by Ross. Douglas had forced Ross to bring action by accusing him of indecencies with boys. Douglas's plea, like his father's, was justification, and shortly before the trial began he collected evidence against Ross from a number of young men. The jury could not reach a verdict, and the case was settled on Ross's plea of nolle prosequi. As a result, Douglas was acquitted and

---

[1] *Without Apology*, p. 60.

discharged, his costs paid and his plea of justification allowed to remain on file at the Old Bailey.

This trial, for the sake of both Douglas and Ross, should never have taken place. It was disastrous for them both. Douglas had cause to complain that Ross had kept private letters of his to Wilde and later produced them as evidence in court; also that Ross used a private document, *De Profundis*, as testimony against him; but his relentless pursuit of Ross cost Douglas sympathy. As for Ross, the trial ended a distinguished career. He was forced to resign his position with the Board of Trade and to retire from public life. Loyal friends solicited a testimonial with over three hundred signatures, an official record of their continuing allegiance and respect (alluded to in Shaw's first letter); but Ross was ruined.

Douglas's bitterness against him and against Wilde's memory continued, and four years later, in June 1918, Douglas offered himself as a witness for Pemberton Billing, the vigilant M.P. and celebrated campaigner for a more vigorous conduct of the war. Billing was being sued for criminal libel by Maud Allan because of his report of her theatre-club production of *Salomé*. When Douglas, on the stand, was asked if he regretted having known Wilde, he replied, "I do. Most intensely. He had a diabolical influence on everyone. I think he was the greatest force for evil in Europe for the last three hundred and fifty years".[1] Billing was acquitted in the war hysteria of the time, and Ross wrote to Vyvyan Holland that the case had destroyed the Wilde estate; everyone had cancelled contracts; there were no royalties.

Ross's own situation was troubled. In late August he tried to enter the Armed Services but was told by his medical board that he was unfit for military or civil duty. So he resumed his plans to go to Australia, where a position in the Melbourne Art Gallery had been offered him the year before. Transport difficulties caused by the war made it impossible to book passage then, but he was now able to buy a ticket and was assured of a sailing date between 26 October and 2 November.

He did not go to Australia. He died on 5 October of a heart attack, at forty-nine.

---

[1] *Bosie*, Rupert Croft-Cooke, London, W. H. Allen, 1963, p. 287.

During the war Shaw turned away from the theatre. The fine period of comedies, of *Fanny's First Play*, *Androcles and the Lion* and *Pygmalion*, was over. He devoted his time and energy to political propaganda and warnings. He urged a pact between the Big Four, though no official attention was paid to his plan. In the *New Statesman* he lashed out against the Minister of Foreign Affairs, Sir Edward Grey. He attacked British policy with *Common Sense about the War*, in which he said that England should have warned Germany that she would fight if Belgium were invaded and France attacked. The Germans were quick to exploit this argument, and Shaw was accused of being pro-German. Friends deserted him, and his plays were no longer performed. His unpopularity became intense when he wrote the speech from the dock for Sir Roger Casement, distinguished servant of the Crown, who was about to be hanged for seeking to 'free' Ireland by inviting German aid.

In 1916 Shaw started to write *Heartbreak House*. Its theme reflected his increasing disillusionment with the war and with the Webbs' belief that world progress would be assured if left to civil servants (he still believed in Communism, however). *Heartbreak House* was not produced until 1920 in New York, 1921 in London. Shaw considered it his best play; Charlotte hated it.

His next work, *Back to Methuselah*, actually five plays to be performed on successive nights, was produced by the Theatre Guild in New York in 1922, and the following year by Barry Jackson in England, at the Birmingham Repertory Theatre. In *Methuselah* Shaw developed the theme that life is not long enough: just as man learns to cope, he dies. Shaw felt this irony himself, for he believed his intellectual powers were still growing though he knew his body was failing. The only way to solve the problem, he claimed, was through Creative Evolution: man must *will* himself to live longer, and he must make himself realize that intellectual passion is indispensable, not physical ecstasy.

Shaw turned to more traditional faith and inspiration in the play which followed, *Saint Joan*. As far back as 1913 he had thought of 'a Joan play' and had written to Mrs Patrick Campbell about it from Orléans (8 September 1913). The idea was revived when Sir Sydney

Cockerell, Director of the Fitzwilliam Museum, gave him a book about Joan of Arc and he was struck with the drama of the trial scenes. Charlotte was enthusiastic and urged him on. *Saint Joan* was produced in New York in 1923 and in London in 1924. In both places it was an enormous success, the favourite of many critics.

In 1926 Shaw was awarded the Nobel Prize for Literature. In the past he had refused all degrees, titles and honours, even the Order of Merit. He still hesitated, but when told that he need not make a speech nor even an appearance, and that his prize money of seven thousand pounds might be used to establish a foundation for translating Swedish literature into English, he accepted.

By the end of the 1920s Shaw was the most celebrated playwright in the world, and in a financial sense the most successful author in history.

13

For Douglas it was a totally different story. His earnings as an author were only fifty to a hundred pounds a year, and although his poetry still had some loyal admirers he was not remembered as a poet. What celebrity he had was as the friend of Oscar Wilde.

Changes in taste during the past twenty years had much to do with the lack of appreciation for Douglas's poetry. Readers had turned away from classical rules and meticulous handling of metre and rhyme to freer forms. Douglas's strength lay in polished lyrics and sonnets, and in these he was a master. Sir Arthur Quiller-Couch, compiler of *The Oxford Book of English Verse*, believed that Douglas wrote the finest sonnets of his time, sonnets that few other English poets had ever equalled. Frank Harris, hostile to Douglas as a man, gave him extravagant praise as a sonneteer, comparing him with Shakespeare. And Shaw compared him with Shelley.

Age was another factor. The sonnets so greatly praised had been written a long time ago, when Douglas was a young man, the time of promise:

> My youth, equipped to go, turns back again,
> Throws down its heavy pack of years and runs
> Back to the golden house a golden boy.

Shaw in his mid-fifties

These lines in the poem 'To Olive', written in 1907, in a way were self-analysis. Childhood had been the happiest time of Douglas's life, and childlike qualities remained with him always. This was apparent to many, and something he himself was proud of: all great poets, he said, had the spirit of a child. He went even further: he believed that because (according to Thomas à Kempis) one could choose one's age in heaven, he would be a child forever.

However, although Douglas chose to be a child at heart, he was at the same time painfully conscious of the fact that he was old. He also knew that he could no longer equal his early poetry and he refused to write inferior verse. So he put all his restless drive, intense emotion and fighting spirit into journalistic writing: argumentative articles, pamphlets, broadsides, letters to the editor—heated, litigious pieces which gained him little respect or praise.

In 1920 he accepted an offer to edit a die-hard Tory journal, *Plain English*, and again employed Crosland as his assistant. The opinions which the two stated were reminiscent of the *Academy*: anti–Lloyd George, anti-Coalition, anti–Sinn Fein and anti-Semitic. After sixteen months a new owner took over and dropped Douglas as editor. Douglas then started a paper of his own, which he called *Plain Speech*, but it survived for only a few months.

In 1923 he resurrected an old article from the defunct *Plain English* files, printed thirty thousand copies of it in pamphlet form, and with the pamphlet and a public lecture launched a crusade against a cabinet minister, Winston Churchill. He declared that in 1916 Churchill had sent out false early reports on the Battle of Jutland, which allowed stock-market profits to be made on the New York Stock Exchange (the British Exchange was closed for the duration of the war) by a small but powerful Jewish group. He also claimed that the sinking of the *Hampshire* (5 June 1916) when it was carrying Field Marshal Lord Kitchener to Russia was the plot of Bolshevik Jewry in which Churchill and other highly placed British officials played a part. Both rumours were baseless but Douglas believed them, and in pressing his accusations publicly forced Churchill to prosecute for criminal libel. In short order Douglas was found guilty and sentenced to a six-month term in Wormwood Scrubs.

Prison had a therapeutic effect on Douglas. He regretted his litigious-ness, regretted the wrong he had done Churchill and changed his atti-tude towards Wilde. He rid himself of the bitterness, anger and sense of betrayal he had felt when the suppressed parts of *De Profundis* were made public. After his release from prison in May 1924 his talk and his writing about Wilde were always without rancour. They were filled again with understanding and deep affection. He was even eager to draw attention to similarities in their experience. He was not ashamed of being a bankrupt and was proud to have been in prison. Once Oscar had been sent to prison, he wrote in his preface to a friend's book, this 'became the obvious goal for any self-respecting English poet, and I never rested till I got there'.[1]

In prison, like Wilde, he wrote an important work, *In Excelsis*, a son-net sequence inspired by *De Profundis*. He was not permitted to take his manuscript from prison when he left, as Wilde had been, but he com-mitted the verses to memory and wrote them down as soon as he was released. The book was published by Martin Secker within a few months.

In the spring of 1925 Douglas went to Nice and while there became reconciled with Frank Harris, to whom he had not spoken since 1916, when Harris's biography of Wilde had been published (privately in New York, because Douglas had threatened a libel suit if the book appeared in England). Harris begged for permission to publish an Eng-lish edition. He promised to write a new preface, to change what Doug-las felt was a villainous interpretation of himself and to correct all lies and misrepresentations. Harris gave him a copy of the second edition (New York, 1918) in which to mark the passages he found offensive.

Both men believed the book would have an excellent sale in England and, as they were both hard up, there seemed a good chance for the success of the project. Considerable progress was made while Douglas was in Nice. He contributed extensive comments and Harris wrote the new preface. But after Douglas returned to England, Harris decided against most of the changes and the British edition did not materialize.

In September of 1925 Colonel Custance died and Douglas tried to re-

---

[1] *Bernard Shaw, Frank Harris and Oscar Wilde*, Robert Harborough Sherard, London, T. Werner Laurie, 1937, p. 14.

establish a relationship with Raymond, his son, who was now twenty-three, but the two did not get on. Olive, though friendly to her husband, continued a completely separate life and soon bought a house on the Isle of Wight.

Little was going well for Douglas, although he had the satisfaction of having his *Complete Poems, Including Light Verse* published in 1928, and his *Autobiography* in 1929, both by Martin Secker. Douglas's *Autobiography* was a lively and entertaining book, but hardly a conventional life story. It consisted mainly of his reminiscences about Wilde, told in the softened words of new understanding. Douglas no longer tried to ward off the shadow of Wilde; he was proud to share Oscar's fame.

When the following correspondence between Shaw and Douglas began in 1931, Shaw was seventy-four and Douglas sixty.

THE LETTERS

In the present edition, addresses have been standardized and salutations and signatures run into the text. Paragraphing and punctuation have also been standardized and abbreviations lengthened. Crossed-out words which have no significance have been deleted, as well as repetitious comments which serve no purpose, and omissions have been indicated by conventional ellipsis marks. Inadvertent misspellings have been corrected and Shaw's eccentric spelling made to conform with standard usage.

Dear Lord Alfred Douglas, It is a pity that Wilde still tempts men to write lives of him. If ever there was a writer whose prayer to posterity might well have been 'Read my works; and let my life alone' it was Oscar.

It is inevitable that you should appear in these biographies as a sort of *âme damnée* beside him, not in the least because you were a beautiful youth who seduced him into homosexuality (how enormously better it would have been for him if you had: you might have saved him from his wretched debaucheries with guttersnipes!) but because you were a lord and he was a snob. Judging from the suppressed part of *De Profundis* (Carlos Blacker[2] lent me his copy) I should say that you did one another far more harm socially than you could possibly have wrought by any extremity of sensual affection. You had much better have been at the street-corner with me, preaching Socialism.

However, you need not worry. Your *Autobiography* and your book anticipating the publication of *De Profundis* in full[3] (I have read both of them attentively) have made your position quite clear; and you need not fear that any biographer will be powerful enough to write you down.

Harris threatens *me* with a biography.[4] I have deleted the allusion to you in the letter which he used as an appendix to his book on Wilde (in case he should republish it). They were not unjust as statements of what we felt at the time. Your hatred of your father may have been very natural, and richly deserved; but you were very young then; and if you had been older and unblinded by that passion, you would have made Oscar ignore the card left at the club as the act of a notorious

[1] The Shaws were in Venice for three weeks on their way home from a Mediterranean tour. Douglas had complained that new printings in America of Frank Harris's biography of Oscar Wilde still contained Shaw's long and laudatory 'Memories of Oscar Wilde', which endorsed Harris's accusations against Douglas.

[2] Carlos Blacker (1859–1928), an English intellectual of means then living in Switzerland. He was a loyal friend to Mrs Wilde and the children and to Wilde while he was in prison but turned against him when the latter resumed his friendship with Douglas.

[3] *New Preface to 'The Life and Confessions of Oscar Wilde'* (2d ed), Fortune Press, 1927.

[4] James Thomas (Frank) Harris (1856–1931) was at work on a biography of Shaw. Harris was very ill and about to die.

lunatic lord, and clear out before the police could be moved to proceed. Consequently we were all rather down on you at the time. Harris's advice was sound. And I still think his memoir of Wilde,[1] and incidentally his revelation of himself (which should have appealed to your sense of humour), much the best intimate portrait that is likely to be drawn. It may be unjust to you; but you have had a very full hearing in defence; and anyhow why should you, who have been so unjust to many good men, expect justice for yourself? Are you not wise enough yet to pray God to defend you from it? Does your conscience never reproach you for the reckless way in which you exploited Crosland's[2] phobia for calumny in the *Academy*?

I have been forced to leave many hundreds of letters unanswered by the limits of time and working power; but I have no recollection of your being among the sufferers. They all have to forgive me; and so must you.

Your picture has not been sent on to me[3]: I shall find it in London on my return presently. I wonder, is there any man alive except yourself who would take such a step as a defence against a diagnosis of narcissism! That flowerlike sort of beauty must have been a horrible handicap to you: it was probably Nature's reaction against the ultra-hickory type of your father.

Ross did not get his testimonial[4] for nothing. Only a great deal of good nature on his part could have won over that distinguished and very normal list of names to give public support to a man who began with so very obvious a mark of the beast on him. A passage in one of my prefaces on the influence of artistically cultivated men on youths who have been starved in that respect, and their liability to be imposed

---

[1] *Oscar Wilde: His Life and Confessions*, 2 vols. (privately printed, New York, 1916). The second edition, containing Shaw's 'Memories of Oscar Wilde', appeared in 1918.

[2] Douglas's assistant editor at the *Academy*, the Yorkshireman T. W. H. Crosland (1865–1924).

[3] Douglas had sent his photograph, taken at the time of the Café Royal meeting (*Autobiography*, p. x).

[4] The public statement issued in March 1915, addressed to Robert Ross (1869–1918), signed by more than three hundred distinguished men such as H. H. Asquith, Edmund Gosse, H. G. Wells and Bernard Shaw, assured Ross of their continued esteem despite his loss of the libel case against Douglas.

Douglas at the time he met Shaw

on by mere style, was founded on a conversation I had with Ross one afternoon at Chartres in which he described the effect produced on him by Wilde, who, in the matter of style, always sailed with all his canvas stretched. Let Ross alone: the world has had enough of that squabble.

Roman Catholicism was not what you needed: you should have turned Quaker. I still hold that Creative Evolution is the only religion in all the associations and implications whereof a fully cultivated modern man can really persuade himself to believe. Unless, indeed, he can content himself with Marxism.

This time you cannot reproach me for leaving you unanswered. Faithfully   G. BERNARD SHAW

15 May 1931   35 Fourth Avenue, Hove, ·Sussex[1]

Dear Mr Bernard Shaw, Forgive me for troubling you again so soon, but I wonder if you are aware that Frank Harris actually printed and sold many thousand copies of his *Oscar Wilde: His Life and Confessions* with your name *alone* on the cover as the author. Thousands of people bought the book thinking it was by you, as Harris's name was not even mentioned on the cover. It does not much matter whether you are aware or not of this piece of sharp practice on Harris's part, but I can assure you that what I tell you is correct. I have seen a whole stack of the books with 'by George Bernard Shaw' on the cover.

What I want to put to you now is that, seeing that Harris used your name in this unscrupulous way to disseminate his admitted lies about me (admitted to be lies by himself in his *New Preface*), you might write a few lines of preface to the new edition of my *Autobiography* which Martin Secker[2] is bringing out in the autumn in a cheaper edition. You say in your letter that I have 'had a patient hearing'. Well, I may have had that (though I got a lot of abuse too) but the hearing I got has, so far, been very limited. I sold less than two thousand copies of the book in London, about five thousand in Germany in the German translation

[1] The house of Douglas's mother, Sybil, Dowager Marchioness of Queensberry, where Douglas was living.

[2] Martin Secker (1882–1978), a scholarly, independent publisher of small means but great vision, taste and courage; a loyal friend to Douglas.

and (up to the present) about four thousand in France in the French translation. Harris told me himself in Nice in 1925 that he had sold forty thousand copies of his book, chiefly in America, where my book, strange to say, has so far practically no sale at all. By this time he has doubtless sold thousands more, although I have kept the book out of this country. If I could advertise my book as 'a new edition of Lord A. D.'s *Autobiography* with a preface by George Bernard Shaw' you know and I know that it would at least double its sale. I would ask you to let me print your letter or extracts from it, but there may be things in it which you would not like to appear publicly over your signature. I put it to you that it would be only fair that you should help me to sell my book as you helped Harris to sell his when, though perhaps you did not realize it, I was 'down and out' and fighting with my back to the wall. If you would do it, it would be a *beau geste* and I would be eternally grateful. I am not thinking, as I am sure you will believe, of money. I have never made any money worth mentioning by any of my writings. All I want is that as many people as possible should read my book about Wilde and myself while I am still alive, because as it now stands it is the absolute truth, and because I have suffered so much from calumny and misinterpretation. Of course if you would do this for me I should appreciate it as a tremendous favour and kindness. Anyhow there can be no harm in asking you. Yours most sincerely   ALFRED DOUGLAS

P.S. I hope you got the picture all right. Your preface might be just a letter to me, or the letter you have already written with any alterations or omissions you care to make. Everyone who has seen it thinks it extraordinarily good and acute.

27 May 1931   35 Fourth Avenue, Hove

Dear Mr Bernard Shaw, I told my publisher, Martin Secker, that I had asked you to write a preface for the new edition of my *Autobiography*. [He thinks] if you will write a preface my book will get the circulation in America which so far has been denied it. As it is precisely in America that Harris's malignant lies about me and my 'ill treatment' of Oscar have been most widely circulated (largely owing to your collaboration with Harris) I appeal to your sense of justice to do this for me. The injury to me in America is *incalculable*, and unless I can get Americans to read my book while I am still alive (I have no fear that it will not be read all over the world after my death) I shall go down to my grave under a burden of false witness and calumny. I don't ask you to 'boost' my book. If you would say substantially what you said in your letter, or give me permission to quote the letter it would be a good action on your part. Yours most sincerely   ALFRED DOUGLAS

29 May 1931   4 Whitehall Court, London[1]

Dear Lord Alfred Douglas, What! YOU among the preface hunters! Have you *no* self-respect? I should like to see the man who would offer me a preface to recommend me to an American publisher.

You are quite welcome to print my letter, but not as a preface, nor in any way that would enable an American publisher to announce me as a contributor, or to play on me the trick you accuse Harris of playing, though in blaming him for it instead of the bookseller or publisher I think you rather underrate his pride of authorship. Only, let me see a proof, as I do not remember it verbatim, and there may be something in it about third parties that should not be published.

Don't fuss about the burden. I have carried a whole haystack on my back for fifty years, sometimes to my heavy pecuniary loss, but I have never wasted five minutes on it, and am therefore alive and reasonably well. The one thing that no man can afford, and that nobody but a fool insists on carrying, is a grievance.

Besides, what claim had Oscar on you or anyone else that it should be a reproach to us that we did not spend the rest of our lives holding his hand after he disgraced himself?

All this maudlin sentiment! Come off it. Faithfully

G. BERNARD SHAW

30 May 1931   35 Fourth Avenue, Hove

Dear Mr Bernard Shaw, You have always been a past-master at confusing issues! Why, if you could write a long screed (not a mere preface

[1] The Shaws' London flat, since moving in 1927 from 10 Adelphi Terrace.

8

Shaw at 4 Whitehall Court

but a whole section of a book running to many thousand words) for Frank Harris, in the course of which you described me as a 'wretched little brat' simply because I did not advise Wilde to run away *after* he had already begun his proceedings against my father, could you not do the same for me (in a very much modified way) without loss of 'self-respect' either on my part or yours? You remind me of the editors of newspapers who in the past used to print insulting things about me in their papers with reference to the Wilde affair, and then, when I replied, write me private letters pleading that it was 'impossible to discuss such a subject in our columns'. Also please allow me to point out that the printed postcard[1] you enclosed with your letter of yesterday's date leaves my withers entirely unwrung. I was not trying to 'ensure the acceptance of an unpublished work'. My book has already appeared in four languages. All I did was to ask you to undo some of the harm you have done me by countersigning Harris's malicious lies and distortions of the truth. However, as you say that I am welcome to print your letter, I must make the best I can of that, and I will send you a proof.[2]

Your suggestion that it was Harris's publisher and not he himself who was responsible for printing a large edition of *Oscar Wilde: His Life and Confessions* with your name alone on the cover as the author will not do. Harris brought out the book himself without a publisher. When I was with him at Nice in 1925 he boasted to me of his 'smartness' in 'roping in' a large section of your admirers. Harris is much more of a crook and a confidence-trickster than a man of letters. In the new American edition of his book he has printed a very private letter of mine about my relations with Wilde, and has added (or forged) a permission to publish the letter which was not contained in it.[3] Yours very sincerely

ALFRED DOUGLAS

[1] Shaw's printed refusal to preface seekers, stating that such a request obliged him to read the book, which was tantamount to asking him for a gift of 'hard professional work'.

[2] Shaw's letter of 16 April 1931, with this answer of 30 May, appeared in the preface to the new edition (1931) of the *Autobiography* (pp. xi–xiv). To Douglas's disappointment, Shaw's letter did not increase the sales.

[3] Undated letter in the Covici Friede edition (pp. xli–xliv) in which Douglas wrote, 'I am now being forced by your widely disseminated accusations, to tell the real truth which, I freely admit, I have not told so far', ending with, 'You are at liberty to make any use you like of this letter and I have no objection to its being published'.

P.S. Have you ever considered what would have happened to Wilde if he had taken your and Harris's advice and run away after starting the proceedings against my father? Where would he have gone? How would he have lived? Would he ever have escaped prosecution? All the evidence would have been handed to the Public Prosecutor, and his failure to go on with his proceedings against my father would have been a complete admission of guilt. How would he have benefited?

4 July 1931   4 Whitehall Court, London

Dear Lord Alfred Douglas, Why has Heaven afflicted me with this infantile complex of yours which keeps you making 'a low-spirited noise', like Mrs MacStinger's baby,[1] down the ages because somebody has been unkind to you—this eternal 'moreover the plaintiff here, the offender, did call me ass',[2] and now this intolerable 'Oo dave Frank a bit of cake and oo won't dive me my piece'. You are worse than the tailor who got into London society on the strength of having once been kicked by Count D'Orsay,[3] because he, poor chap, had nothing else to say for himself, whereas you started with all the advantages, social and personal. You are the literary Man from Shropshire,[4] who died, a universally execrated nuisance, of his grievance. I tell you, you must never have a grievance. Never excuse yourself, never deny, never explain, never moan; and seize every opportunity to apologize (the most effective and popular of public attitudes) and to embrace every accusation and expose yourself to every reproach until your enemies are tempted to shift all the sympathy to your side by slapping your always-turned-other-cheek as hard as they can while you are good-humouredly knocking them out with the disengaged side.

I have revised your two galley slips;[5] and on your life, do not restore a word I have struck out or alter a word I have put in. If you cannot

[1] The wails of young Alexander fill the pages of Dickens's *Dombey and Son*.
[2] Dogberry, the constable in *Much Ado About Nothing*, Act V, scene 1.
[3] The Victorian dandy who lived with Lady Blessington at Gore House in London.
[4] A background character in *Bleak House*.
[5] Of Shaw's letter, 16 April 1931, for Douglas's *Autobiography*.

produce an impression that I am on your side, don't advertise me as being against you.

As to that notice of *Getting Married*,[1] I honestly believed that you had not written it; and when, to my genuine surprise, you said you had, I said:

> If boozy be bosie, as some folks miscall it
> Then Bosie is boozy, whatever befall it.[2]

You must have been as drunk as a boiled owl on that occasion; and if you were to tell the whole story, couplet and all, exactly as it occurred, it would amuse your readers much more than your allusion to it as it stands. But I shall never make a good controversialist of you. You will always raise that wail ———!

By the way, that retractation [the *New Preface*] that you induced Harris to perpetrate was judged from its style as being the work of Alfred Douglas, the signature alone being Frank's. And if you want to convince your readers that Frank is unscrupulous, you could do it much more effectively by owning up to the dictation than by implying that the retractation has the smallest value to you. In great haste—don't be so ungrateful as to reply and argue.   G. BERNARD SHAW

6 July 1931   35 Fourth Avenue, Hove

Dear Mr Bernard Shaw, Thanks for the proof, which I will leave exactly as you have corrected it. No, I was not 'drunk' when I wrote the notice of *Getting Married* in the *Academy*. (By the way, you don't specify whether you assume that I was 'drunk' when I wrote the notice or when I saw the play or both.) Why should you suggest that I was drunk then or at any other time? I will not say that I have never been drunk in my

---

[1] Shaw's play *Getting Married* opened at the Haymarket Theatre in London on 12 May 1908 and on 23 May was given a hostile review in the *Academy*, the weekly journal edited by Douglas. See the Introduction, p. xxxi, and Appendix I.

[2] A parody on the jingle, about Sir Thomas Lucy, absurdly ascribed to Shakespeare caught deer-poaching in Lucy's park at Charlecote. It ran: 'If lousie is Lucy, as some volke miscall it/ Then Lucy is lousie whatever befall it'. With this rhyme Shaw put his foot into it again, for Douglas did not place the couplet.

life (donkeys' years ago) but I have certainly never been drunk when I was sitting in the stalls of a theatre, nor when I was writing an article in my editorial office. I hated your play. It bored and exasperated me, and I expressed exactly what I thought about it at the time. In the notice you will perhaps remember it is explained that I only lasted through two acts. Talk about narcissism! You are such a mental Narcissus that you cannot believe that anyone who is not drunk can possibly fail to fall down and worship you. You have the advantage of me in this sort of 'back-answering' because I am politer and more tender-hearted than you and cannot bring myself to be rude or to say wounding things except when I am really angry (which never happens nowadays).

I never know whether what you say is meant to be taken seriously (you probably don't know yourself), but in case you really mean what you say about Harris and the preface, I will give you my word of honour that I did not write or dictate a solitary word of it (leaving out my letter to Harris of course).

I am sure you are right about my infantile complex which makes 'a low-spirited noise'. You will find the same phenomenon in most of the great poets, not excluding Shakespeare (in the sonnets). All real poets have an infantile complex. Also, there is the best authority for believing that the possession of an infantile complex is the only way to get into the Kingdom of Heaven. Yours very sincerely   ALFRED DOUGLAS

19 November 1931   35 Fourth Avenue, Hove

Dear Mr Bernard Shaw, Many thanks for sending me Harris's book.[1] I read it right through yesterday. I know next to nothing of your life and I really wanted to find out something about it. Harris's book gave me very little enlightenment. He has all the faults that a biographer could possibly have. As you point out, he is reckless in his statements and does not verify his facts. He jumps to all sorts of conclusions which

[1] *Bernard Shaw*, Frank Harris, London, Gollancz, 1931. The copy was inscribed by Shaw 'to Lord Alfred Douglas, another victim of Frank's failings as a biographer'. Despite the limitations and unfriendliness of the book, Shaw, in a kindly effort to help Harris's widow, edited the manuscript, corrected proof and saw it through the press.

are quite unjustified (or at any rate liable to be quite unjustified) and he is all the time blowing his own trumpet and posing as a righteous large-hearted man. Whereas he was a liar, a thief (both literary and otherwise) and an unscrupulous blackguard. I happened to be with him at the time he started to write his idiotic play about Joan of Arc.[1] It is quite untrue that he wrote it (as he declares) before reading your own play. I was seeing him daily at the time (1925) at Nice. He asked me all sorts of questions about Joan of Arc and about the Catholic attitude towards her which I answered to the best of my ability. He then told me that he was going to write a play about her which would 'knock spots' off yours. I afterwards read the play and I thought it beneath contempt. Not that I am such a very great admirer of your own play on the same subject. I take my Catholicism too seriously to approve of your flippant treatment of a martyr and saint. But your play is of course brilliant and original whereas Harris's is simply the sort of thing a rather dull fifth-form schoolboy might write.

To return to the biography. He seems to have started off with the intention of writing a panegyric and as the book goes on he gets less and less enthusiastic. Then comes his 'quarrel' with you about Joan of Arc and from that time on the book is simply an essay in denigration.

In my own autobiography I deliberately left out what I could have said about Harris's shameless theft of Wilde's play *Mr and Mrs Daventry*.[2] I did not want to appear to be attacking him all the time. But the facts of that episode are damning to Harris. They were lately put into the form of an article by a man called Bell (a very charming Scotsman), who was Harris's private secretary at the time. The article appeared in the New York *Bookman*,[3] and I believe it is to be published as a booklet in a French translation by Jacques Bernard in Paris. Harris ruined Wilde's play (the full story of which, act by act and scene by scene, I heard from Wilde's own lips about twenty times). Wilde died cursing Harris about it. In fact it was his rage and indignation at the way Harris swindled

[1] *Joan la Romée*, printed in Nice in 1926, three years after the first production of Shaw's *Saint Joan*.

[2] *Mr and Mrs Daventry*; see the Introduction, pp. xxiv–xxv. The play was published by the Richards Press (Martin Secker), 1957.

[3] 'Oscar Wilde's Unwritten Play', T. H. Bell, *Bookman* LXXI, no. 2 (1930).

him over the business after ruining his play which killed him. It is the irony of Fate that Harris should be accepted all over the world as Wilde's great friend and champion. The best part of Harris's book about you (which is well written and entertaining in parts) is your letters.

I did at least find out from the book, what had always puzzled me before, namely the reason for your going on sticking to Harris as you did after he disgraced himself by his *Life and Loves*.[1] Evidently he was at one time a good friend to you and I suppose he was useful, and you were grateful. All this is a good trait in your character and I am glad to hear the explanation. Yours very sincerely   ALFRED DOUGLAS

[June 1933]   4 Whitehall Court, London

Dear Lord Alfred, Your book on the sonnets is by far the best of all those known to me. Nobody else has understood the case of Mr W. H.[2] in the least; and nobody else has understood the case of Shakespeare so naturally and unstudiously. The first success is the more important; and the explanation is that you yourself have had the experience of Mr W. H.: men fell in love with your personal beauty; and you learnt thereby what neither Wilde nor Butler[3] had discovered, that the attraction of beauty is entirely distinct from the homosexual attraction, and that the one is no evidence of the other. And you are poet enough to move easily in the Shakespearean atmosphere and not be oppressed by the awful duty of worshipping a panjandrum in a sarcophagus.

I don't think I can say anything more or less than this of any importance; but if the book runs to a second edition I advise you to read Thomas Tyler's book on the sonnets if you can hunt it up at any of the

[1] Four volumes of Harris's autobiography were privately printed in his lifetime and a fifth, based on unpublished material, after his death. All five are in the Obelisk one-volume edition, Paris, 1949.

[2] Douglas had sent Shaw a copy of his *True History of Shakespeare's Sonnets* (Martin Secker, 1933). Like Wilde, Douglas identified the person to whom the sonnets were dedicated as Will Hughes, a presumed boy actor in Shakespeare's company, although there is no contemporary record of any boy actor so named.

[3] Samuel 'Erewhon' Butler (1835–1902), painter, scholar and writer. In his *Shakespeare's Sonnets Reconsidered* (1899) he identified Mr W. H. as the son of a sea cook.

•

libraries.[1] If you were the best-looking man of our time Tyler was certainly the ugliest; but he was a very honest gentleman and serious scholar; and he was certainly right on a point or two which you have foozled. You will find a thrilling personal description of him in the preface of my play *The Dark Lady of the Sonnets*, which also deals with our late friend Frank Harris, whom you handled with unnecessary violence.

You are clearly wrong about the rival poet. Minto[2] and Tyler identify him beyond all reasonable question as Chapman. I put this confidently because you have forgotten that theatres in Shakespeare's time did not give 'nightly' performances: there were too many footpads about. The performances were in the afternoon. As to Marlowe's Mephistopheles, who carried hell about within him, being 'an affable familiar ghost' you have only to read the play to dismiss it as impossible. But the crowning evidence is that Chapman did actually claim that his Muse came to him by night and inspired him. So you may wash out Marlowe. I can understand the young Shakespeare being imposed on by the scholarly pretence and tremendous self-assurance of Chapman; but he must have been conscious that he could outmarlowe Marlowe without turning a hair.

Wilde's surmise that W. H. was an actor is to my mind absolutely ruled out by the famous lines about the dyer's hand and the degradation of making himself a motley to the view. Nobody, least of all Shakespeare, would have written such a confession to an actor, nor to anyone who was not above the rank of an actor.

I do not think the case for William Herbert is either so weak as you think it, or so strong as Tyler thought it. The Hewes pun is not at all convincing: there is just as much to be said for Tyler's contemptuous rejection of it as for Wilde's and Butler's acceptance. Noblemen of Pembroke's type have always been accessible to literary geniuses. And what about that amazing first batch of seventeen sonnets urging W. H. to get married and have children. They must all have been delivered in a lump. I cannot exorcise a vision of 'Sidney's sister, Pembroke's mother'

[1] Thomas Tyler (1826–1902), in his facsimile edition of *Shakespeare's Sonnets* (1886), suggested that Mary Fitton was the dark lady, a theory he elaborated upon in the 1890 edition. Tyler suffered a goitrous disfigurement from birth.

[2] William Minto (1845–1893), in his *Characteristics of English Poets* (1874), pp. 289–292.

coaxing or even tipping a young poet with whom her son was struck, to get him married and settled. Of course W. H.'s mother need not have been a countess; but it seems utterly impossible that Shakespeare should have had businesslike parental anxieties about his friend. Can you suggest any other explanation?[1] . . .

The sonnet about the mortal moon raises the difficulty that neither by the Armada nor by the Essex rebellion was Elizabeth in the least eclipsed: the Armada was gloriously defeated and Essex never had a dog's chance. As the Armada was followed by several British failures, for the first of which Drake was sacked and in disgrace for five years, and as Elizabeth had severe illnesses from time to time, it is easy to produce half a dozen much more possible eclipses than either the Armada or Essex.

I think your view of Shakespeare's complaints of senile decay and decrepitude as proofs that he was a very young man indeed when he wrote them is brilliantly sound; but you had better keep at the back of your mind the fact that such complaints have two characteristic ages. One of them is twenty and the other forty. Forty, which decisively ends all pretension to youth, makes a fearful impression. If I were you I should take the complaint as proving that Shakespeare was either twenty or forty, and then show that forty is out of the question. My own feeling without studying dates is that the sonnets are the work of a young man self-destined to be a poet and write Venus-and-Adonises and such like, and that the theatre caught him as being the only place where he could earn a living, and presently compelled him not only to gobble up Henry VI and become an adapter of other men's inventions, but to make himself a motley to the view, which was extremely hurtful to his dignity. I know too well the snobbery of a man in Shakespeare's social position.

I think you are hasty in removing the sonnet-sermon on lust from the list of those addressed to Mr W. H. I suggest that it was just the very thing to send him at the moment when he was falling to the lure of the dark lady. It was a warning, ineffectual of course, but very timely. I

[1] 'Yes I can', Douglas noted on a typed copy he made of this Shaw letter, now in the Columbia University Library: 'Shakespeare's pretext for urging the young man to marry as an excuse for extolling his beauty, had worn out. Thereafter he expressed his feelings openly'.

cannot believe that it was an arrow shot into the air: there must have been some urgent occasion for it. Why not then attribute it to this fairly obvious emergency? It could not have been addressed to the lady herself: it is not personal enough, and would have been quite thrown away on her. . . .

Your statement that Shakespeare was brought up as a Catholic is made without any reference to a book published not very many years ago in which the author showed that the Shakespeares were a Catholic family; but why *should* you refer to it even if you had read this book and remembered it? Literature is too full of 'acknowledgments' and squabbles about originality, which are in bad taste in a work about Shakespeare. Never mention a rope in the house of a hanged man.

Reverting for a moment to Wilde's notion that W. H. was an actor, it does not make sense of the 'millions of strange shadows'. It has an air of doing so at first sight, just as it has an air of reproach to W. H. for being all things to all men. If it were addressed to Shakespeare by someone who knew all his then unwritten works it would be quite intelligible. But as it is, the more carefully you parse it, the less you can make of it.

The length of this letter, and the fact that the writing of it is a busman's holiday for me, not to mention that I was far away on the Pacific when your book arrived, explains my long delay in writing to you about it. Many thanks for it and for the inscription. Faithfully

G. BERNARD SHAW

P.S. The sonnets contain no explicit evidence as to the social standing of Mr W. H. He may have been only the son of a prosperous bourgeois, well dressed and nice as to his person. But he was certainly not Shakespeare's social inferior.[1] Butler's son of a sea cook reminds me that the most convincing pamphlet I ever read demonstrated that *Romeo and Juliet* was a fine dramatic poem edited by a conceited stage-struck butcher. Hence 'and madly play with my forefathers' *joints*'!

---

[1] 'In spite of what Mr Shaw says I still incline to believe that [Mr W. H.] was an actor', Douglas noted on the Columbia typescript.

Dear Mr Bernard Shaw, I am pleased to get your long letter and I am especially pleased to find that you have appreciated the point about the difference between the attraction of beauty and the homosexual attraction, and that the one is no evidence of the other. I think this is my most important contribution to the subject and no one else but you has 'spotted' it. It is quite true that I am not properly speaking a Shakespearean scholar. I mean that in writing my book I relied far more on my poetical instinct and my knowledge and understanding of Shakespeare's text than on the other commentators. Although I read a great many of them, I no doubt missed much that I would have absorbed if I had been more of a scholar.

My argument was: 'There is no evidence about the sonnets except what is contained in the sonnets themselves and in Thorpe's dedication. Consequently the best way to arrive at a solution is to try to get it out of the sonnets themselves'. I feel so sure that the sonnets were not written to Southampton or Pembroke or to any great nobleman but to someone of Shakespeare's own class and station in life, that when I find anyone (e.g., Tyler) assuming that they refer to Pembroke or Southampton I am apt to dismiss his conclusions impatiently as unworthy of consideration. You yourself agree that Shakespeare may have been in the early twenties (you actually say twenty) when he wrote them. When Shakespeare was twenty Pembroke was about eight, and Southampton about twelve. So, if my argument about Shakespeare's extreme youth when he wrote the sonnets is correct (and you seem to think it is) that completely disposes of Pembroke and Southampton. . . . As to Marlowe being the rival dramatist, if you look again carefully at what I say, you will see that I myself say that the rival poet was probably Chapman. . . .

I have no doubt that Harris got his Mary Fitton idea from your review of Tyler's book.[1] Harris always got *everything* he wrote from someone else! He got most of his theory about the sonnets from Richard

---

[1] 'The Truth about Shakespeare', an unsigned review in the *Pall Mall Gazette*, 7 January 1886.

Middleton (in fact I believe Middleton actually wrote it), as I only found out accidentally about three weeks ago.[1]

My ideas about Shakespeare being brought up a Catholic were largely derived from a book called *Shakespeare et la Religion* by Camille Looten of Lille University,[2] a most brilliant book. Nobody seems to have read it. I wanted Secker to publish a translation of it. Have you seen it? It was published in Paris about nine years ago. Perhaps that is the book to which you are alluding. But others have said the same before, e.g., the late Father Sebastian Bowden[3] of the Oratory. So I did not think it necessary to make any acknowledgment. Yours very sincerely

ALFRED DOUGLAS

P.S. I really am quite delighted and flattered that you say my book on the sonnets is 'by far the best of all those known to you'. This is really generous praise and gives me great gratification. The book was very well (though often very unintelligently) reviewed. But it does not sell much. Secker however says that it will go on selling for a long time.

3 January 1936   1 St Ann's Court, Hove[4]

Dear Mr Bernard Shaw, I am sending you under separate cover the new edition of my poems (in two volumes, *Lyrics* and *Sonnets*) published by Rich and Cowan. I would like you to have them as you have really been very kind to me lately, and the whirligig of Time now surprisingly exhibits you in the light of a friend. I saw your friendly

[1] When Douglas worked on the introduction for *The Pantomime Man*, miscellaneous writings by Richard Middleton (1882–1911).

[2] Published by Perrin et Compagnie, Paris, 1924.

[3] Father Sebastian Bowden (1836–1919), better known for his connexion with Wilde. Douglas claimed that after leaving prison Wilde sought Father Bowden to receive him into the Roman Catholic church (*Oscar Wilde, a Summing-Up*, p. 132). See a conflicting account of Wilde's enquiry in H. Montgomery Hyde's *Oscar Wilde*, New York, Farrar, Straus and Giroux, 1975, p. 324.

[4] Douglas's mother had given up the Fourth Avenue house in the summer of 1934. Early in 1935, Francis, the Marquess of Queensberry, Douglas's nephew, made him a gift of the ground floor flat at 1 St Ann's Court (paying the rent of £130 a year). Douglas's mother had another flat in the same building until she died on 31 October, 1935.

reference to my book on Shakespeare's sonnets in the article you wrote in the *Manchester Guardian* on Samuel Butler, sent by my press-cutting agency. I appreciated it very much. You will never convert me to your views, or to Socialism, but at any rate now you have succeeded in turning me into one of your admirers! Yours ever sincerely

ALFRED DOUGLAS

P.S. My poems have been almost completely boycotted by all the London reviewers (I presume because in my preface to the poems I have attacked their reigning tin idol T. S. Eliot) but they are selling vigorously and I have had enough praise and appreciation from judges of poetry anytime these last forty years to satisfy me. So my withers are unwrung.

11 May 1936   1 St Ann's Court, Hove

Dear Mr Bernard Shaw, I hope you got the new edition of my poems which I sent you many months ago. Please do not think that I am expecting a *critique raisonnée*, but I would like to be sure that the books reached you, and you have always acknowledged my former communications, which makes me fear that you have not got the books. I know you have been abroad and that probably huge piles of books have been accumulating for you in your absence.

Did I tell you that I had found fresh evidence about Master W. H., that is to say Will Hughes? If my clue turns out to be correct it will simply settle the question once for all that W. H. was Will Hughes. I am keeping it for a new edition. Yours sincerely

ALFRED DOUGLAS

8 October 1937   4 Whitehall Court, London

Dear Lord Alfred, Nellie Harris is on the rocks, as you may imagine, having sold everything saleable that Frank left.[1] I cannot adopt her, but

---

[1] Frank Harris had died in Nice on 26 August 1931, leaving his widow destitute. His copyrights were her only asset and she appealed to Shaw to write a preface and to try to have the Wilde biography published in England. Shaw was sympathetic and agreed to help. By mid-September he had virtually finished the preface and he then approached Douglas, to whom he had not written in more than four years.

that funny book of Sherard's[1] has given me a cue for a preface to a new edition of the *Life and Confessions of Oscar Wilde*.

This book, as you know, has never been published in England because the publishers were afraid of litigation from you. I can quite easily edit the book so as to make it quite inoffensive to you; or, alternatively, delete all references to you, if you would prefer that. But on examining the last American edition (1930, Covici Friede) I find that you actually contributed a long letter[2]—practically a very readable chapter—to this edition. Do you wish this to be included in the English edition; and, if so, will you give Nellie the necessary authorization?

Both the style and the matter of this letter make it a valuable attraction, but much as I appreciate its extraordinary candour I am not sure that some of it will not suggest more than it really means. And Frank's reply, to say the least, is not gracious.

Anyhow, let me know how you feel about the matter.

By the way, I have owed you a letter about the poems for a long time; but it is quite a job, and I have not yet had time to sit down to it. You certainly have a first-rate talent for the most difficult forms of verse: sonnet sequences come from you as easily as limericks; but where's your epic? If I could sing like that in words I should by this time have left more verses than Shelley did. It is not as if, like poor Henley,[3] who had a bit of a gift too, only coarser, you had nothing to say. Are you lazy? Faithfully   G. BERNARD SHAW

12 October 1937   1 St Ann's Court, Hove

Dear Mr Bernard Shaw, Let me just add to what I said in my letter of last Saturday that I think you would be well advised to wait till *Without*

[1] Robert Harborough Sherard (1861–1943), a great-grandson of Wordsworth, had met Wilde in Paris in 1883. Sherard, though strongly opposed to homosexuality, was a devoted friend and had already written three books about Wilde. The most recent, *Bernard Shaw, Frank Harris and Oscar Wilde*, was a defence against Harris's biography, which Sherard claimed was a malicious book, filled with plagiarisms, fictions and lies. He disproved many of Harris's best stories by researched facts. The preface to Sherard's book was by Douglas.

[2] Douglas discussed this (see 30 May 1931).

[3] William Ernest Henley (1849–1903), poet, journalist and editor.

Apology comes out before coming to any decision about reissuing Harris's book. Mine will be out in less than a month and it contains a lot about Wilde and also about Harris. I have said something about Mrs Harris's visit to me about eighteen months ago when she asked me to consent to a reissue of Harris's book.[1] I also saw Allen Lane,[2] who came to see me about it a year ago. He was quite keen to do a new edition of Harris's book, but after I had had an hour's conversation with him he changed his mind and said that he had definitely decided not to do it, although I told him (as I did in the case of Mrs Harris) that if my conditions were observed I would not take any legal action. [*The next sheet of this letter is missing.*]

I have not got a copy of the Covici edition. I don't think I have ever seen it. I would rather like to see a copy of what I said about my father before giving my consent to its being reproduced. I may tell you that A. J. A. Symons and Vivian[3] (that is the way to spell his name, at any rate that is the way his father spelt it though he now calls himself 'Vyvyan') Holland are strongly opposed to the re-publication of Harris's book. But this is no affair of mine. I think it shows that I am not a person who makes mischief that I did not reveal the contents of your letter to Sherard. If I had done so he would have certainly been out for your blood by this time! I think you are unfair to him and I think his devotion to Oscar is really touching. Of course, as I have frequently told him, he knows *nothing at all* of at least half of Oscar's life and character. There is quite a lot about you in my new book, I dare say you won't like some of it! But *que voulez?*

[1] See Douglas's *Without Apology*, pp. 288–289.

[2] Allen Lane (1902–1970, knighted 1952) had resigned as managing director of the Bodley Head in 1935 to found Penguin Books, which venture created a publishing revolution.

[3] A. J. A. Symons (1900–1941), director of the First Edition Club, was writing the official life of Oscar Wilde and editing the definitive edition of his works.

Vyvyan Holland (1886–1967), Wilde's younger and only surviving son, a Cambridge man, a barrister until the Great War, a major in the Royal Air Force, was now a journalist and translator. He was not told the reason for his father's disgrace until he was grown up. "Is that all?", he said. "I thought he had embezzled money". Holland was devoted to the memory of his father and watched over the publication of his works with concern beyond his interests as owner of the copyright. As for the spelling of his name, though his parents had usually written 'Vivian', he was christened 'Vyvyan' and preferred that form.

Did I tell you that I have discovered proof of the existence of 'Master Will Hughes'? My book on the subject only sold about five hundred copies, but I dare say I shall bring out a new edition sooner or later. Yours sincerely   ALFRED DOUGLAS

2 November 1937   4 Whitehall Court, London

Dear Lord Alfred, It is clearly not possible to prevent publication of Harris's book now. Nellie must live, even if you and I have to support her; and an advance of three hundred and fifty pounds on a fifteen per cent. royalty has already been offered; so that the tea-shop in Nice promises to materialize.[1]

I was greatly relieved to learn that your letters in the Covici edition were not intended for publication. But they contain a description of your father which is not only irresistible as literature but is a vital part of the history of the Wilde affair. I should very much like to work it in somewhere.

It is, as I said, possible to cut you out of the book altogether if you feel that way about it; but it would make a frightful hole in it; and it would miss a chance of setting you right at last. I still stick to my old opinion that Harris's portrait of Oscar is by far the most vivid we have. Ransome's is far more respectable and judicial;[2] and Sherard's little account of the spaniel-like attachment that made him at last unbearable is pitiful and sincere; but neither of them can push the trenchant Frank off the stage; his power of assertion and readability will carry the day with posterity if posterity ever troubles itself about any of us. It is important to get Harris right: he is unsuppressible.

I must go over his stuff and see what can be done to make it harmless to the innocent. As you know, I have already had the job of editing his biography of myself so as to get the facts right without taking out the pepper and salt. As the man was dying, the book fell to pieces at the end; and at the beginning it was full of stupendous inventions, as he

[1] Shaw had arranged with Constable, the publisher, for profits to go to Nellie.
[2] Arthur Ransome (1884–1967), Oscar Wilde, a Critical Study, London, Martin Secker, 1912.

knew nothing about my early life. Consequently a good deal of it is autobiography on my part, with the advantage of making Harris say one or two things that I could not decently say myself.

But before I tackle this job (I have already written a preface in which I have great fun with R. H. S.) I should like to know whether you wish me to depict you as well as I can and let Frank have the credit of it, or else leave you out of the saga altogether, which would be a great pity and would not remedy the wrong done you by the previous edition.

I must congratulate you on the sale of five hundred copies of the book on the sonnets. I should have put the number of people interested in them to the extent of buying a book about them at fifty as an outside figure. If you succeed in tracking down Mr W. H., a second edition or even a new book must appear at all hazards.

I agree that to ask a poet to write an epic is rather like asking an explorer to live all his life on the summit of Mount Everest. There are scraps of downright doggerel even in Shelley's *Prometheus*; and Scott's worst is laughable. Still, there is plenty of good music in the middle of the voice, and much to be said for the idle singer of an empty day.[1] I knew him, by the way, pretty well. Faithfully G. BERNARD SHAW

25 January 1938   Ayot St Lawrence,
                                                    Welwyn, Hertfordshire[2]

Dear Lord Alfred, At last I have finished this job for Mrs Harris.[3] By this post I send to the publishers (Constable's) the edited copy for Frank's *Oscar Wilde*, with a preface by me running to eighteen thousand

---

[1] The description William Morris (1834–1896) gave of himself in the prefatory verses to *The Earthly Paradise*.

[2] The country house which the Shaws leased in 1906. They did not like it, but after the outbreak of the Great War, when the owner gave them the alternative of moving or buying, they purchased the house. It was to be their residence as long as they lived.

Their 'omnibus round', as they called it, consisted in spending Thursday morning to Saturday afternoon in London, the rest of the time at Ayot.

[3] On the same day Shaw wrote: 'Dear Constable's. Here at last is this accursed job finished. I think it is lawyer proof now. Far from libelling Douglas, it gives him his first coat of whitewash'.

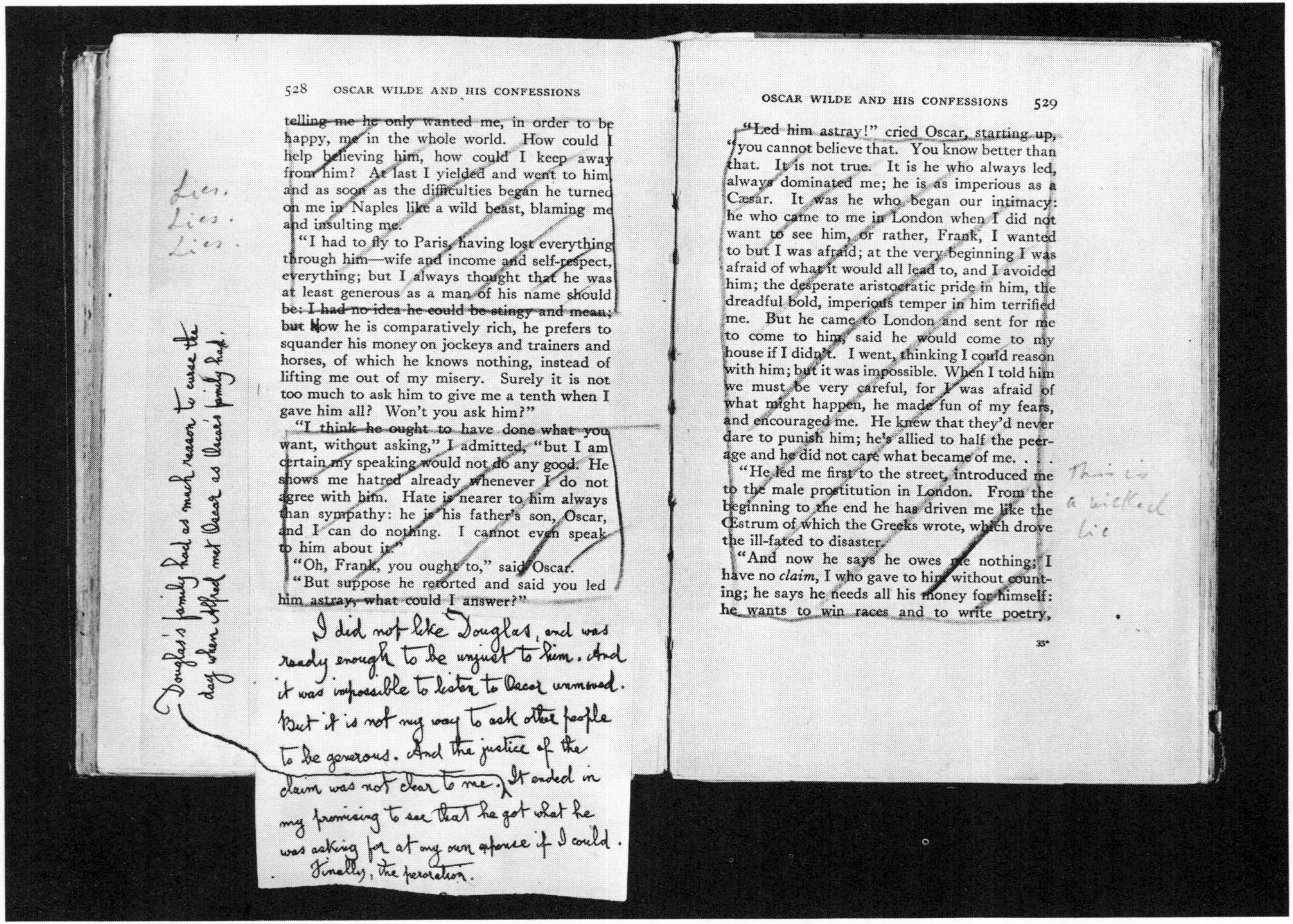
528 OSCAR WILDE AND HIS CONFESSIONS

telling me he only wanted me, in order to be happy, me in the whole world. How could I help believing him, how could I keep away from him? At last I yielded and went to him and as soon as the difficulties began he turned on me in Naples like a wild beast, blaming me and insulting me.

"I had to fly to Paris, having lost everything through him—wife and income and self-respect, everything; but I always thought that he was at least generous as a man of his name should be: I had no idea he could be stingy and mean; but Now he is comparatively rich, he prefers to squander his money on jockeys and trainers and horses, of which he knows nothing, instead of lifting me out of my misery. Surely it is not too much to ask him to give me a tenth when I gave him all? Won't you ask him?"

"I think he ought to have done what you want, without asking," I admitted, "but I am certain my speaking would not do any good. He shows me hatred already whenever I do not agree with him. Hate is nearer to him always than sympathy: he is his father's son, Oscar, and I can do nothing. I cannot even speak to him about it."

"Oh, Frank, you ought to," said Oscar.

"But suppose he retorted and said you led him astray, what could I answer?"

Lies. Lies. Lies.

Douglas's family had as much reason to curse the day when Alfred met Oscar as Oscar's family had.

I did not like Douglas, and was ready enough to be unjust to him. And it was impossible to listen to Oscar unmoved. But it is not my way to ask other people to be generous. And the justice of the claim was not clear to me. It ended in my promising to see that he got what he was asking for at my own expense if I could. Finally, the peroration.

OSCAR WILDE AND HIS CONFESSIONS 529

"Led him astray!" cried Oscar, starting up, "you cannot believe that. You know better than that. It is not true. It is he who always led, always dominated me; he is as imperious as a Cæsar. It was he who began our intimacy: he who came to me in London when I did not want to see him, or rather, Frank, I wanted to but I was afraid; at the very beginning I was afraid of what it would all lead to, and I avoided him; the desperate aristocratic pride in him, the dreadful bold, imperious temper in him terrified me. But he came to London and sent for me to come to him, said he would come to my house if I didn't. I went, thinking I could reason with him; but it was impossible. When I told him we must be very careful, for I was afraid of what might happen, he made fun of my fears, and encouraged me. He knew that they'd never dare to punish him; he's allied to half the peerage and he did not care what became of me. . . .

"He led me first to the street, introduced me to the male prostitution in London. From the beginning to the end he has driven me like the Œstrum of which the Greeks wrote, which drove the ill-fated to disaster.

"And now he says he owes me nothing; I have no *claim*, I who gave to him without counting; he says he needs all his money for himself: he wants to win races and to write poetry,

35*

This is a wicked lie

Harris's biography of Wilde, annotated by Douglas, edited by Shaw

words or so in the form of a reply to Sherard's Shaw-Harris-Wilde explosion.

Your marginal notes[1] and letters have been of great assistance. I agreed with all of them practically. What I cannot understand is why Harris would not accept them and get rid of the libellous character of the book.

I think Wilde took you both in by the game he began to amuse himself with in prison: the romance of the ill-treated hero and the cruel false friend. Once you see the character of this make-believe, all his lies and your imaginary crimes become merely comic.

I take it that the book of which you wrote to me—or shall I say threatened me with—is not yet published? So much the better: you had better hold it back until mine is out; for not only will you have the last word but, as I have made out a much better case for you than you can decently make out for yourself, you will be able to avoid spoiling it.

Is that portrait of you in the volume of *Poems* available? And is there such a thing in existence as a portrait of Thersites Crosland? Constable's may want both.[2] In great haste   G. BERNARD SHAW

29 January 1938   1 St Ann's Court, Hove

Dear Mr Shaw, You certainly are 'one of the ones'! The way in which you calmly go ahead and do what you intend to do 'in the matter of Frank Harris and others', without paying the slightest heed to the howls of protest arising from Oscar's literary executor and official biographer, Symons, and his son, Vyvyan Holland,[3] really arouses my admiration.

[1] Douglas's notes in the two volumes of Harris's *Life of Wilde* (1918). Shaw had done his editorial work with dispatch, for it was as recently as 18 December that Nellie Harris had written, 'I have been ill with a terrible cold for over two weeks. I just managed to get the two books corrected by A. Douglas off to you. I hope you received them all right. I think I told you that Frank said nearly all Alfred Douglas's statements on investigation were untrue. I wonder what you think of the corrections and notes of A. D. I would awfully like to know' (British Library Add. Mss. 50538).

[2] The drawing by Walter Spindler in Douglas's *Poems* (1896). Shaw was seemingly unaware of W. Sorley Brown's *The Life and Genius of T. W. H. Crosland* (1928), which contained a number of striking photographs of Crosland.

[3] Holland, through his solicitors, notified Constable's and Shaw that he would not allow inclusion of any part of *De Profundis*; other Wilde copyright material he would

As far as I am concerned I don't mind at all, especially as I have every confidence that you have treated me fairly, and I agree entirely that it is far better for me to be defended against Harris's and Oscar's abuse and calumny by you than by myself.

My own book, *Without Apology*, has been held up in the most exasperating and idiotic way because the solicitors of the printers (who reside in Bungay and are evidently the village idiots of that place) said it was 'dangerous', which is, I assure you, utter nonsense. I carefully refrained from making it dangerous and it is really mild and genial. As my publishers' solicitor read the book and passed it as perfectly safe and went out of his way to say he admired it very much, and as the publishers thereupon paid me a hundred and fifty pounds advance royalties, it does not really much matter to me except for the irritating delay, as if Rich and Cowan won't publish it (it is already printed and could have come out last October) I have another publisher who is panting to get it.[1] So no doubt from my point of view your getting your new edition of Frank's fairy tales in first is really entirely providential. As you say, I shall now get the last word, and I may tell you that, recognizing your good will in all this business, I have carefully gone over again what I wrote about you and removed or modified even what little there was that might have annoyed you, a thing I would certainly not have cared to do unless I could do it 'with ample satisfaction to myself'. I shall look forward with great interest to your new preface, which like everything you write (even when it maddens me) is bound to be brilliant. Yours very sincerely   ALFRED DOUGLAS

consider upon application. Shaw replied (21 April) that *De Profundis* had been expunged en bloc from the revised *Life of Wilde*, together with all matter not the copyright property of Mrs Harris or himself. He further explained that the book had been undertaken only because of the straitened circumstances of Mrs Harris and the recklessly rough handling of her husband by Sherard and Douglas. He hoped Mr Holland would be reassured by the fact that the present book 'might have been in worse hands than ours'. Holland's solicitors responded with a friendly letter saying that their client was satisfied.

[1] Martin Secker published *Without Apology* on 6 April 1938.

Pencil drawing of Douglas by Walter Spindler

Dear Lord Alfred, The book is extremely readable: I enjoyed reading it very much.[1] And it is quite convincing as to your entire sincerity as a writer of confessions and your innocence in the Wilde affair and generosity in your relations with him.

But you have not got the hang of Harris. There are in the story two George Washingtons: one who could not, and the other who would not tell a lie. One was Harris: the other was yourself. In your case this dangerous virtue was a trifle compared to the tragedy produced by your father. But Harris was ruined by it. Sherard describes him as trumpeting lies all over the place. That is exactly what he should have done to establish his place in London society. What he did do was to trumpet the truth all over the place and make himself quite impossible.

All the recriminations about lying are traceable to the lying of Wilde (his bread depended on it) when he gave up writing. He was living on you, on Harris, on Ross, on Turner (who was Turner?),[2] on all his old theatrical friends to whom he sold the Daventry plot exactly as Sheridan sold shares in Drury Lane Theatre. It was a necessary part of the game that you should each be persuaded that all the others had left him to starve. He convinced Harris that you had never given him a penny. He convinced you that Harris had cheated him basely over *Daventry*. And so on with all the rest. Harris believed him when he wrote his life of Wilde. You still believe his tales about Harris. And Harris died convinced of your mendacity. In truth there was only one master-liar in the case; and he was Oscar.

Let me again remind you that I am an Irishman. I know that there is

---

[1] Douglas wrote comments on Shaw's letters on separate sheets of paper (see the Postscript, pp. 200–201). His note here was that *Without Apology*, though it contained 'some pretty severe criticism of Shaw (which he took in the most good-natured and friendly way), was the actual cause of the subsequent very friendly and affectionate relations which are revealed by this correspondence'.

[2] Reginald Turner (1869–1938), illegitimate son of Lionel Lawson, originally Levy (1824–1879), part owner of the *Daily Telegraph* and builder of two London theatres, the Queen's and the Gaiety. See Introduction to *Max Beerbohm: Letters to Reggie Turner*, ed. Rupert Hart-Davis (1964). Turner was always loyal to Oscar. He not only met him at Dieppe after his release from prison, but also was with him when he died in Paris. By the 1930s Turner was living in Italy.

Shaw at Ayot St Lawrence

no beggar on earth as shameless as an Irish beggar. I have seen them beg when they are perfectly well-off—beg from poor people. And I know that flexibility which enables an Irishman to charm you to your face, and tear you to pieces the moment your back is turned. When I said that Oscar was incapable of friendship (as you understand it) I knew what I was talking about.

Harris disliked you, and said so frankly. Another man would have disparaged you to gratify his dislike. Harris alone placed you at the top of the tree, and never retreated a step from that estimate. It was this knowledge of the difference between chalk and cheese, and this courage in trumpeting his opinion that made Harris's editorship of the *Saturday Review* the success it was. Whatever he was he was neither a liar nor a hypocrite; and you and Sherard owe his ghost an apology for dismissing him as a combination of Pecksniff and Montague Tigg.[1]

But there is one thing that you perhaps do not know. You accuse him of a specific attempt to blackmail you. His notions of business morality were so American that it is possible that he regarded blackmail as one of the legitimate ways of making money out of journalism. But he behaved exactly as if he knew nothing of the attempt. He took no notice of your attacks in your paper; and was genuinely astonished and hurt by your treatment of him at the Café Royal.

Perhaps you do not know that Harris collapsed as a writer very much as Wilde did. He was the nominal editor of at least four papers after the *Saturday*, and no doubt drew a salary for the goodwill, such as it was, of his name in the bill. But that was all they got out of him. The first of them, the *Candid Friend*, engaged him for a day or two in a vain attempt to rally his old *Saturday* staff round him; but it was run by Lady Jessica Sykes,[2] a clever woman and a heavy drinker, until it perished. As to *Vanity Fair*, it contained an article abusing me up hill and down dale over the signature 'F. H.' It did not contain a sentence that he could have written or would have written. Finally he found himself in prison for stuff that he knew nothing about.

[1] Mr Pecksniff, the arch-hypocrite, and Montague Tigg, adventurer and swindler, characters in Dickens's *Martin Chuzzlewit*.

[2] Anne Christina Jessica (1856–1912), daughter of George Augustus Cavendish-Bentinck, married Sir Tatton Sykes in 1874. She was a journalist and author.

Are you quite sure that he knew anything about the attempt to black-mail you? When he was banished by the war and had really to edit a rag called *Pearson's Magazine* he reprinted any mortal screed of his sooner than write fresh stuff. The *Saturday* finished him as a writer just as Wormwood Scrubs finished Oscar.[1] [Frank's] attempt to write a book about me was pitiable. Drink and pneumonia disabled him. He was never drunk to my knowledge; but then he was never sober in my fashion.

As to your final denunciation of me as a dangerous man, you are quite right: I am as fatal to retired majors and pensioned governesses as I could possibly desire to be, though they won't die, damn them! How is it that the fragment of mind that you exercise is so first rate whilst all the rest prefers the *Patriot* to the *New Statesman*? But I bear no malice: I am used to it; and the Harris preface will be my revenge. By the way, it ought to be issued as edited by Lord Alfred Douglas; for I agreed with all your notes and made no attempt to improve on them. The book is now perfectly presentable; and I hope its publication will do you a service as showing for the first time that the Queensberry affair was your tragedy and, comparatively, Wilde's comedy.

I enclose a little present.[2] Einstein is a poet.   G. B. S.

20 April 1938   1 St Ann's Court, Hove

Dear Mr Shaw, Thanks for your letter and for the Einstein book. I haven't read a line of the latter yet. When I do read it I'll write and tell you what I think. As to the Wilde business, the trouble with you is that you don't know the facts and I do. It is absurd to say that I 'believed Wilde's tales about Harris'. It was not a question of believing any tales. I was with Wilde in Paris the whole time the *Mr and Mrs Daventry* business was going on and I was also at the time continually with Harris. Oscar told me the story of the play, act by act, at least a dozen times before Harris had ever heard of it. I was present, exactly as described in my book, at Durand's restaurant, when Harris persuaded him to

---

[1] Shaw is mistaken: Wilde was never at Wormwood Scrubs.
[2] *The Evolution of Physics*, Albert Einstein and Leopold Infeld (1938).

consent to his (Harris's) writing the play and sharing the profits. The rest of the story is just history. The play was produced and ran a hundred and fifty nights. Harris took all the credit of authorship and all the profits and did not give Oscar a penny after the fifty pounds he gave him at Durand's. Then Oscar died, chiefly of rage because of this. That Oscar was unscrupulous about money after he came out of prison I have never denied. I said so myself in my *Autobiography*, but you are unfair to him and you always have been, just as you are unaccountably prejudiced in favour of Harris. I don't agree that Harris was not a liar and a hypocrite. I think he was both! However this sort of argument is futile at this stage. I must read your preface and say what I think after I have read it.

As to the *Patriot*[1] (does it still exist?) and the *New Statesman*, I never read either of them if I can help it. I bought a copy of the *New Statesman* the other day because it had an advertisement of my book in it. Having bought it I read it and was bored and irritated by its stupidity and denseness and its one-note howl. There was an article by Leonard Woolf[2] (or is he Wolfe?) which seemed to me to be so stupid and senseless that I could not understand how any editor could bring himself to print it. I have not seen a copy of the *Patriot* for at least ten years, and I doubt if I ever read it more than two or three times in my life. I read a brilliant article by you in the *London Mercury* about a month ago about *Cymbeline*.[3] I thought it extraordinarily good though it did not *quite* convince me.

As you ask, 'who was Turner?', he was a great friend of Max Beerbohm and he lived for years in the same house as Robert Ross and More Adey. He now lives in Florence. You are wrong again when you say that Wilde 'lived on (among others) Ross'. Ross in those days was

---

[1] A conservative weekly published from 1922 to 1947.

[2] A review of G. G. Coulton's *Inquisition and Liberty* (9 April 1938) to the effect that the barbarous methods of the Catholic church's Inquisition were now being practised in the name of Fascism, National Socialism and Communism.

[3] 'Cymbeline Refinished: A Variation' (February 1938) was Shaw's new and, he claimed, better final act for Shakespeare's play. 'It bore the test quite well', he commented, 'when it was pluckily produced at the Embassy Theatre' in London, though Stratford 'funked it at the last moment for fear of shocking their American patrons, to whom the text of Shakespeare is supposed to be sacred'.

almost penniless. He began to make money (chiefly by his able exploiting of Oscar) only about five or six years later.

As to the blackmail business, how could I be mistaken? The man who came to see me from Harris was Edgar Jepson. I had his name in my original manuscript of *Without Apology* but the publishers (who were then Rich and Cowan) made me take it out.

When is the Harris book coming out? I look forward to your preface.[1] Your theories are brilliant and stimulating, but as I've already said they are more often than not (in this particular business) refuted by hard facts and what actually happened. Yours sincerely

ALFRED DOUGLAS

24 April 1938   Ayot St Lawrence

Dear Lord Alfred, If your bank account will stand it don't think of fighting [Rich and Cowan]. Even if you win hands down it will cost you in time and worry and collection of evidence a thousand pounds. There is nothing like a lump of solid gold straight in the face to put this sort of assailant on the spot. Cheap that, I assure you, at a hundred and fifty pounds.

Besides, it is not certain that you will win, though I do not know enough for my opinion to be worth anything on that point. The law of libel is very tricky. Almost any remark that you can make about a living man may be construable as a libel. I, as a critic, have been libelling people all my life. What has protected me is partly the fear of the boycott which pursues a litigant (you have suffered from this yourself) and partly the possibility of a farthing damages. Also there is the curious privilege of 'vulgar abuse', under which you may vituperate with impunity provided you do not suggest that your adversary has had his cheque dishonoured, or carries on two domestic establishments: above all, that you have not done him out of his job, which a jury never pardons.

[1] Nellie Harris had returned the preface proof to Shaw, saying in her note of 12 March, 'I have read it several times with absorbing interest. It is a masterpiece, you certainly have made mincemeat of Sherard in a very lovely way. Only you in all the world could have done this'.

Unfortunately these protections do not operate as between publisher and author. If a publisher buys a pig in a poke to the extent of advancing a hundred and fifty pounds on a manuscript which he has not read, the author, in accepting the advance, gives an implied undertaking that he will deliver a lawfully publishable book. And if this condition is fulfilled the publisher is bound to publish the book within a reasonable time if none is specified.

Therefore the case turns on whether your manuscript is lawfully publishable; and here is where the extreme indefiniteness of the law comes in. Rich and Cowan (alias Strabolgi and Company)[1] will have to produce passages from your manuscript, publication of which would expose them to prosecution for seditious, obscene or blasphemous libel or a civil action for damages. If they can do this (which is probable enough, as you are a hard hitter and rather a reckless one) you are done for: they will get a verdict with costs; and you will be heavily down on the cash balance. They must have taken counsel's opinion on the point.

If not, their action is unaccountable and unintelligible. Have you had any quarrel with them? They cannot complain of *Without Apology*, which will certainly pay its way if it is fairly advertised. I cannot help concluding that there is something that they are really afraid to publish; and what frightens them will frighten the jury.

But anyhow you had better play the haughty aristocrat and fling the money back in their faces, even if you have to borrow it for the purpose. You should know better than most people how much time and worry a lawsuit costs even if you are the victor.

This is all I can say in my ignorance of the particulars. In great haste

G. BERNARD SHAW

P.S. I had forgotten that Jepson was Harris's ghost on *Vanity Fair*. Jepson was *capable de tout*.

I always made a point of treating Wilde with great respect as a serious writer, scrupulously avoiding the current Oscar-Jimmy [Whistler] badinage in the fashionable weeklies. Oscar made a point of doing exactly the same with me. The consequence was that when we met, which was

[1] Lieutenant Commander Joseph Montague Kenworthy, R. N., tenth Baron Strabolgi (1886–1953), a Labour M.P. and a director of Rich and Cowan.

seldom, we put one another out absurdly until at last we met accidentally in an exhibition in Chelsea, when he entertained me with a first-rate performance as raconteur. After his imprisonment I sent him all my books as they came out, thus keeping up my policy of distinguished consideration; and he sent me all his. The only jar in our relations was when I denounced *The Importance of Being Earnest* for the mechanical farce which it is. But I don't think that rankled for very long. You must always remember that we were Irishmen, resenting strongly the English practice of making pets of Irishmen. We understood one another on this point, and thereby made our relationship quite unintelligible in England.

25 April 1938 [postcard]   Ayot St Lawrence

I forgot to say that the Einstein book is not a joke. Just put it by until you feel the necessary curiosity about the revolution in physics which has taken place in our time. You see, the whole Catholic philosophy is founded, on its scientific side, on Aquinas, who was founded on Aristotle, a pagan whose works were made virtually canonical in the thirteenth century. Nowadays a Catholic who is ignorant of Einstein is as incomplete as a thirteenth-century Dominican ignorant of Aristotle.

The protest against scientific physics was led by Luther, Melanchthon and the Protestants generally. Religion without science is mere small-mindedness.   G. B. S.

26 April 1938   1 St Ann's Court, Hove

Dear Mr Shaw, It is very kind of you to write and give me what might be good advice if it were in my power to carry it out. Unfortunately however I haven't got a hundred and fifty pounds or anything like it. Moreover Rich and Cowan are suing me not only for that but also for sixty-five pounds (the printers' bill) and for damages for the 'loss they have sustained by their non-publication of the book' (which they themselves refused to publish)! This sounds quite crazy, but it is the fact nevertheless. However the case won't cost me a thousand pounds to fight. Bitter constraint and sad occasion have taught me how to fight cases on the cheap. When I got a thousand pounds damages from the *Evening News*[1] (three days in court and cross-examined for six hours by the subsequent Attorney General and Lord Chancellor, Hogg) the whole thing cost me exactly seventy-five pounds, which I recovered with the costs when I won the action. My counsel Comyns Carr's fee was twenty-five pounds, Hogg had five hundred and refreshers. If I had only a hundred pounds now I should be quite at ease. But for the moment I don't know where to get it. The case is much simpler and much more favourable to me than you imagine. Rich and Cowan asked me to write the book and accepted it, when I delivered the manuscript, with great satisfaction. Their own solicitor read it and passed it as perfectly safe after I had at his request 'modified' about half a dozen passages. They then gave me a hundred and fifty pounds advance royalties. It was all printed and the proofs revised and ready for publication when the *printers* suddenly announced that it was a 'dangerous book' and that they declined to print it (that is to say machine it off, for it was already set up and completely printed). Thereupon Rich and Cowan calmly told me that under the circumstances they could not proceed with the publication. Naturally I told them that if they didn't publish it I would sue them for breach of contract. Then Secker (quite miraculously and in reply to prayers!) came to the scene and took it over. So I came to the conclusion that I would not sue for breach of contract although I certainly had a very strong case, and I was content to keep the hundred and fifty pounds (which by that time was all gone) and let them off any further damages. Secker printed the book without altering a word exactly as it left Rich and Cowan's hands, which in itself proves that it is a perfectly 'safe' book.

I don't think I can possibly lose the case, and my only trouble is where to get the small sum I need to go through the preliminary business which solicitors have to do and pay the fee for counsel. I was relying

[1] On 4 February 1921 this paper printed a false report of Douglas's death and an unfriendly obituary, written by Arthur Machen, who said among other things that, 'poetry excepted', Lord Alfred 'did nothing and worse than nothing'. Douglas sued for libel. He received a favourable verdict, costs and damages of a thousand pounds.

on my nephew Queensberry but he has let me down.[1] I am going to try to soften his heart. He has heaps of money, but 'things have been going badly in the City' lately and he is having a fit of meanness. On other occasions he has been very kind and generous. I am full of troubles and very worried and meanwhile my book is apparently being boycotted by the reviewers. I would be only too glad to avoid the action but, unless I fight it, Rich and Cowan will get judgement against me and sell me up! I only have five hundred pounds a year. So what can I do? Poets in England invariably get this sort of treatment (that is, of course, if they are real poets). Yours very sincerely

ALFRED DOUGLAS

27 April 1938   1 St Ann's Court, Hove

Dear Mr Shaw, What on earth induced you to send me that ghastly book *The Evolution of Physics*? *Pour qui me prenez vous*? If I were stranded on a desert island with the book and had nothing else to read I still would not read it. I would rather pass the time saying a few rosaries for your conversion to Catholicism. It deals with subjects which have no interest for me at all. You say that Einstein is a 'poet'. Well, all I can say is that he evidently belongs to the school of T. S. Eliot and Auden, or perhaps it would be more correct to say that they belong to the school of Einstein. Come off it! Or perhaps the whole thing is an elaborate joke, and I have missed the point. If so, consider my infantile complex and explain.

I am going through fearful tribulations because [of] the firm of publishers, Rich and Cowan. . . . This morning I received a letter from their solicitors claiming *damages* for their loss in not having published the book!! They having refused to publish it on the ground that it was full of libels. This sounds quite fantastically insane, but I can assure you that it is sober truth, and that in their letter this morning they ask for the name of my solicitors who will accept service of a writ. I suppose I shall

[1] Francis Archibald Kelhead Douglas (1896–1954), educated at Harrow, an officer in the Black Watch in the Great War, in peacetime a stockbroker. Francis became the eleventh Marquess of Queensberry in 1920, upon the death of his father, Douglas's brother Percy.

now be let in for another lawsuit. I shall of course defend the action and counter-claim for damages for breach of contract. The only consolation I can find is that it will make great publicity for my book.... There was a favourable and fairly lengthy review in the *Times Literary Supplement* [9 April 1938] two days after publication, but since then almost a complete blank. I got a wire from James Agate saying 'many thanks for the delightful book' but not a word of notice from him so far in his *Express* weekly columns.[1] It is really very exasperating. Not that I care a hoot what they say but because I want a few people to read my book. (This isn't true, I *do* care in some cases, and I have a high opinion of Agate as a critic.) Secker however tells me that it is 'going well'. I make a joke of it but really I am *fearfully worried* about Rich and Cowan's threatened action. I was hoping that I would never have another action, although I don't see how I can possibly lose this one, even if I conduct it myself without counsel.

Really, of course, it was kind of you to send me the Einstein nightmare, as the dedication from you makes it valuable and atones for the fearful boredom of the text, which I need not read anyhow, or must I?

I have just realized that in my book I referred to *Cashel Byron's Profession* when I meant *The Admirable Bashville*, also I said Mrs Quickly when I meant Doll Tearsheet (apologies to you and Shakespeare).[2] I wish I saw you sometimes as although we disagree about nearly everything I believe you would give me good advice on mundane affairs.
Yours most sincerely   ALFRED DOUGLAS

28 April 1938   1 St Ann's Court, Hove

Dear Mr Shaw, 'And which of you if he ask his father bread, will he give him a stone? Or a fish will he give him a serpent? Or if he ask for an egg will he reach him a scorpion?' I quote from the Douai Version (Luke XI:11 and 12).

You reach me a scorpion in the shape of that book by Einstein and his

---

[1] Agate (1877–1947) was drama critic of the *Sunday Times* and literary critic of the *Daily Express*.
[2] See *Without Apology*, pp. 28 and 85.

partner in crime, when what I obviously wanted was an egg or something of a comfortable nature. It would have been far more to the point if you had offered to lend me a hundred pounds to enable me to repel the utterly unprovoked and really brutal attack of the firm which you rightly call 'Strabolgi and Co'. I had vaguely noticed that Strabolgi's name was printed at the head of Rich and Cowan's notepaper, as one of the directors, but, till you rubbed it in, the true explanation of the whole business was not brought home to me. You certainly have (to return your compliment to me) 'an efficient and acute mind'. I suppose Strabolgi (whom I met and took a deep dislike to some years ago, at a country house in Scotland) read my book, after the comparatively innocent Commander Rich and Mr Cowan had accepted and liked it very much, and said, "I object to publishing this foul attack on all the principles which I hold most dear". They then proceeded to do their damnedest to squash my book and me. Then when the prayers of the Franciscans at Greyfriars (Oxford) miraculously brought forth Martin Secker out of the void to take over the book which they imagined they had scotched, Strabolgi and his partners naturally got very angry and said, "If we can't squash his book, we can at least give him a very bad time by forcing him to defend a bogus action and throwing mud at him in the law courts". Charming gentlemen these Left-Wingers! What on earth you are doing *dans cette galère* I have never been able to understand. I shall continue to say rosaries for your conversion to Catholicism. I said the whole fifteen decades for you about ten days ago late at night in bed after I got your really very kind first letter on receiving my book, which is still being boycotted by all the reviewers. I am going up to London tomorrow to see the solicitors who are representing me in this action, Gilbert Samuel and Co of Great Winchester Street. They are Queensberry's solicitors. If—or I suppose I must say when—the case gets into court I will deal with Strabolgi in the witness box and apply the principles of 'le système Douglas'[1] to him. He may get an unpleasant sur-

---

[1] His method for defeating cross-examination; to tell 'the exact truth' and even to volunteer added admissions in anticipation of the examiner's next questions. Of one opposing counsel he said, 'My instant and fierce reply flabbergasted him and immediately won the sympathy of the jury. . . . To win a case, all you have to do is to "get" the jury' (*Without Apology*, pp. 206–207).

prise. At any rate the case will be a huge advertisement for my book.

Another perfectly imbecile book about Shakespeare's sonnets by a Mr. Thomson has, I see, appeared and is reviewed in tonight's *Evening Standard*, and the reviewer brings in two references to me and my book on the same subject.[1] When I picked up the paper tonight and saw my name, I thought, "Hurrah, here at last is a long review of *Without Apology*". So you can imagine my disgust when I saw that it was merely a quite brainless 'boost' of Thomson's half-witted book. Yours very sincerely   ALFRED DOUGLAS

29 April 1938   4 Whitehall Court, London

Dear Lord Alfred, This beats me. A printer should read his copy before he sets it up.

For the moment I have no time to say more than that your banker will let you overdraw by one hundred pounds if I guarantee it. If the worst comes to the worst Queensberry may be persuaded to liquidate an overdraft for the credit of the family. He certainly will not put his hand in his pocket to oblige me; so do not let me appear as your backer.

I will send you proofs of the Wilde volume and preface as soon as I can get a clean copy. You had better have a look at it.[2] In haste to catch the eleven o'clock post   G. BERNARD SHAW

29 April 1938   1 St Ann's Court, Hove

Dear Mr Shaw, I have just got back from London and find your letter. I am *deeply* touched by your kindness. In fact I hardly know what to

---

[1] *The Sonnets of Shakespeare and Southampton*, by Walter Thomson (1938). Mr Thomson suggested that a hundred of the sonnets were written by Shakespeare, the rest by Southampton and constituted 'comment and reply exchanged between loving friends'. 'Mr W. H.' stood for 'a compound of William and Henry'. The reviewer commented that Mr Thomson has proved his case and left Willie Hughes a discredited claimant.

[2] On 8 April, Otto Kyllmann, who was in charge of Harris's book at Constable's, had written to Shaw saying it was essential that Douglas read the preface and 'write that he will not take action about it'. He also thought Douglas should read all Shaw's revised text.

say at present. I must write again when I have had time to consider what I ought to do. My solicitor (Mr Hart of Gilbert Samuel and Co) gave me a fairly strong hint this afternoon that it was quite likely that nothing may come of the case after all. He said he could not say more at present, but that he inclined to think that Rich and Cowan and their solicitors, with whom he seems to be rather 'thick', were beginning to realize that the nature of my financial position was such that they might come to the conclusion that they would have very little chance of getting any-thing out of me even if they succeeded in winning their case. All my income (apart from the trifles I earn by writing) is derived from what are called 'voluntary allowances'. This may be rather an inglorious way of getting out of trouble, but if Rich and Cowan drop the proceedings against me I in turn shall certainly not continue my claim for damages for breach of contract. Anyhow whatever happens I shall never forget your kindness. It ought to make Francis Q. blush if he ever hears of it! You really are an *angel*.

I see that Harold Nicolson, in a very fine notice of my book in today's *Daily Telegraph*, says that you emerge from my book as 'an imp of Charity'.[1] Substituting 'angel' for 'imp' this is a prophetic utterance. Yours ever sincerely   ALFRED DOUGLAS

30 April 1938   1 St Ann's Court, Hove

My dear Mr Shaw, I am rushing this off early to catch the post. I will write again tomorrow. On the other question and your generous offer I will give you my matured thought. I find it difficult to write to you now without getting 'sloppy', which I know you would hate. But it's a fact that when I got your letter last night (being then worn out and fatigued and having just received the blow of getting the enclosed wire

[1] Nicolson (1886–1968, knighted 1953), a diplomat, author and critic, said in the re-view that the 'pre-eminent poet' had written a 'generous and urbane' book, much more than 'random recollections of [his] stormy life', for in it 'he makes peace with society' and is now 'kind even about Frank Harris and André Gide. Mr Shaw comes out of the volume as an imp of charity. And to the memory of his own father Lord Alfred makes generous amends. . . . He disproves—and I trust forever—the legend that he deserted Wilde in his ordeal'.

from my poor darling wife at Bembridge) the tears ran down my cheeks.[1]
Beautiful actions, like beautiful music, always make me inclined to cry.

The preface is *immense*. You have never done anything better.[2] Yours
ever   A. D.

P.S. Please send me another copy of the preface.

2 May 1938   1 St Ann's Court, Hove

My dear Mr Shaw, I have been thinking over this Rich and Cowan
business and I feel certain that while there is a good chance that they
will drop the action *eventually*, it would be fatal for me to show any
sign of weakening. This means that my solicitors . . . must put all my
case forward, including my claim for damages for breach of contract,
and also of course accept service of the writ for me and put in the statement of claim on my side. I must have money to do this (and moreover
it is still quite possible that the case *will* go on) and as you so nobly
offer to help me by guaranteeing a hundred pounds overdraft at my
bank, I will, with your permission, see the manager of the bank (The
National Bank of Scotland, 37 Nicholas Lane, Lombard Street) and
arrange it. I suppose he will write to you and ask you to sign a guarantee.
Please let me know if this is all right. It is impossible for me adequately
to express my gratitude. Yours ever   ALFRED DOUGLAS

P.S. I have written to Sherard and told him that when he sees your
preface he will be convinced that he has profoundly misjudged you, and
I have told him (what is the truth) that you have treated him most
kindly. I feel sure that this will be a great relief to his mind as the poor
old chap has been worrying himself, I know, and he is pretty ill and, as
he says, feels that his 'number is up'. You have really left him nothing
to feel indignant about and you have demolished his case so completely

---

[1] 'TERRIBLY UPSET BY YOUR LETTER TOO ILL TO WRITE BUT SURELY FRANCIS WILL HELP
FONDEST LOVE AND SYMPATHY'

[2] Douglas wired Constable's: 'THE PREFACE IS SUPERB POSTED PROOF WITH MARGINAL
NOTES'. Douglas's numerous notes were sent on to Shaw to deal with, but he accepted
very few of the suggestions.

(and yet in such a genial friendly way) that I shall be very much surprised if he does not 'forever hold his peace' hereafter about the whole business.

4 May 1938   1 St Ann's Court, Hove

My dear Mr Shaw, The enclosed copy of a letter posted this morning to the author of that perfectly idiotic book about the sonnets may amuse you. All the ridiculous reviewers, including Ivor Brown, have been praising the book and saying that it 'solves the problem of the sonnets'!

I see your delightful play *You Never Can Tell* was revived last night. Congratulations, but please don't forget that till I hear from you in confirmation of that amazingly kind offer of yours I am on tenterhooks, and that anxiety, like a worm in the bud, feeds on my damask cheek to the great detriment of my peace of mind and my ability to sleep of nights. My solicitors sent me a copy of the letter they have addressed to Rich and Cowan's solicitors. I was much pleased with it, as it shows that my solicitor, Mr Hart, is an intelligent man and that he has completely grasped my case, which was just what I feared he had not done when I saw him. I had a barrister lunching with me here last Sunday and he assured me that Rich and Cowan have no case. All the same I fully expect them to take it on to the last stages, if not right into court. Yours ever   ALFRED DOUGLAS

P.S. I hope you don't mind my quoting (in the letter to Thomson) your praise of my book about the sonnets. It's no use getting testimonials from the great and good if one does not use them.

4 May 1938 [postcard]   4 Whitehall Court, London

Quite right. Give my bank as a reference: The Westminster, 109 New Oxford Street.

I must make some changes in view of *Without Apology*. The breakdown at Naples (the correspondence with your mother is extraordinarily touching)[1] is a major incident in the *Life*. Which of the twain was the impossible person to live with?   G. B. S.

6 May 1938   1 St Ann's Court, Hove

My dear Mr Shaw, A thousand thanks for your card. I have now written to my bank manager and told him what you say. You really are an angel.[2] I have been trying to think of a good name for you. I hate writing 'Mr Shaw'. I think 'St Christopher' is about the most appropriate one. May I use it when writing to you? Also, I know it's all rather foolish, but I would much rather you didn't go on calling me 'Lord Alfred'. Couldn't you drop the 'Lord' and call me 'Alfred' (or 'Bosie' if you don't share my grandfather's objection to the name, see page 232 of *Without Apology*)? 'Alfred' is really a good name and I sometimes wish it was more used for me.

I feel bound to pass on to you what my wife, Olive, wrote to me when I told her that you had so gallantly come to my rescue, because in her letter she says, '*Do please tell him what I say*'. Here it is: 'Bernard Shaw is really a Darling. . . . I have always admired him as a great man of genius. . . . but now I simply love him for his kindness to you'. (The dots, ..., are not indicative of words omitted, she always has used them instead of commas or semicolons.) I am delighted to hear that you are going to add to the preface in the light of what I have added to the story of the Wilde business in *Without Apology*, and particularly in relation to those old letters to my mother.[3] This will be an additional thing to look forward to in connection with the publication of your splendid preface. When will the book be out? Yours ever

                                                 ALFRED DOUGLAS

[1] Two letters which had been written by Douglas to his mother in December 1897, bearing overwhelming evidence of his loyalty to Wilde after he had left Oscar in the villa at Naples, had 'turned up almost miraculously out of the ashes of the past' (*Without Apology*, pp. 297–305).

[2] When Rich and Cowan heard of Shaw's backing they gave Douglas no further trouble.

[3] Despite what he had written on 4 May, Shaw never found time to mention Douglas's letters to his mother nor even *Without Apology* in his preface. He was driven beyond endurance by his own work and was on the point of physical collapse.

Olive Eleanor Custance Douglas

P.S. It's amazing and satisfactory beyond words that you should turn out, after all, to be a sort of saint. I never could really love anyone unless he or she were good, however brilliant and gifted and clever. Nearly all the men I have been devoted to have been really, I fear, rather bad, though I have always tried to 'kid' myself into thinking that they were really good at the back of it all.

In church last Sunday when the priest read the Gospel, which was that beautiful passage 'I am the Good Shepherd, I know my sheep and mine know me' (I quote from memory), when he came to 'other sheep I have which are not of this fold' I immediately thought, 'That's dear Bernard Shaw'. It explained everything about you in a flash and showed that I had always misjudged you, though (honestly) I always did like you without knowing why.

8 May 1938   Ayot St Lawrence

Dear Lord Alfred, Don't quarrel with a good name: it would come very well in a ballad epic by Walter Scott. The only practicable alternative is Childe Alfred, which is out of date. Alfred has been appropriated by the costermongers;[1] and Alph is the name of an immortal river.[2]

As to Bosie, half your misfortunes are due to it. Your grandfather was right about it. It always sets a jingle going in my head:

> If boozy be bosie, as some folks miscall it
> Then Bosie is boozy, whatever befall it.[3]

I prefer Childe Alfred to the dark tower came,[4] which has excellent initials, C. A. I can use these if you like.

As for me, I am Mister to the mob, and G. B. S. to everyone else.

Your banker, instead of sending the bond straight to me, has sent it to my banker, who will no doubt send it on to me.

---

[1] Alf or Alfie and Liza or Eliza were common cockney names. The Doolittles in Shaw's *Pygmalion* are examples.

[2] In Coleridge's 'Kubla Khan'.

[3] The jingle is inked out by Douglas but can be read.

[4] As in 'Child Rowland to the dark tower came', *King Lear*, Act III, scene 4.

The Oliviate [Olive's] system of punctuation is an admirable one. H. G. Wells found out the value of dots, but makes only one use of them. Yours, devilishly old   G. B. S.

10 May 1938   1 St Ann's Court, Hove

Dear St Christopher, (I refuse to call you 'Mister' or even 'G. B. S.') I don't like that 'jingle' of yours. It sounds to me much more like Frank Harris than Bernard Shaw, and in any case I don't see much point in it, or why you should quote it at me as you have done once before. I think it's distinctly unkind. But I accept 'Childe Alfred' as a name, and I think it is really rather appropriate (partly because I often come to dark towers, though I generally get out of them all right and escape by magic casements) and partly because it has a pleasant sound and nimbly and sweetly recommends itself. I continue to say rosaries for you and to put you on pedestals.

I have just returned from Olive in the Isle of Wight. I find a long letter from Abbot Sir David Hunter-Blair[1] in which he tells me that my account of the incident at the Catholic Poetry Society's meeting is 'quite accurate' except that he denies that it was Noyes who 'frighted' him with 'false fire'. The culprit, he says, was Lord Edmund Talbot (now Lord Fitzalan). The Abbot is now evidently much 'worked up' by the whole thing and asks me if I can arrange another meeting where he could deliver his lecture on 'Oscar Wilde as I Knew Him'. Unfortunately, however, the Catholic Poetry Society is now dead and buried. The Abbot really pretty well killed it himself by his failure to turn up at that meeting, as I think there were only about three more meetings after that. I think he now realizes that he was very foolish and weak to allow himself to be bullied, and the fact that the process was performed by Lord Edmund Talbot instead of Noyes (who, however, he says he

[1] Hunter-Blair (1853–1939), Wilde's close friend 'Dunskie' at Oxford, was converted to Roman Catholicism while there. He became a Benedictine and rose to become Abbot of Fort Augustus. For the sudden cancellation of his lecture, see *Without Apology*, pp. 254–264. The Abbot finally told his story of Wilde as an essay in *Victorian Days and Other Papers* (1939).

knows was 'bitterly opposed' to his lecturing) doesn't let him out very much. On the contrary, Noyes at least is a sort of semblance of a minor poet while Lord Fitzalan is merely a bore of the first water, and his objection to the lecture on Wilde stamps him as a hypocrite and bankrupt of charity. I have told the Abbot that he had much better write the whole story in a book or pamphlet and I have offered to ask Secker to publish it which I feel sure he would do. In fact the Abbot says, "I still intend to do it either in writing or by word of mouth. Of course I am under no obligation to Lord Fitzalan and the story ought to be told, and soon or I shall be dead".

I don't accept you as being 'devilishly old' or old at all. You are distinctly of the genus Phoenix. In fact you are obviously *the* Phoenix. Yours ever   CHILDE ALFRED

12 May 1938 [postcard]   4 Whitehall Court, London

I signed up this morning [the guarantee]; so all is in order.

G. B. S.

13 May 1938   1 St Ann's Court, Hove

Dear St Christopher, It was very kind and thoughtful of you to send me that card which I got this morning. I was expecting a letter from my bank and was wondering when it would arrive, and then your card came. A thousand thanks. Yours ever   CHILDE ALFRED

P.S. I am greatly looking forward now to the publication of Harris's new edition with your preface. I see the papers have been writing about it. I suppose you do not know yet when it will be out? I hope soon. I would greatly appreciate seeing a proof of the preface with the additions you have made. I was to have gone on Monday to my niece (or ex-niece!) Lady Dunn at Norwich House, Norfolk Street, Park Lane, but this morning I had a letter from her putting me off till the following week. So I shall come on Tuesday the 24th and remain a few days. She was Queensberry's first wife and left him and married Sir James Dunn.[1] That's why I call her my 'ex-niece'.

I sent a copy of my book to Lord Fitzalan, as the Abbot told me that it was he and not Noyes who had squashed the Abbot's lecture on Wilde at Shane Leslie's[2] house (chap. xxx of my book) and have just had a formal letter of thanks from him. Chap. xxx will probably give him a *mauvais quart d'heure*, as he will realize that the Abbot has 'spilled the beans' and that this is why I have sent him the book. 'Shake quoth the dove-house.'[3]

16 May 1938   1 St Ann's Court, Hove

Dear St Christopher, I have just made the discovery, to my great surprise, that in three editions I have here of Shakespeare '*Child* Rowland to the dark tower came' is printed as I have written it. I always thought it was 'childe'. I have now looked the word up in the dictionary, which I find makes no distinction between the two words, merely gives 'child' in its sixth or seventh sense as 'a youth of gentle birth', and adds at the end 'sometimes childe or chylde'. I don't suspect you for a moment of not knowing all about this, and doubtless you were punningly referring back to my 'infantile complex' which is a thing I don't deny and am really rather pleased to have recognized (especially by saints who spend more than half their time carrying children across deep rivers) so please don't think I am complaining. Quite the contrary. But in your letter you quoted 'Childe Alfred to the dark tower came'. Perhaps it is printed like that in some edition of *Lear*. Please elucidate this point.

I have sent a long letter to the *Times Literary Supplement* in reply to a

---

[1] Francis Queensberry [1896–1954] in 1917 married a Gaiety actress, Irene Richards, and by her had a daughter, Patricia Sybil. The marriage was dissolved in 1925; in the following year the Marchioness married Sir James Dunn, a Canadian financier, and the Marquess married an artist, Cathleen Mann.

[2] Sir Shane Leslie (1885–1971), graduate of Eton and Cambridge, a versatile author and a man of remarkable personality. A first cousin of Sir Winston Churchill.

[3] Nurse to Juliet, *Romeo and Juliet*, Act I, scene 3.

peculiarly imbecile article[1] on the subject of the sonnets and 'W. H.' which appears in the current number. I hope they will print my letter. Probably they will, because the editor, Bruce Richmond[2] (though I don't know him personally), has always been very kind and friendly to me in the pages and has never yet failed to print any letter I wrote to him. Perhaps you will 'butt in' when you see my letter (in which I have quoted you). I hope so. The nonsense which is written about the sonnets really makes me sick with irritation.

Just had a gloomy letter from my stock-broking nephew Q., who says he is on the verge of ruin. However I am not unduly perturbed, as I have noticed that all people who have anything to do with 'the City' always go on like that. My nephew came into nothing at all, as my father and my brother Percy got rid of seven hundred and fifty thousand pounds as well as all the landed property in Scotland. So, as he made himself a rich man out of nothing in about twenty years, I think he will come out all right. Yours   CHILDE ALFRED

20 May 1938   1 St Ann's Court, Hove

Dear San Christophero, You never write to me now. Why is this? But of course I know you are always frightfully busy. I expect you will have seen my letter about Shakespeare and W. H. in today's *Times Literary Supplement*.[3] Since I wrote the letter a week ago, I also wrote to the Dean of Canterbury and asked him if he would help me to find a reference in the archives of the cathedral of 'Will Hewes'. With great kindness the Dean put on his librarian to search the records for it, and this morning I have a letter from the librarian saying he has *got it*!!

He sends me the copy. This is a *terrific scoop*, as it establishes a real

---

[1] The anonymous article (14 May 1938) said that 'the claim of Southampton to be the poet's friend seems to be gaining ground' whereas that of 'Willie Hughes, the pretty actor boy, has nearly faded out'. See p. 42, n. 1.

[2] Richmond (1871–1964, knighted 1935) had been on the staff of *The Times* since 1899 and was editor of the *Times Literary Supplement* from 1903 to 1937.

[3] Douglas said the claim that Southampton wrote some of the sonnets was 'preposterous' and demanded to know on what grounds the claim of Will Hughes 'has nearly faded out'.

Will Hughes at the exact date and links him (or Hews or Hewes) with Marlowe and therefore, of course, with Shakespeare. He was apprentice to John Marlowe, the father of Christopher. Don't pretend that this is not exciting! I do wish you would let me come to see you next week. I want to consult you about this W. H. business. Should I write a letter to the *Times Literary Supplement* about it, or shall I keep it dark till I can get out a new edition of my *True History of Shakespeare's* . *Sonnets*? Do please advise me. Your   CHILDE ALFRED

P.S. A review of my book by James Agate in yesterday's *Express*[1] quoting your Mrs MacStinger's baby jest. It's a rotten review and deliberately misleading about the nature of my book, but I don't mind at all, as it will sell the book more than if it had been a 'boost'.

P.P.S. I am going away tomorrow for the week-end. Back here for one night on Monday. Then going next Tuesday for the whole of the rest of the week to Norwich House. If you don't write to me I shall start making a low-spirited noise again.

22 May 1938 [postcard]   Ayot St Lawrence

For the moment (I hope) I am seriously ill. My head is all right, and my organs are all sound; but I can hardly walk. At eighty-two that may mean anything. So all appointments are impossible: we must put off meeting until you are in London next time, unless you have to substitute a sonnet entitled 'Poor Old Shaw'.

The *Literary Supplement* has done you handsome in its featuring of your letter.

The Canterbury news is very decidedly exciting. W. H. was bound to turn up some day; but it might easily have been a thousand years hence. If the date fits, the Marlowe connexion almost settles the case.

The temptation to forge the entry was so enormous that it will have to be most carefully authenticated.

[1] 'An intensely readable and human book', Agate said, 'a record of some pretty good quarrelling'. However, he concluded, much can be forgiven an author 'who can see a joke against himself. And see it to the point of quoting Mr Shaw's remark that Lord Alfred Douglas reminded him of Mrs MacStinger's baby'.

Muggeridge is another Crosland. His father is a Fabian whom I knew of old.[1] As a warning to us old uns that we are obsolete, it was a good article.

G. B. S.

It was Byron who re-established Childe. C. Harold filled the poetic horizon when I was a child.

23 May 1938   1 St Ann's Court, Hove

Dear St Christopher, I am very distressed to hear of your being ill. I have just got back from a week-end visit to a country house and found your card in your wonderful clear writing, which seems to flout anything like illness or weakness. I shall resort to all sorts of supernatural means to get you well and shall say the rosary for you and also have Mass said for you. Also I believe there is a statuette of St Christopher in the Sacred Heart Church here, or did I dream it? If it is really there I shall light a candle for you and in any case shall light a candle for you to St Anthony of Padua.

I have written to the *Times Literary Supplement* about the Canterbury discovery, and my letter should be in next Friday's issue. I thought I had better quickly nail it down as *my* discovery, as I had rather rashly mentioned it to several persons and it would have been annoying if someone else had got in first with the news. Really it's a disgrace that I did not follow up the clue four years ago or more. I've had it all this time, but somehow I never really expected the confirmation would materialize so promptly and easily. As you say, it might have lain there for another thousand years, and when I wrote to the Dean and asked him to try to unearth the entry I thought of it as a thousand-to-one chance.

I suppose you saw my reply to 'Comrade Muggeridge' in *Time and Tide*.[2] I am now told by a friend of his that he had no intention of being

---

[1] The father of Malcolm Muggeridge was H. T. Muggeridge, Fabian lecturer, City businessman and M.P. (1929–1931) for Romford, in Essex.

[2] Malcolm Muggeridge said in his review (30 April 1938) that 'in reading Lord Alfred Douglas's entertaining volume of reminiscences' he had the sensation of rustling through fallen leaves of a remote past, another world in which ' "genius", "artist" and "beauty" had as rich a content as, now, words like "proletariat", "class-war", "Communism" and

rude or offensive to me, but I can hardly swallow this. I go to Norwich House tomorrow till Saturday. It's a disappointment that I shall not see you. But I shall ring up and ask how you are. Yours

CHILDE ALFRED

P.S. I *am* going to write a sonnet about you, if I can. I tried for an hour the other day but couldn't get a line out.

23 May 1938   1 St Ann's Court, Hove

My dear San Christophero. I *did* dream that statuette of St Christopher. I went to the church after posting my other letter to you and asked one of the priests if there was a shrine of St Christopher or if I'd dreamt it, and he said, "You must have dreamt it, because there isn't one". So I put up a candle for you to St Anthony of Padua, and also arranged for a Mass to be said for you (through my intention); and the priest (a young Irishman) told me that he couldn't work it before Thursday, but, when I expressed disappointment and said it was urgent, as an afterthought he said, "I'll say Mass myself for your intention tomorrow morning at 7:15". I told him it was for you and for your speedy recovery from an illness. Your   CHILDE ALFRED

30 May 1938   1 St Ann's Court, Hove
My dear St Christopher, Thanks for your delightful card, which I got before leaving Norwich House on Saturday. I do *violently* hope you are better. I shall show your card to the priest who said the Mass for you. I

―――――
"Fascism" '. Douglas replied (*Time and Tide*, 7 May 1938) that his 'autobiographical books seem to have a peculiar effect upon your reviewers, male and female'. He had received 'a very spiteful and offensive notice' of his *Autobiography* by Sylvia Lynd, and now '*Without Apology* appears to have had a disastrous effect on the proletarian mind of Comrade Muggeridge'. What was back of 'this strange exhibition of utterly unprovoked malice and stupidity'? And why must he drag in a totally unconnected obscene passage from *Lady Chatterley's Lover*? It is difficult to account for the review 'unless Mr Muggeridge was drunk'. Following the text of the letter, Malcolm Muggeridge replied, 'I was not drunk'.

went to see him this morning for that purpose, but he was out. I expect you *are* better really, aren't you?

I got the enclosed from the *Times Literary Supplement*. They seem very friendly and considerate. I suggested, in a private letter to the editor, that he had printed the letter from 'Mr Cripps', immediately after mine, as 'an example of the imbecility which overtakes most people when they discuss the sonnets'. He admits this, as you see, and I am glad to know that he realized the absurdity of Cripps's effort.[1]

I already have evidence that the Will Hewes discovery is shaking the dove-house of Shakespearean circles. I expect there will be several letters about it in next week's *Times Literary Supplement*. Would that there might be one from St Christopher. Your   CHILDE ALFRED

P.S. I have just remembered (in an 'intellectual vision') that the statuette of St Christopher which I thought was in the church here is really in Westminster Cathedral. It suddenly flashed upon my inward eye with daffodil-like brilliance!

9 June 1938   1 St Ann's Court, Hove

My dear St Christopher, Do let me know how you are, or shall I have another Mass said for you? When are your new edition of Harris and the preface coming out? I am anxiously awaiting them.[2] I had a very

[1] Simon Nowell-Smith apologized (28 May 1938) for the editor's having shortened Douglas's letter, explaining that it was not more conspicuously placed because such great prominence had been given his letter in the preceding issue.

Mr A. R. Cripps of Worthing had made the ingenious suggestion that 'HEWS' might well stand for 'HE[nry] W[riosthesley, Earl of] S[outhampton]'.

[2] Shaw had not sent the proofs as promised, and Otto Kyllmann was uneasy about the matter, for Constable's solicitor, H. F. Rubinstein, warned that Douglas had possible claims for libel. Shaw, ill and flat on his back, in a letter dictated to Charlotte, assured Kyllmann on 4 June that there was no cause for alarm: 'Your legal adviser is an idiot: it is quite impossible to ask A. D. to initial the proof sheets. Besides, I have a bushel of letters from him which are more conclusive than any initials'. The correct thing to do, Shaw said, was to send Douglas a letter, and he enclosed a draft. The final sentence read, 'May we have your assurance that our efforts to avoid any damage or injustice to you have been successful?' On 7 June Constable's sent this letter to Douglas (without the change of a word). Douglas's reply of 8 June was friendly, though he complained that he had not yet seen a copy of the revised preface.

amiable letter from Constable's which made me suppose that the book was on the eve of publication, and since then I have been hoping that the book would appear every day. I replied at length to Constable's. I have written a very short letter to the *Times Literary Supplement* and hope it will be in tomorrow's issue.[1] So please look out for it.

I liked the enclosed review[2] published in a Scottish paper which comes out in the 'Douglas country', as that part of the Border is still called, especially the last paragraph, which confirms your dictum about the 'infantile complex'! Do *please* let me know what date I may expect the new preface to appear. Your   CHILDE ALFRED

22 June 1938   1 St Ann's Court, Hove

My dear St Christopher, I do hope you are better. The last I heard (from your secretary) was that you were 'looking decidedly better'. That was more than ten days ago. So I hope by now you really are recovered or on the way to recovery. I feel sure the Mass was efficacious. I *knew* it would be, and besides it was for you altogether and not only for your recovery from an illness.

I myself have been in bed for the last three days with a sort of influenza. At least it had all the usual symptoms but I know very well it was brought on by worry because a friend of mine, a retired doctor (Dr Orme) whom I consulted, told me I must have an operation for a rupture which I have had for more than a year. It has caused me endless misery as I've had to wear a strap. I was not in the least afraid of the operation, which is quite simple and can be done with a local anaesthetic, but I was utterly unable to see how I was going to pay for it. It's all right now, or I wouldn't be writing this to you. My nephew Queensberry, poor chap . . . told me he *couldn't possibly* help me. Now, however, he writes that he can get the operation done by a leading surgeon

---

[1] It was.

[2] By W. Sorley Brown in the *Border Standard*, stating that Douglas was 'one of the first of living poets'; the 'emotion of the small lost boy that lingers forlornly in the memory of each of us has never altogether departed from the character of the author of this book'.

for 'practically nothing' in a private ward in what he calls 'my hospital' [St Mary's, Paddington] or in St George's. He is a governor of these two hospitals and has supported them very generously, so he has the power to do this for me. This is a great relief. You will probably say, "Why on earth should he bother me with all these sordid details?" Why indeed? I can't give any proper excuse for it. It's simply that I feel I must write and tell you because as you have been so kind to me I am constantly thinking about you, my dear St Christopher. You can put it down to my 'infantile complex'.

Constable's sent me the proof of your brilliant preface[1] in which you said such kind things about me. I can't agree that Harris's picture of Wilde is as good as you think it, but that really doesn't matter, as your preface is the main point of the new publication. I think Harris makes Oscar out much too 'soft' and weak. He really wasn't like that. He had a 'ferocious will' about many things. As for Harris himself, I don't think even you will succeed in whitewashing him, though I have come to think lately that a great part of his apparent villainies were due to sheer stupidity. You are very light on his sexual enormities. They *were* enormities. (I know of things he did which are perfectly horrible.) His character and his outlook on life and his judgement of men and women were of course affected all the time by this, just as you say is the case with a man who is never quite sober, which might, as you point out, be truthfully said about both Harris and Oscar.[2] You probably, in fact certainly, don't know as much as I do about Harris's excesses. He wasn't homosexual, simply because it was not in his nature, but he was all the same a sort of Minotaur and devoured female children in a wholesale

---

[1] On 9 June. The following day Douglas returned it with a few corrections for 'Mr Shaw's attention'. On 13 June Constable's wrote that Shaw was too ill to deal with his comments, but that 'we have made certain slight corrections, for your approval' and were sending the preface 'once again'. Douglas returned this immediately, saying that he found it satisfactory.

[2] Douglas's comments on the page proof: 'Oscar was often drunk even before the catastrophe. He drank more than any man I ever knew, but till the *débâcle* he never showed a sign of it. He could "carry" any amount' (p. xxxv); Harris 'was the only man I ever met who could "carry" liquor as well as Wilde could' (p. xxxvii); 'I myself drank "like a fish" when I was young, but my splendid constitution and the exercise (particularly riding) which I took preserved me from harm' (p. xxxviii).

way. Not that I think one ought to put such things into a biography, but I at least can never forget them.

When I think of Harris and all his nauseating 'Jesus' stuff it really makes me sick to read. I am still 'laid up', though not actually in bed as I write this, but I hope to be up tomorrow. Your

CHILDE ALFRED

25 June 1938   4 Whitehall Court, London

Dear Childe Alfred, I have pernicious anæmia[1] and am for the moment forbidden to write anything.

I also have to deal with a rupture. I have tried all sorts of appliances and prefer a belt buyable at Beasley's Ltd, 45 Conduit Street. It is quite comfortable and slips on and off in a hand's turn.

A private ward in a hospital is far superior to most nursing homes you cannot do better.

I quite understand about Oscar's 'ferocious will'. He went to the devil his own way in spite of everybody. What you say about his and Harris's drinking is interesting. Frank, exactly like Wilde, could not (except for his *Life and Loves*) or would not write after his success with the *Saturday Review*. Of his career as the Minotaur[2] I know nothing; but I don't doubt your description of it in the least, though I always doubt the virility of sex-obsessed literary people.

I expect to be an invalid for a month or so.   G. B. S.

27 June 1938   1 St Ann's Court, Hove

My dear St Christopher, I am delighted to get your letter, and it is very kind of you to write (or dictate) a letter to me when you are still so ill. I can't believe you have really got 'pernicious anæmia' as I always under-

[1] Diagnosed by Dr Geoffrey Evans (1886–1951), the eminent pathologist. The prescribed cure was complete rest and massive injections of liver extract, a treatment humiliating to the vegetarian Shaw.

[2] Douglas noted on his comment sheet that at one time Harris was very nearly 'lynched by the angry population near Éze'.

stood it was a most dreadful thing, whereas you say you 'expect to be an invalid for a month or so' which doesn't sound too bad. Your letter is epoch-making for me because you actually for the first time address me as 'dear Childe Alfred'. You have never done this before. You bestowed the name on me but up till now you have never used it. This, no doubt, was because all your last communications have been on cards, and not letters. In any case I am delighted to be confirmed as 'Childe Alfred' though I hope it won't be necessary for me to come to any more dark towers just now, as I've really been having a very bad time and have only just (not quite) recovered from an attack of influenza. I am going to St Mary's Hospital, but I still don't know where that is except that it is in London. I expect I shall hear definitely tomorrow.

Harris did write a certain amount after the *Saturday Review* (e.g., besides *My Life and Loves*, his *Life* of you and that quite appalling and ridiculous play about Joan of Arc) whereas Oscar literally never wrote another line after *The Ballad of Reading Gaol*.

Is there such a thing as a complete edition of all your works at any sort of reasonable price? Because I feel that I don't really know them half as well as I ought to do. I am determined to write a sonnet about you sooner or later. Your   CHILDE ALFRED

4 July 1938   1 St Ann's Court, Hove

My dear St Christopher, I am going this afternoon to London to the Almroth Wright Ward, St Mary's Hospital, Paddington. Operation tomorrow, I suppose. I don't mind *much* though I feel slightly frightened. Please say a prayer for me! As Bernard Shaw you wouldn't do this I know, but in your capacity of St Christopher you might rely on the powerful efficacity of your prayers. I expect your preface will be published by the time I get back here in two or three weeks. I hope you are rapidly getting well again. Your   CHILDE ALFRED

6 July 1938   1 St Ann's Court, Hove

My dear St Christopher, If you *did* say a prayer for me the effect was stupendous and shattering! I lay shivering in bed for eighteen hours in what was called 'a private ward' at the hospital (it was much more like a public lavatory) and after being reluctantly washed by a nurse who commented unfavorably on the absence of muscle in my arms, and having undergone other indignities, the surgeon at last 'showed up' and rapidly inspecting me said that an operation was *quite unnecessary and not to be thought of*!! (I realize that my grammar has gone wrong in these last sentences but I refrain from attempting to correct it.) So I arose feeling like a criminal who is reprieved on the scaffold and departed with great joy. I spent last night at my favourite hotel, The Shelleys, at Lewes and came back here tonight. Can you beat it? Your

CHILDE ALFRED

P.S. Did you or did you not say a prayer for me? Please send me your photograph if you will be so kind.

11 July 1938   1 St Ann's Court, Hove

Dear St Christopher, I was pleased to get a letter this morning from Doctor Porteous of St Mary's Hospital telling me that you had written to Sir Almroth Wright[1] about me while I was at the hospital. This compensated me for not hearing from you which rather hurt my feelings, as I quite expected to get a card of condolence (or congratulation on my escape). But I expect I am rather a nuisance to you by this time.

I hear this morning from Sherard that Werner Laurie, the publisher of his last book about Wilde and Harris and yourself, told him that "anyone could buy the American edition of Harris's book in England for 7/6". This is rather startling, as I fondly imagined that I had stopped the sale when I got damages for selling it from Hatchard's and Harrods' about ten years ago. However, I imagine that Bonny Werner Laurie (of

[1] Wright (1861–1947, knighted 1906) was an eminent bacteriologist, a Governor of St Mary's and Professor of Pathology there since 1902, with the exception of the war years, during which he carried on remarkable work in wound infection, initiating a salt treatment for the early closure of wounds. Sir Almroth was a friend of the Shaws and his remark (on saving a man's life by this new opsonic system) "Is he worth it?" was the inspiration of *The Doctor's Dilemma*. The play's Sir Colenso Ridgeon is modelled on Sir Almroth.

Clifford's Inn where early fa's the dew[1]) was exaggerating, and in any case it will be your preface and not Harris's unpleasant fairy tales that will be the attraction of the new edition.

What about that photograph of you? I think you might send me one. You will remember that I sent you mine years ago. Are you well again yet? Your   CHILDE ALFRED

P.S. Your letter to Sir Almroth Wright did not reach him (Dr Porteous tells me) till after I had left the hospital.

14 July 1938   4 Whitehall Court, London

Dear Childe Alfred, I talked the matter over with the Holy Ghost, who told me not to be a damned fool and to write at once to Almroth Wright, recommending you to his special care.[2] He replied, 'As to your man Lord Alfred, we gave him a little ward by himself; and our best surgeon saw him and thought an operation would be inadvisable; and so he promptly went out of hospital and I never saw him'.

So that is all right. But what is the matter with you? Or what *was* the matter before our prayers intervened?

I have had a set-back from a brief but very weakening attack of the King's complaint[3] which has kept me in London until tomorrow.

[1] When Werner Laurie, the publisher of Crosland's *The Unspeakable Scot* (1902), commissioned him to write *The Wild Irishman* (1905), Crosland penned the following verse on Clifford's Inn note paper:

> O, Clifford's Inn is bonnie
> When lightly fa's the dew;
> For 'twas there that Werner Laurie
> Gie'd me his promise true.

The Life and Genius of T. W. H. Crosland, W. Sorley Brown, London, 1928, p. 161.

[2] Shaw wrote to Sir Almroth on 5 July 1938, asking that he be kind to Lord Alfred Douglas, whom he described as the 'very beautiful youth' and 'quite considerable poet' who 'stuck to Wilde through thick and thin'. Douglas, he said, 'still has an infantile complex that is amusing, especially as he is quite conscious of it himself. Tell the students that he is not a homosexualist, and that his [nephew] the Marquess is a great figure in the hospital world'. (In the collection of Dr Ernst Jokl, University of Kentucky Medical Center.)

[3] An attack of gastric influenza from which George VI had recovered just in time to pay his state visit to President Lebrun of France, 12–22 July.

I will send an assortment of portraits from the country. I am not so presentable as we all were in the *fin de siècle*.

We had taken tickets for the Glyndebourne Festival, and intended to stay at Hove for a week; but my collapse put a stop to that.

Constable's are arranging with Dodd, Mead of New York for simultaneous publication of my edition of Harris's *Life of Wilde*. This will involve their buying out Covici and buying up their reprint, which could hardly be worse from your point of view. When it is got rid of (pulped) the smugglers can get nothing but my edition, which will be equally available in Constable's edition, so that there will be no point in smuggling it.

Until the 27th my address will be Ayot St Lawrence   G. B. S.

14 July 1938   1 St Ann's Court, Hove

My dear St Christopher, This letter will reach you before you start for Ayot St Lawrence. I was enchanted to get your letter. Your writing on my behalf to Sir Almroth Wright was a very Christopherian gesture for which I am very grateful. I *had* a rupture, but the surgeon (Professor Pannett) said it was "very slight" and not at all likely to get worse even if it didn't disappear altogether. He told me it would be a great mistake to have an operation and that by wearing a different kind of 'support' I would be perfectly comfortable and safe. So of course I cleared out of the hospital at once.

My niece Lady Queensberry,[1] telephoned asking me to go to her house in Cheyne Walk, but I had left before her telephone message came, and I went for one night to the Shelleys Hotel at Lewes (a most lovely old house and garden which belonged to Sir Timothy Shelley) and then returned here.

I am greatly looking forward to the 'assortment of portraits' which you promise me.

The stars in their courses seem determined to prevent me from meeting you. If you had come to Hove for Glyndebourne I would *surely*

---

[1] Cathleen Mann, the painter, married Queensberry in 1926. They lived at 5 Cheyne Walk.

have seen you, and I might perhaps have persuaded you and Mrs Shaw to lunch here with me. I *am* sorry to hear you got that set-back just as you were making such a good recovery. I had the same complaint just a week before my abortive operation, and I was feeling pretty ill before I got to the hospital. So it was all the more cheerful to escape the operation.

What you tell me about the American edition of your new Harris is very good news. You certainly have performed a miracle, because I despaired of ever getting even a hearing on the Wilde matter in America. There was an American edition of my *Autobiography* but it was published by a rotten firm of publishers and had no success at all.[1] In fact after its publication I never heard a word more about it nor collected one cent of royalties from it.

The late Monsignor Bickerstaffe-Drew,[2] who received me into the church, told me that he once received an old peasant woman, and that at the last minute he asked her if there was anything she would like to have explained to her. To which she said, "Well, Father, there *is* one thing that has been troubling me. The Holy Ghost, now, Father, would that be a lady or a gentleman?"

There is a very pleasant article by D. B. Wyndham Lewis[3] about *Without Apology* in today's issue of the *Weekly Review* (G. K.'s *Weekly*). I expect you will see it, as your name appears two or three times in it, so your press cutting agency will certainly send it to you. It is three columns and a great 'boost' for me. It is moreover a very witty and well-written performance.

I am looking forward with the greatest excitement to those portraits. So please don't delay sending them. Your   CHILDE ALFRED

---

[1] *My Friendship with Oscar Wilde*, New York, Coventry House, 1932. A thousand copies were printed, the first hundred signed by the author.

[2] Bickerstaffe-Drew (1858–1928) served for twenty years as Chaplain to the Forces in Plymouth and in Malta, and was Private Chamberlain to both Pope Leo XIII and Pope Pius X. He wrote fiction under the name John Ayscough.

[3] Dominic Bevan Wyndham Lewis (1891–1969), columnist and biographer. He found *Without Apology* a 'candid and cheerful book of memories and impressions', free from hypocrisy and bitterness.

15 July 1938   1 St Ann's Court, Hove

Dear St Christopher, I got a copy of the Harris book today.[1] It was a distinct shock to find that you have not altered a word of Harris's malicious (and really so *idiotic* that nobody but a fool would believe it) account of our interview at Chantilly when he accuses me of, among other things, running down the *Ballad of Reading Gaol*! (The true account of this interview is in my *Autobiography*.) Considering that Harris himself accepted my correction of all his poisonous nonsense and incorporated it in his *New Preface to 'The Life and Confessions of Oscar Wilde'* I cannot see why you should have left it untouched. I understood you to say (in fact it's not a question of 'understanding', because I have your letter where you distinctly say it) that you had 'accepted all' my 'emendations and corrections'.[2] A cursory glance through the book gives me the impression that most of Harris's most offensive attacks on me remain exactly as they were. However I am not going to quarrel with you about it. It's my own fault for being such a mug as to agree to your reissuing the book without insisting on seeing the proofs and on your printing Harris's own admissions that nearly everything he said about me in the book is false. I have also a whole stack of letters he wrote me from Nice which you have never seen. In one of them he says that his revised book will do me far more good than his original book did me harm. Your preface certainly provides an antidote to Harris's poison, and in any case I console myself by reflecting that Harris has already done his worst and that this reprint of his dishonest book cannot induce reasonable people to believe his story as far as it concerns me against my own story in my *Autobiography*. My idea of Harris's book is that it is not only false and malicious and full of obvious 'fakes' but that it is a very stupid book. I shall be very much surprised if even the magic of your name can bring about any revision of the general verdict on Harris as a blatant fraud.

[1] *Oscar Wilde* was published on 18 July (price ten shillings), without the sub-title '*His Life and Confessions*'. Shaw had written on the proof, 'I think this Newgate Calendar sub-title should be dropped. It was one of Frank's less reputable tricks'. The book was now in one volume and the lengthy section of *De Profundis* was deleted. There was no Appendix. Illustrations had been vetoed and there was still no Index.

[2] Shaw to Douglas, 18 April 1938: ' . . . I agreed with all your notes and made no attempt to improve on them'.

your main object was to help poor Nellie whom I always liked, but you will remember that I told you from the beginning that I thought it was a beastly book & that it was a great pity to give it another lease of life. So lets leave out further reference to it in distinct for your preface.

your Childe Alfred.

1, ST ANN'S COURT,
NIZELLS AVENUE,
HOVE 2, SUSSEX.

Dear St Christopher.

July 15. 1938.

I got a copy of the Harris book today. It was a distinct shock to find that you have not altered a word of Harris's malicious (& really so idiotic that nobody but a fool would believe it) account of our interview at Chantilly when he accuses me of, among other things, running down the Ballad of Reading Gaol! (The true account of this interview is in my autobiography). Considering that Harris himself accepted my correction of all this poisonous nonsense and incorporated it in his "New Preface To The Life & Confessions of Oscar Wilde"

Childe Alfred to St Christopher, 15 July 1938

People will buy the book simply to read your preface, which is brilliant, but apart from sheer pornography hunters the public will (at this time of day and after all that is now known about the story) be disgusted and repelled by the book itself. As I have said often before, it is as unfair and misleading about Oscar as it is about myself. I really don't think I can bring myself to read the damned stuff again. In fact I would not even have started to read it at all if I had not done so in the hope of finding the 'emendations' and 'corrections' and editing which you led me to expect. Your motives in reissuing the book are I know entirely altruistic, and I realize that your main object was to help poor Nellie, whom I always liked, but you will remember that I told you from the beginning that I thought it was a beastly book and that it was a great pity to give it another lease of life. So let's leave out further reference to it as distinct from your preface. Your   CHILDE ALFRED

17 July 1938   Ayot St Lawrence

Dear Childe, What is done is done: no plangency of low-spirited noise can avail any more.

You said not a word about the *Ballad*. *All* your notes were acted on.[1]

It is of no importance in comparison to the main drift of the edition, which clears you for the first time of your father's innuendo and of the reproach for having left Wilde penniless, besides giving you your proper prominence in the tragedy. Be content with that; and don't spoil it all by joining Pearson, Kingsmill, Sherard and the rest in the hullabaloo against Harris.[2] It is your cue to back this edition up for all you are worth. At least it does not ignore you.

Besides, *critically* (you have some reputation as a critic to lose) Harris's

[1] This statement is not borne out by the two 'marked-up' volumes.
[2] R. H. Sherard's book had exposed Harris's mis-statements; the review of Harris's biography by Hugh Kingsmill in the September *Fortnightly* was scathing; so was that by Hesketh Pearson in the *Observer* of 17 July. 'There are liars and liars', Pearson said, 'but only Rousseau and Casanova are Harris's equal. His biography is not the story of Oscar Wilde but the story of Frank Harris'.

book has very considerable literary merit in its Plutarchian way; and its effect is, on the whole, true as corrected as far as you are concerned. It was always true of Wilde.

Anyhow I have done my best for Nellie, for you and for the ghost of Harris; and I can spare no more of the remnant of my life for the subject. I have not seen MacCarthy's article yet,[1] only Pearson's.

It will relieve your feelings to tear up the enclosed clearing-up of an ancient drawer.[2] Like St Christopher I find the Childe suddenly becoming frightfully heavy in midstream.   G. B. S.

18 July 1938   1 St Ann's Court, Hove

Dear St Christopher, It is bewildering that you can have ignored (as you have done) Harris's own corrections and admissions of the falsity of a number of his statements, which corrections and admissions were made in his *New Preface to 'The Life and Confessions of Oscar Wilde'* of which I know you have a copy and of which I lent my own number one limited *edition de luxe* copy to Nellie Harris when she visited me here two years ago. Practically everything he said about me in his original book is corrected in his *New Preface*. Moreover I know you have read my *Autobiography*, and you wrote and told me at the time it came out that, in effect, you accepted it as the truth and that it 'made my position perfectly clear'. My account in the *Autobiography* of the interview Harris had with me at Chantilly, when he came to dine and sleep as my guest at the Hotel Condé, contradicts his (now reprinted) account in every particular. It was at this interview that, after agreeing with everything I said about Wilde and the unreasonableness of his demands for two or three thousand pounds out of my small capital, he invited me to stay with him at Monte Carlo where (a few weeks later) he relieved me of the two thousand pounds by a blatant fraud. I took it for granted that

---

[1] Desmond MacCarthy in his review (*Sunday Times*, 17 July) thought Constable's should withdraw the book. Despite Shaw's emendations, the book 'remains misleading and mendacious; while Mr Shaw's preface strikes me, not as important, but as discreditable'.

[2] The promised photographs of Shaw, a bundle of about twenty.

you would not allow Harris's exposed and admitted (and now universally recognized) lies and mis-statements about myself to remain exactly as they were in his first edition. But there they nearly all are still. It is really incredible that you should be capable of behaving in such a way. I trusted you *blindly* and you have let me down terribly. How *could* you?

I cannot agree to the continued dissemination of all these lies about myself. Even your preface, kind and friendly as it was to me, does not outbalance the frightful injury to me and my reputation caused by this revised broadcasting to the world of baseless accusations, faked conversations and malignant falsifying of the whole story. I feel all this as a terrible blow, for I had got to feel real love and affection for you, and I was, and still am, most grateful to you for your defence of me and your kindness over the Rich and Cowan business.

I have told you over and over again that I do not agree with your literary estimate of Harris's book, but that is really neither here nor there. Even if Harris were as good a writer as you are yourself his malignant lies and libels could not be justified or condoned. And when he himself has admitted the untruth of what he said about me and explained that he was misled into saying it by Robert Ross, how can you defend your reissuing of it in this book? I wish I could think of any way out of the situation that has arisen, short of withdrawing the book from circulation. But I fail to see what else there is for it. I have written to Constable's. I wrote the letter late last night and went out to post it at four A.M.[1] Yours sorrowfully   CHILDE ALFRED

P.S. It is not correct to say as you do that your preface 'clears me from my father's innuendo and from the reproach of having left my friend penniless, *for the first time*'. Harris himself in 1925 cleared me from these

---

[1] 'I have now had time to read the text of Harris's book as issued by Mr Bernard Shaw and yourselves', Douglas wrote. 'To my amazement I find that it is full of the most foul and abominable libels on me. Relying on Mr Shaw's word of honour that he was "editing" the book in such a way as to make it quite inoffensive to me, I did not think it necessary to insist, as I might have done, on seeing the proofs'. The 'whole book is a great deal worse than my recollection of it (I had not read it for twenty years). Under these circumstances you can hardly suppose that I am going to allow its continued circulation. I am considering what steps I can best take'.

accusations and nobody, as far as I know, has believed them now for thirteen years at least. I refer you to Vincent O'Sullivan's book, to Sherard's last book, to Léon Lemonnier's *Vie d'Oscar Wilde* and to the other (Dutch) biographer, whom Sherard attacks and whose name for the moment I have forgotten.[1] Also the question was fought out in the law courts, where I got a verdict and a thousand pounds damages from the Northcliffe Press. The reprinting of my father's abusive letter is also an outrage, as the jury at that trial, of their own accord, said in a rider to their verdict. In Brasol's new life of Wilde he has reprinted my father's abuse and blatant mis-statements. I allowed him to do so only on condition that he also published a note from me. The book is not yet out and will contain my note.[2]

P.P.S. Desmond MacCarthy is no friend of mine. On the contrary he is hostile to me, so please do not imagine that the devastating 'press' you have had so far for the book is in any way connected with me. For months past I have been going round praising you to the skies and telling everyone that you had 'edited out' all Harris's libels on me. My friends naturally are now bewildered.

19 July 1938   Ayot St Lawrence

Dearest Childe, You will drive me crazy.

Don't blather like all the rest of them about Harris's malicious lies. They are imaginary. Put your finger on one of them; and I shall know what grievance you have left.

I have all your notes made when you went through the text. They were very useful: I did all you required and more. I must now have something definite to bully you about.

I never read Harris's preface.[3] I have read the sulky and hostile letter

[1] Vincent O'Sullivan, *Aspects of Wilde* (1936); Robert Sherard, *Bernard Shaw, Frank Harris and Oscar Wilde* (1937); Léon Lemonnier, *Vie d'Oscar Wilde* (1931); and the Dutch biographer Gustav Renier, *Oscar Wilde* (1933).

[2] Boris Brasol, *Oscar Wilde, the Man—the Artist* (1938); Queensberry's letter, pp. 253-254; Douglas's note, p. 362.

[3] He had in fact read it (see earlier letters).

AYOT ST LAWRENCE, WELWYN, HERTS. 19/7/38
STATION: WHEATHAMPSTEAD, L.& N.E.R. 2¼ MILES.
TELEGRAMS: BERNARD SHAW, CODICOTE.
TELEPHONE: CODICOTE 18.

4, WHITEHALL COURT, LONDON, S.W.I.

Dearest Childe

You will drive me crazy.

Dont blether like all the rest of them about its malicious lies. They are imaginary. Put your finger on one of them; and I shall know what grievance you have left.

I have all your notes made when you went through the text. They were very useful: I did all you required and more. I must now have something definite to bully you about.

I never read Harris's preface. I have read the sulky and hostile letters with which he introduced the two awful letters from you which appear in the Covici edition.

Do you want that to hold the field?

Why did you not agree to an English editor when you and he apparently had it out at Nice?

I am completely done up — too much work this morning — and can no more.

G.B.S.

St Christopher to Childe Alfred, 19 July 1938

with which he introduced the two AWFUL letters from you which appear in the Covici edition.

Do you want that to hold the field?

Why did you not agree to an English edition when you and he apparently had it out at Nice?

I am completely done up—too much work this morning—and can no more.[1]   G. B. S.

20 July 1938   1 St Ann's Court, Hove

My dear *darling* St Christopher, I am deeply grieved to hear you are ill and so worried, but truthfully it is not my fault. Please get this: when Nellie Harris came to see me here two years, or more, ago (long before you wrote to me about your new edition of Harris's book), she begged me to let her bring out an English edition. In reply I said I would not raise any objection (although I did not like it) provided that the new edition should contain Harris's own *New Preface to 'The Life and Confessions of Oscar Wilde'* published at the Fortune Press in 1925.

Nellie Harris said "of course it shall be included in every copy of the book, and you can also, if you like, write a note or additional preface yourself". (She also offered me half the profits, which of course I declined.) She went on to say that she had not got in her possession a copy of the *New Preface*. I then gave (or rather lent) her my last copy of the book and told her I *must* have it back. I heard no more from her and I assumed that she could not get any publisher to issue the book with the author's own admission that a great deal of it was utterly false and 'a caricature of the facts' (Harris's own words). So when you wrote and asked me to consent to an English edition and promised me that there should not be a word offensive to me in it, I naturally took it for granted that any alterations you made in Harris's text would be taken direct from his own written and published words of recantation and apology. He actually ended the preface by the words: 'That I should have misjudged the foremost poet of this time is my keenest regret'.

[1] Kyllmann called on Shaw at Whitehall Court on 18 July. Constable's, Kyllmann felt, had done nothing wrong. The conflict was between Shaw and Douglas.

Your memory has betrayed you over this. In 1931 you wrote me a letter [4 July 1931] about this preface, and it may remind you of this if I recall to you that you (I presume in joke) said that you supposed that I had really written the preface myself. (I have not got your letter because two or three months ago I entrusted it and other letters including one from Wilde to have copies made, to A. J. A. Symons. I have just written to him to send it back to me.) But I have a copy of the reply I sent you dated July 6, 1931. . . . So you see you *have* read the *New Preface*, and you are far too honest not to admit that it was natural that I should take it for granted that you were using it as the basis of your 'corrections and emendations' of Harris's text.

Nellie Harris is greatly to blame, because it was sheer bad faith on her part not to have told you that the *New Preface must* be included, or at any rate a précis of it. She had my copy given to her for that very purpose.

Need I say more to convince you that you are honourably bound to withdraw the book (which of course can be reissued with corrections and explanations)? Your still quite devoted   CHILDE ALFRED

P.S. I am in the dark about your references to my 'AWFUL letters' to Harris. I have not seen the Covici Friede edition. Obviously, from what you say, the letters must be forgeries or fakes. When will you realize that Harris was a complete scoundrel and capable of any villainy?

P.P.S. I have telegraphed to Caton of the Fortune Press to send you a copy of Harris's *New Preface* and also one to myself.

20 July 1938   Ayot St Lawrence

Dear Childe, Thanks for the Sherard letter, a very amiable and sensible one under the circumstances. I did not mean to attribute corrupt motives to him but to reproach him for having, on exactly the same evidence, attributed them to Harris.

And I cannot understand how he could ask Sarah[1] for an advance on

[1] Desperate to raise money for his legal defence in August 1895, Wilde (through Sherard) begged Sarah Bernhardt to purchase the world rights for *Salomé*. After a tantalizing hesitation, she refused.

a play which no manager would touch if Wilde were convicted. It was heroic, but crazy.

I left the Chantilly interview in after some consideration because it was so obviously true. I rather admired you for not objecting to it. But when Wilde made the monstrous demand that he should be supported by your family for the rest of his life (as he very largely was) you MUST have said exactly what Harris represents you to have said. And as to the *Ballad*, you, as an authentic poet, as distinguished from an Irishman with a good ear for metre and an acquaintance with *The Ancient Mariner*, most certainly said just what he represents you as saying.

If this is the only 'foul and abominable libel' of which you complain, nothing is easier than to cut out the last half of the chapter.[1] I shall then have the ecstasy of being able to say that the only passage I had to cut out was not because it was false but because it was unbearably true.

If I were as thin-skinned as you I should have been dead long ago; but I suppose you must be indulged. Weakness on my part, eh? In great haste   G. B. S.

20 July 1938   Ayot St Lawrence

Dear Childe, I forgot to say that the words 'Fortune Press' brought back to my utterly untrustworthy memory that Harris's preface had actually been in my hands. But that preface was written under duress; and when your consent to publication, which was the price of it, was still withheld (for some reason which I could never understand) he retracted it and expressed his opinion of you with his accustomed trenchancy.

But in any case the notion of crying stinking fish by publishing a book with a preface by the author describing it as a tissue of falsehoods is one that could have been conceived by you only in one of your most impossible moods. Would you really prefer that preface to mine?

I will hunt out the Covici edition and send it to you. There is no mis-

---

[1] On Douglas's comment sheet: 'Ultimately the Chantilly chapter was cut out. . . . I could have forced a lot more deletions or had the whole book suppressed, but out of consideration for G. B. S. and in view of his kindness to me I contented myself with this one correction'.

take about the authenticity of your letters in it. Harris's powers of forgery did not run to that. It contains also a quotation, pages and pages long, from *De Profundis*, which is in this country the copyright of Vyvyan Holland.

I have had to spend the day writing to the *Sunday Times* about Desmond's amazing splutter,[1] also to you. I can no more today.

G. B. S.

21 July 1938 [telegram]   Hove

ALL RIGHT WILL ACCEPT WITHDRAWAL OF PAGES 360 TO 367 LETTER
FOLLOWS   CHILDE ALFRED

21 July 1938   1 St Ann's Court, Hove

My dear St Christopher, Thanks for your letter in which you say that you can easily cut out the last half of that Chantilly chapter. (Please read again my account of the incident in my *Autobiography*, page 163 to the end of that chapter, and you will then realize how impudently Harris has perverted the truth and why I feel indignant about it.) I will accept that offer of yours, and the only thing I would ask of you is that the offending pages may be cut out *immediately* and that as far as possible copies of the book containing them may not be circulated. There are other passages which I dislike intensely and which contain deliberate malice and falsehood on Harris's part, but they are less important, and I certainly agree that your preface more than counterbalances these passages, so I will say no more about them now or at any future time.

Please note, by the way, that Harris's 1925 *New Preface* did not con-

---

[1] Shaw's reply was printed in the *Sunday Times*, 24 July 1938. He said he did 'not understand why the mention of Frank Harris or Oscar Wilde sends so many normally sane people clean off their heads'. He offered to give Mr MacCarthy 'a penny for every lie of which he can convict Harris'.

A letter from Douglas in the same issue expressed gratitude that Shaw had written 'most kindly and sympathetically'; however, Douglas felt that the book was 'still full of libels'.

tain my 'Note to the Second Edition' which will be in the copy sent to you. I had really forgotten all about this 'Note' and I think it was a mistake to print it. I especially regret that it should have contained a nasty remark about the (then unrevealed) St Christopher.[1]

The last three or four days have been a nightmare, and my hair is showing slight signs of going gray (which it has never done before) in consequence! Your   CHILDE ALFRED

P.S. Why do you say in your remarks reported in today's *Daily Herald* that I threatened your publishers with a libel action? I did nothing of the kind and carefully refrained from making any threats. I merely said I could not consent to the continued dissemination of libels on me and that I was 'considering what steps I ought to take'. I couldn't possibly bring myself to take an action against *you* under any conceivable circumstances as you know very well. And as for poor Messrs Constable I am very sorry for them. Their good faith is quite evident and shining. I have just heard from Harold Nicolson that he is doing the book in tomorrow's *Daily Telegraph*.[2]

23 July 1938   1 St Ann's Court, Hove

Dear St Christopher, I have just written to Constable's that I will agree to let the rest of the objectionable matter stand, provided pages 360 to the end of the chapter are cut out. They had already this afternoon wired me agreeing to this. What the h—— you mean by saying that Harris wrote the preface 'under duress' I cannot even guess. Show it to any honest man and let him judge. You admit that you had forgotten

[1] When Harris delayed publication of the *New Preface* and the English edition of his biography of Wilde, Douglas published the *New Preface* himself (Fortune Press, 1925). And when, in 1927, it became apparent that Harris had no intention of publishing the revised edition of the Wilde biography, Douglas added a scathing prefatory 'Note', ending with the remark that 'Mr Harris insists upon placing me in the uncongenial company of his bosom friend and fellow libeller, Mr George Bernard Shaw'.

[2] In his review Nicolson agreed with Desmond MacCarthy that the Wilde biography should not have been published in its present form. As for the preface, he noted the miraculous fact that Shaw managed to be loyal to Alfred Douglas, to Wilde, to Frank Harris and to Robert Ross. 'The dexterity of this combination of incompatibles leaves me agape'.

all about it when you wrote your 'duress' nonsense. So far from my exercising 'duress' on Harris the exact opposite was the case. He *pestered* me and importuned me repeatedly to meet him, and when at last very reluctantly I did (at lunch as a guest of a Mr Chance, an American[1]) he told me his one object was to correct his lies about me, which he said had all been practically dictated to him by Ross, except when they had been told him by Oscar himself. After we had agreed that he should make the corrections and I had written him the long letter in the preface and also given him a book with marginal comments, I did not see him again for a week, when he wrote that he had finished the preface and asked me to go and stay with him at Boulevard Edouard VII. I stayed there for a fortnight and he and Nellie overwhelmed me with hospitality and he professed the greatest affection and friendship the whole time I was there and in many subsequent letters. The story is related minutely in the book I sent you two days ago. I have besides twenty letters of his and numerous witnesses. If you persist in doubting the truth I can only say that this is very injurious and unfriendly. The reason he did not carry out his promise (which you say you can't understand) is clearly explained in my 'Foreword'. So please don't be insulting or unkind. I am at the end of my tether and feel deeply depressed and ill. *Everyone* has been urging me to fight and to get the book suppressed, but I felt I could not possibly fight *you* after the great kindness you showed me over the Rich and Cowan affair and since.

So for God's sake let's not argue any more about the wretched business. Time will show how much or how little I shall have to suffer for it. Perhaps I am needlessly alarmed, but the revival of the whole horrible scandal (millions of people nowadays have hardly heard of it) is very dreadful and Olive also is dreadfully upset by it. Your

CHILDE ALFRED

P.S. I only remember *one* very indiscreet letter I wrote to Harris. That I should have been so foolish as to write it surely *proves* that I believed his desire to right me to be perfectly genuine.

[1] Wade Chance, originally from Canton, Ohio. Through an advantageous marriage to an older lady of position and means (a grand-niece of Washington Irving) he was able to become a conspicuous socialite and clubman, at home in New York, Newport, London and the Riviera. He was a collector of important persons.

23 July 1938   1 St Ann's Court, Hove

Dear St Christopher, I have just come in and found your quite 'dotty' telegram (lying on the mat) in which you speak of the '*1825* (sic) preface' and refer me to the 'postscript on pages *46 and 47*', whereas the postscript is on pages *54 and 55*. The correct version of what happened at Chantilly is given, as I have already told you (only evidently you don't read my letters), in my *Autobiography* . . . and relates how Harris got two thousand pounds out of me after agreeing that I had been most generous to Wilde and that it would be lunacy to give him the two thousand pounds he was demanding. Harris said, "Give *me* the two thousand pounds and I will invest it for you and you will get cent for cent, or two thousand pounds a year for life". When I saw Harris at Nice I did not say anything about this, as I had just been reconciled to him and did not want to stir up old sores, but I gave the full account of the whole business in my *Autobiography*. I sent you the *Preface* so that you might appreciate that the book in its present form is still full of malicious lies about me. You are very lucky that I have not insisted on the alteration of many more passages or the complete suppression of the book. I was far too soft really. I see your telegram reached Hove at 5:14 by which time Messrs Kyllmann and Arnold[1] had left and I had gone up to my wife's in Chichester Terrace. Your

                                                              CHILDE ALFRED

24 July 1938   1 St Ann's Court, Hove

My dear St Christopher, Your letter in the *Sunday Times* is very nice and kind about me though you (once more quite unconsciously) do

---

[1] On his own initiative Otto Kyllmann had gone to Brighton with Ralph Arnold, a young member of the Constable firm, for a talk with Douglas, who finally agreed not to demand the recall of the first edition. This was their first meeting with Douglas, and Kyllmann reported to Shaw that Lord Alfred 'treated us both with the greatest courtesy and was really very pleasant and interesting'. Ironically, the same day (Saturday 23 July) Shaw sent Kyllmann a blast, saying that Douglas 'has grossly libelled your firm by accusing you of "foul and abominable libels". . . . It was I who proposed to delete the pages, as they must be very unpleasant to Vyvyan Holland, and Alfred is now horribly ashamed of them. You must on no account either call in, or refrain from issuing, or in any way admit that you have libelled him or anyone else. Don't go to Brighton unless you mean to kick him. . . .'

me an injustice when you say that I regarded all Harris's other friends as 'shameless liars' on the money question. On another page I give an extract from my *Autobiography* which settles this, and I may also point out that in that same *Autobiography* I accepted Harris's story of the yacht without any qualification. Since then I have been led to doubt it[1] (as well as many of Harris's alleged money gifts to Oscar) by Sherard. But in my *Autobiography* I accept this without question, and speak highly of Harris's generosity in money matters.

As to the discrepancies between what I wrote about Chantilly in my letter to Harris in the 1925 *New Preface* and what I wrote later in my *Autobiography* (and I freely admit that there are discrepancies) I could easily explain them in half an hour's conversation viva voce. . . .

The discrepancies between the two accounts of the Chantilly affair are chiefly explained by the fact that when I was with Harris in Nice in 1925 I was still *raging* against Oscar (over the *De Profundis* letter) and that my only object was to clear myself from Harris's lying charges. Also I was very anxious to avoid offending Harris and starting a new quarrel, which would have been inevitable if I had flatly told him that he was a liar and that his account of the Chantilly interview was a malicious misrepresentation. I might of course easily have denied that I had ever compared Oscar to an 'old prostitute' but knowing how angry I was at the time of the interview I did not trouble to dispute it. . . .

Anyhow I do now violently object to those seven pages and if you had shown me the text before publishing it (as I can't help thinking you ought to have done) I would have told you that nothing on earth would induce me to consent to their republication. This also applies to other pages, but I say no more about them. I did not get your telegram till three and a half hours after it was delivered, so in any case there was nothing I could do about it, and I could not even answer it. I went to the post office and found it shut. Yours   CHILDE ALFRED

---

[1] Sherard disproved Harris's claim that he had had a yacht waiting at Erith for Wilde's escape to France; *Bernard Shaw, Frank Harris and Oscar Wilde*, pp. 189–203.

Dear St Christopher, I send on the enclosed from Robert Sherard as representing the pretty general opinion of my friends (and also of some of my enemies, with whom I classed Desmond MacCarthy until I read his article in yesterday's *Sunday Times*). As to what Sherard says about page 76 in my *Autobiography* (he might more correctly have said pages 75, 76 and 78) there is no denying it.[1] I made those admissions because (although you sometimes seem to cast doubts on my veracity) I am really wedded to the truth, and as soon as I possibly could I told it. I *could* not tell the exact truth in 1914 when my *Oscar Wilde and Myself* appeared. At that date it was *impossible*, except of course that I could plead 'not guilty' in the same sense as Wilde did (see your preface[2]). But there are all sorts of ways of telling the truth, and even the small amount of truth which is contained in Harris's ordurous book is told in the most hostile, unfair and misleading way, while there are whole passages and pages which are deliberately false. One of these days you will begin to realize what a bad turn you have done me by republishing Harris's book, even allowing for your very kind defence of me in your preface. However, I appreciate that you meant all for the best for me and I remain devoted to you. Your   CHILDE ALFRED

P.S. One of these days when I (at last) see you and am able to talk to you I will explain that there is really nothing quite *untrue* even in that first book of mine and Crosland's. I repudiated it because it conveyed a false and misleading impression *on the whole*. It is simply that there are at least two ways of telling the truth and in *Oscar Wilde and Myself* I told it in the bitterest and most uncharitable way, whereas in my *Autobiog-*

---

[1] Sherard's letter assured Douglas that his response in the *Sunday Times* (24 July 1938) was dignified and conciliatory, but he wondered if 'certain plucky admissions' in Douglas's *Autobiography* might not now be used against him, such as his statement that after heavy siege from Wilde, ' "familiarities" (to use Harris's word)' did take place about nine months after meeting, even though these 'familiarities' never included sodomy and they ceased six months before Wilde's trial and were never resumed.

[2] Shaw had stated on p. xxvi that 'Guilty or not guilty is a question not of fact but of morals', and since Wilde believed that homosexual love was the noblest form of passion he could 'plead not guilty with perfect sincerity, and indeed could not honestly put in any other plea'.

raphy I told it much softened and with a great deal of charity. No one more than you knows how to tell essential truth kindly and charitably, so you will understand what I mean.

27 July 1938   1 St Ann's Court, Hove

My dear St Christopher, Why don't I hear any more from you? I have selected four of those photographs of you. Will you please sign them for me if I send them?

The enclosed,[1] which I have just laboriously copied from the copy which I took at the time I wrote it in 1925, will, I think, perhaps make you feel that you have not always been very kind in your judgements of your   CHILDE ALFRED

P.S. Don't drop the childe half way across the river, St Christopher. This is, or might be, the basis of the sonnet I have been trying to evolve about you.

28 July 1938   1 St Ann's Court, Hove

My dear St Christopher, I heard yesterday (rather to my dismay) from Olive that she had sent you a telegram on your birthday! I suppose you know that we don't live together, though on the best of terms. She has a flat here, in the other part of Brighton, as well as one in London, so I see her nearly every day when she is here. I have not shown her the Harris book. I would not like her to see it, as it would frightfully upset her and she is in a very bad state of health. I shall cut your preface out and consign the other part of the book to the kitchen fire.[2]

I wish you would write and tell me how you are, and also what

[1] An angry answer (16 September 1925) to Harris's blackmailing threat concerning his relations with Wilde. For the text see Appendix III.

[2] Five days later Douglas wrote to Otto Kyllmann, 'I would be greatly obliged if you would send me a copy of the Harris book in its altered form with the seven pages removed. I have destroyed the first copy you sent me. That is to say I cut out and preserved Mr Shaw's preface and destroyed the rest'.

about my photographs that I want signed? Are you in London or still at Welwyn? You said you were there till the 27th so I presume you are back in London. Your CHILDE ALFRED

28 July 1938   4 Whitehall Court, London

Dear Childe, Yes: send anything you want signed.

St Christopher has carried the childe safely over and landed it safe and dry on the bank. If the little devil rushes back into the mud and throws lumps of it at the too officious saint, screaming, 'I WILL be drowned; and nobody SHALL save me', what more can the saint do?

I can protect you against everyone except yourself, except yourself, except yourself.

The letters in the Covici edition are now explained. It may have been heroic to put your head into the lion's mouth; but why, oh why did you proceed to kick him?[1]

You and Constable have now taken the case out of my hands. Go your own ways; but don't repeat your unfortunate indication of the suppressed too-true passage. That was wicked.

I can't write until I am better. I had a partial relapse on Monday. And it can't be good for you, this correspondence. I shall not write again (look at my handwriting!) for at least a month.[2]   G. B. S.

28 July 1938   1 St Ann's Court, Hove

My dear St Christopher, I *was* glad to get your letter just now. I have been feeling miserable for the last week, and I feel better now. Do you

[1] Douglas's letter to Harris, see Appendix III.

[2] Shaw wrote to Douglas's wife on this day, relieved that she was not upset by the new edition of Harris's *Life of Wilde* but annoyed that Douglas continued to identify the suppressed pages: 'Please tell him that if he lets the identification go any further you will divorce him. Do this for me and I will promise not to write to him again for a month. With all his gifts and charm Alfred is a psychological curiosity. Sometimes he is possessed by his father, sometimes by his mother; often by both simultaneously. Add to this that his age varies from five to fifty without a word of warning. But this you know a thousand times better than I do' (Clark Memorial Library).

really think that I am safe now? I don't feel as if I were at all, but perhaps you may be right. At any rate I am glad that you are not angry with me as I feared, and that you now understand why I wrote the letter which that beast Harris used in his own characteristic, ignoble way. I still can only remember writing one, but I suppose there must be two.[1] It really doesn't matter much. I feel utterly worn out and am now going to bed although it is only 9:30. I will send your photographs to be signed tomorrow (four of them). The others I will send back in another envelope. I feel sure you will get well now quite soon, and I shall put up a candle for you tomorrow early in the morning to St Anthony, dear St Christopher. Your devoted   CHILDE ALFRED

29 July 1938   1 St Ann's Court, Hove

My dear St Christopher, Here are the four photographs which you kindly promised to sign for me. I will return the others in another envelope. I hope you are better today. I lit a candle for you at eight o'clock this morning. Your   CHILDE ALFRED

P.S. I am trying to find a photograph of myself taken about four or five years ago. It's the latest, and doesn't look *too* awful. But unfortunately the only known copy still in existence I gave to our old cook, Mrs White, when she left us from my mother's house. However, I think I can borrow it from her (she has retired from 'service' but lives in Hove) and have a copy made. It originally cost a shilling in the Western Road here! You have already got one of me in my youth and also the one in *Lyrics*. I wish I still looked like that or, better still, that I had died thirty years ago.

2 August 1938   1 St Ann's Court, Hove

My dear St Christopher, Many thanks for autographing the photographs. Olive wants me to give her one of them, but (as I only have

---

[1] There were two in the Covici Friede preface: pp. xvi–xxxiv and xli–xliv.

four!) I really cannot spare it. So will you be angelic enough to auto-graph another one for her? The one she wants is the one of you leaning forward with your hands clasped.

I have recovered that photograph of myself from our ex-cook, Mrs White, and I am going to get Pannell the photographer here, who is really very skilful, to do some copies of it, one of which I will send you. I shall also get a copy from him of the photograph he did some years ago of the portrait (by Graves) of me at the age of eight, for you. This is really the most appropriate one for you to have as you always treat me as if I were about eight or less, and refer to me in the same way to others (e.g., in your letter to Olive). Of course I don't mind at all, really, though it does *sometimes* cause me to gnash my teeth. I would be very angry if anyone else did it, but of course there is nobody else like you. You seem to be having a great success with your new play[1] but I gather that you are not at Malvern. I hope you are better. Your

CHILDE ALFRED

5 August 1938   1 St Ann's Court, Hove

My dear St Christopher, Your letter in the *New Statesman* is fine. If I had known you were writing I would probably have held my peace, but my letter really corroborates yours entirely.[2] I wrote to Mr Kyll-mann and asked for a copy of the emended edition. I have not yet received it nor any reply to my letter, but I expect he is away on a

[1] Shaw's *Geneva*, a satire on the League of Nations, had opened at the Malvern Festival the night before.

[2] Both Shaw and Douglas replied (6 August 1938) to Raymond Mortimer's review in the previous issue of Harris's *Life of Wilde*. Mortimer had complained that eight thousand of Harris's words had been omitted and that Shaw often put his own words into Harris's mouth, giving an insulting account of Ross.

Shaw cited the *New Preface*, with Harris's 'ungrudging and complete' withdrawals. Douglas said that Harris's condemnation of Ross in his *New Preface* was even more severe than Shaw's. In Ross's defence, however, he noted that though Ross induced Wilde to prosecute Queensberry, he (Douglas) had long before urged the same action. Mortimer replied to both in the same issue, that he had not read Harris's *New Preface*, which was nowhere mentioned in the book he was reviewing, and that he was still not satisfied with Shaw's rewriting of Harris's biography.

Douglas at eight, a pastel by Henry Graves

holiday, and there is no hurry. I have ordered those photographs for you and will send them as soon as I get them.

Two awful misprints in my letter to the *New Statesman*, *Bayeux* for *Bagneux* and *Père Lachaix*(!) for *Père Lachaise*. I can visualize the clever compositor thinking that as *Père* is masculine it must be *Lachaix* and not *Lachaise*! He had also of course heard of the Bayeux tapestries. I have been driven nearly mad by the ingenious imbecility of compositors in my time, when I was editing the *Academy* and *Plain English*.

I see you are now being accused of being on the side of the dictators [his play, *Geneva*]. I am *simply delighted at this*. Of course in the long run you would be bound to see that 'Democracy' is a ludicrous fraud. I have known it and said it all my life. You will certainly end up in the Catholic church. Your⠀⠀⠀⠀⠀⠀⠀⠀⠀⠀⠀⠀⠀CHILDE ALFRED

11 August 1938⠀⠀⠀⠀⠀⠀⠀⠀⠀⠀⠀⠀⠀⠀1 St Ann's Court, Hove

My dear St Christopher, I gnashed my teeth with jealousy yesterday when I saw Olive's photograph of you inscribed 'to Olive', whereas those you sent me are merely signed. Why didn't you put 'to Childe Alfred' on at least one of them? It is very unfair. . . .

I have purchased for a guinea a complete edition of your plays. I am now going to read them all (I know most of them already of course).

I had a letter from Coleridge Kennard[1] at Deauville saying that he has written to the *New Statesman* confirming what I say about Harris. Doesn't it show how abominably I have always been treated by the filthy English press that when in 1925 Harris's *New Preface* was published in London . . . not one single paper in England took the slightest notice of it though at least fifty copies were sent out for review, and it was (obviously) a first-class literary sensation? Can you be surprised that when I had the chance I hit out hard at everyone all round in view of the way I have always been treated?

Without Apology I fear is already as good as dead. Secker is a charming fellow but he has no business instincts (and precious little money)

[1] Sir Coleridge Kennard (1885–1948) denied that he had witnessed the transfer of Wilde's body at Père Lachaise, as Harris claimed.

whereas if Rich and Cowan had published the book they would certainly have sold at least five thousand copies. Secker has sold about a thousand. I shall be lunching with George Sylvester Viereck[1] tomorrow or Saturday and I shall consult him about the possibility of an American edition.

I have not yet got those photographs of myself for you. The tiresome Pannell has not yet even started to make the copies, apparently.

I read *Arms and the Man* last night (of course I knew it before and saw it acted). I think it is *quite delightful*. I discovered a split infinitive in one of your prefaces by the way. Not that I was looking for it, but it hit me in the eye. For my views on split infinitives see page 284 of *Without Apology*.[2] I know lots of the best writers have used them, but I maintain that they did so simply by carelessness and not on purpose. Oscar has a lot, but he always winced when they were pointed out! I found one of my own in an article I wrote in the *Spirit Lamp* in 1893, the other day.

Has the new edition of Harris yet appeared in the U.S.A.? Please write to me and do send me a photograph inscribed like Olive's. Your

CHILDE ALFRED

P.S. I enclose the photograph I like best so that you may add the inscription if you will, please. . . .

12 August 1938 [postcard]   4 Whitehall Court, London

A law reporter of my acquaintance tells me that Clarke[3] told him that he surrendered on an understanding that the affair would go no further.

The American edition has collapsed. Covici's affairs are in confusion.

---

[1] Viereck, German-born American, poet and novelist, a pro-German propagandist during the Great War, who became the leading exponent of Hitler in America. 'My three ideals', he once wrote, 'were Christ, Napoleon and Oscar Wilde'.

[2] Douglas objected to split infinitives on aesthetic grounds. They were ugly. He knew of only one in Shakespeare (in the sonnets), plainly a printer's error.

[3] Sir Edward Clarke (1841–1931, knighted 1886), Wilde's counsel in all three trials. Shaw was offering an explanation for Clarke's withdrawal from the prosecution in the first trial. See the Introduction, p. xv.

Alfred Douglas.
May. 1932

Douglas at sixty-two, a photograph by Pannell

He is practically bankrupt. A recent well-written life of Oscar flopped dead. Dodd, Mead offers to publish my preface, but not the book. Ridiculous. But Dodd insists that there is no interest in Wilde in America.

You are lucky to have sold a thousand copies of your book. People are not buying dear books. There has been a rush for *Saint Joan* at two shillings; and of course my Pelicans are selling at sixpence. The rest don't sell: they only dribble out.

You must take account of the inevitable press boycott of the litigious. Every criticism is a libel if it is not unmixed eulogy. Do you remember Mrs Weldon, a singer with a grudge against Gounod (she had him beaten up)? When she died her name had not been mentioned in a newspaper for twenty years because she was always rushing to the courts.[1] Lottie Collins, the Tarara lady, took an action against a critic and instantly vanished from the press.[2] You paid the same penalty. In great haste   G. B. S.

12 August 1938   1 St Ann's Court, Hove

My dear St Christopher, Many thanks for the photographs and the inscriptions. . . . I am delighted with them and as I have now got five and Olive only one, I am quite happy about it and I shall have a special frame made to hold them all, because if one leaves photographs unframed they end by getting dirty and tumbling to pieces. I shall have the two of myself (one at the age of eight and the other at the age of sixty-two!) for you tomorrow. If I really looked sixty-two, or anything remotely like it, in the photograph, I wouldn't send it to you. I fear it flatters me and it was taken five years ago. Olive however says it is still very like me.

I enclose a copy of my letter to the *New Statesman*.[3] Clarke was a

---

[1] Georgina Weldon (1837–1914), a most litigious woman, was at one time involved in seventeen legal actions, all conducted by herself. See *Letters of Oscar Wilde*, p. 202, n. 1; also *Storm Bird: The Strange Life of Georgina Weldon*, Edward Grierson (1939).

[2] Lottie Collins (1866–1910) was a music-hall performer who became famous for her song and dance, 'Ta-Ra-Ra-Boom-De-Ay'.

[3] This was Douglas's answer to Sir Edward Clarke's letter, dated 16 September 1929 (Clarke had died in April 1931), but his letter had just been sent to the *New Statesman* by

humbug and a twister of the deepest dye. How could he be anything else with that face and those whiskers? I am convinced that he didn't *want* to win Oscar's case against my father. He was a frightful snob and (like many, I might say most, other counsel whom I have experienced) he thought chiefly of himself and only secondarily of his client. My father was a wealthy Marquess, and public opinion was entirely on his side. Clarke refused to lift a finger to show up my father in his true colours. It is absurd to say as Clarke does in his letter in today's *New Statesman* that my father's character was 'quite irrelevant'. Theoretically it may be Clarke could not 'attack' his 'character', but he was entitled to show 'malice', and to expose his *motives*. Actually and in effect he might have launched a deadly attack on my father's character, just as Sir Ernest Wild[1] did on mine in the Ross case (only in my case it didn't succeed because, as you acutely point out, I really was innocent; and not a person of bad character at any time of my life). I am seeing a well-known K.C. here tomorrow morning and I am going to show him my letter and if he thinks there is anything in it which will put me in the wrong I will of course alter it. The fact remains that Clarke *did* promise to put me in the box and it is a piece of sheer impertinence of Sherard to contradict me. How can he possibly know what happened at the 'consultation'? Sherard's assumption of universal and exclusive knowledge about Wilde is very irritating. If I cared to do it I could riddle his book *Bernard Shaw, Frank Harris and Oscar Wilde* with criticism. It is full of ridiculous mistakes and absurdities, though I still think (as I always told you) that there is enough left in it, even allowing for this, to prove Harris a complete liar and faker. If Sherard doesn't take care I shall arise and smite

---

L. Wallace James. In it Clarke categorically denied having promised to put Douglas in the witness-box at Wilde's first trial; the brutalities of the Marquess of Queensberry to his family were 'quite irrelevant to the case' and 'if an attempt had been made to give such evidence the judge would of course have peremptorily stopped it'.

Douglas's reply to Mrs James appeared in the *New Statesman* of 20 August. It was Clarke's word against his, he said, and his recollection of the incident ' had never varied for forty years'. His own character was relevant in the libel case Robert Ross brought against him in 1914, and there was an exact parallel between the two cases.

[1] Wild (1869–1949, knighted 1919) was counsel for Robert Ross in his libel suit against Douglas.

him! You could have made your reply to him in your preface much more effective if you had consulted me about details.

What you say about the American edition is curious. . . . All the same, I hope you will at least publish your preface, which remains, when all's said, a brilliant performance. Your   CHILDE ALFRED

20 August 1938   The Impney Hotel,
Droitwich, Worcestershire

Dear Childe, The portraits had to chase me round a bit before they overtook me; and when they did I was disabled by packing and travelling. The infant one explains why you were so frightfully spoiled by your mother and probably everyone else. The other reminds me of Shackleton[1] the explorer: he had the same sort of eyes.

Clarke's hoity-toity letter probably meant that your father's character was irrelevant in the particular case in question because nothing could have saved Wilde in the face of the Savoy evidence, which must have knocked Clarke end-ways; for I cannot believe that he would have taken the case on if he had foreseen it, especially if, as it is now alleged, he did it for nothing (Why?!!!).

I never read *The Little Duke*. In my childhood I could not endure boys' or children's books (bar fairy tales). Still I have met adults who had liked *Eric* (I never read him, though I read and loathed *Tom Brown*) and adored *Alice in Wonderland*.

My wife is strong on *Water Babies*.

Now I must go off to the theatre to see the Bergner Saint Joan.[2]

How I hate looking at my plays when I cannot work at them!

G. B. S.

3 September 1938   1 St Ann's Court, Hove

My dear St Christopher, I have not written for a long time but this is not because I do not often think of you. I think Hugh Kingsmill's

[1] Sir Ernest Henry Shackleton (1874–1922, knighted 1909), Antarctic explorer of vision and courage.

[2] Elisabeth Bergner was playing the part at the Malvern Festival.

article in the *Fortnightly*[1] is unfair to you in the matter of myself and Mr W. H. Obviously the question of birth did not arise, and you merely pointed out that like W. H. I provoked flowery tributes from poets and others in my youth.

The idiotic Rich and Cowan, who have remained dormant for three months, suddenly flared up again a few days ago and their solicitors wrote to mine still harping on their 'claim' and suggesting that I might write a book for them 'for nothing'!! They really seem to be out of their minds, but until a little more time has elapsed I shall not feel safe from them. I really believe that it would have been better for me to sue them for breach of contract on the principle of attack being the best defence. There is no question but that if they had carried out their contract and published my book they would have sold at least five or six thousand copies. Rich told me (before the trouble about the book began) that they would sell anything from five to ten thousand, and perhaps more. They have a tremendous organization and an army of canvassers, and producers and publicity agents, in contrast to Secker whose business is distinctly 'one-horse'. Rich told me they were 'sitting on the top of the book trade' and could place any book they published with the booksellers all over the country. So if they had published my book I would have made several hundred pounds as I had fifteen per cent., rising to twenty after the first thousand. However I don't like to start an action as the worry of it is so great, and I shall not do anything about it and just wait and see what happens. If they *did* sue me I would certainly beat them and win on my counter-claim for damages, but I hardly think they will do so now. *Nous verrons*.

I have been trying to write a sonnet about you. I haven't got it yet, but it may come out. My standard for sonnets is very high, and unless I can do something up to my best form I will not let it go out.

Are you going to let the American publishers do your preface without the text of Harris's book? I hope so. I fear that book has caused you nothing but trouble. I warned you that even you couldn't whitewash Harris. His book and reputation are dead and buried.

---

[1] September 1938. Kingsmill asserted that 'Shaw had not read Douglas with much attention, or he would not have thrown out the suggestion that Lord Alfred was the plebeian Mr W. H. redivivus'.

I go on reading your plays. You may be pleased to hear that I have come right round about *Saint Joan*. I have never seen it acted, but I have now read it several times and think it splendid. I was prejudiced against it at the time you wrote it.

What do you think about Noyes? I can't help being rather pleased, after the way he behaved about the Abbot's lecture on Oscar, that he should now get rapped over the knuckles.[1] It's a good example of poetic justice. He is a fifth-rate poet anyway. I have not read his *Voltaire*.

Are you quite well again yet? Do let me know. Secker wants me to bring out a new edition of the Harris 1925 *Preface* with a new 'note' by me. But I don't think I am keen about it. What do you think? Your

CHILDE ALFRED

P.S. There is a letter of mine in the [September] *London Mercury*, containing a reference to you.[2]

P.P.S. I am deeply in love with a little girl called Norma[3] (aged eleven). She lives with her parents in an adjacent flat. She began by asking for my autograph and she is now bringing out a magazine! The first number is written out by hand in printed characters, and only two copies were issued, of which I had one. The circulation is however going up by leaps and bounds and there will be four typed copies of the next number.

7 September 1938   1 St Ann's Court, Hove

My dear St Christopher, I have written that sonnet about you (as St Christopher) but I fear it is not up to the mark. I've looked at it now

---

[1] It was Lord Edmund Talbot, not Alfred Noyes (see Douglas to Shaw, 10 May 1938).
    Noyes's argument in *Voltaire* (1936) that the philosopher's deism was more Christian than agnostic aroused controversy. A second edition was causing further tremors in Roman Catholic circles. The matter was being dealt with firmly by the Archbishop of Westminster, Cardinal Hinsley (1865–1943).
[2] Saying he accepted Shaw's comment on his 'infantile complex' as a compliment. Hugh I'Anson Fausset had said that Douglas's childish claims for superiority as a poet were 'self-applause'.
[3] Norma Reeves.

several days and know that it is bad. So unless I can improve it I shall not let it go out. Still I don't despair of ultimately getting it right.

I am going tomorrow to stay for a week with Augustus Ralli[1] at The Grange, Weston Park, Bath. I wish you would write to me, but I don't suppose you will. I have also written a poem for Norma and her magazine, but I have just read in the current number the following devastating *'rule for competitions'*: 'Only people aged eighteen or under can enter. Age will be taken into consideration'. Your   CHILDE ALFRED

P.S. You might let me know how you are.

15 September 1938   1 St Ann's Court, Hove

My dear St Christopher, I have just got back from Bath and find no letter from you. In addition to this disappointment I had the pain of being greeted with marked coldness by Norma when I saw her just before dinner in 'the park' (as St Ann's Walk Gardens, which face my flat, are called by the youth of Hove), although I had sent her an expensive box of chocolates from Bath, besides contributing a sentimental (not to say soppy) 'poem' to her magazine! Altogether life is full of bitterness.

Do let me know how you are. What do you think about Hitler et cet.? I am entirely on his side, but in any case I feel perfectly certain that there will not be any war or anything like it. If I am wrong I am prepared to eat my hat. Your (depressed)   CHILDE ALFRED

17 September 1938   1 St Ann's Court, Hove

Dear St Christopher, I forgot to tell you in my letter yesterday that Olive has given up her flat in Brighton and has moved to London. So I am left alone here, which is very depressing and conducive to low-spirited noises. If you don't write to me soon I shall begin to suppose that you are annoyed with me. You have never told me what you are doing about the American edition of your preface. Is it to be issued by itself? Also are you cured of the anæmia? Your   CHILDE ALFRED

[1] Ralli (1875–1954) was the author of a monumental *History of Shakespearian Criticism.* He shared Douglas's interest in religion, poetry and Shakespeare.

15 October 1938 [written on a   4 Whitehall Court, London
circular of the Arts Club]

Beginning Tuesday October 25th and onwards

OSCAR WILDE
a play by Leslie and Sewell Stokes

Francis L. Sullivan as Oscar Wilde
Peter Osborn as Lord Alfred Douglas!!!
Alan Wheatley as Frank Harris
Leonard Coppins as *Charlie Parker*???
Earle Grey as Sir Edward Carson
Francis James as Dijon

[emphasis and punctuation by Shaw]

Have you seen this and sanctioned it?
I like not Charlie Parker.

G. B. S.

16 October 1938 [postcard]   Ayot St Lawrence

I forgot to point out—though no doubt you know it—that as the Arts
place is by way of being a private club, the Lord Chamberlain's writ
does not run there. Otherwise he would act on your application: at least
he did when he made me change Saumarez into Summerhays [in *Misalliance*] on the application of a real Lord S. But the club, the actor and
the author are vulnerable if they damage a plaintiff or bring him into
hatred, ridicule or contempt.   G. B. S.

18 October 1938   Greyfriars, Iffley Road, Oxford

Dear St Christopher, Here I am among the holy friars, and last night I
dined with Father D'Arcy[1] and the Jesuits at Campion House. So I am
in the odour of sanctity. I go back to Hove on Friday. I should be much

[1] D'Arcy (1888–1976) had been Master of Campion House since 1933 and was inter-
nationally known and respected.

interested to hear what you think of the Oscar Wilde play, which I have not seen myself. Do tell me what you think of it. I am full of melancholy here in Oxford. Yesterday I walked round the cloisters of Magdalen and the whole place was peopled with the ghosts of my boyhood friends, most of whom are dead. I seem to be going through a sort of dark night of the soul just now. I can only hope that I shall emerge into the light soon. This morning I am going over to Stratford with an American friar who is taking a degree here in English Literature. He is motoring me over; I haven't been there for twenty years and have never yet seen the new theatre. Your   CHILDE ALFRED

27 October 1938   1 St Ann's Court, Hove

My dear St Christopher, Do tell me if you saw the Wilde play and what you thought of it. As a matter of fact it was first produced at the Gate Theatre by Norman Marshall *two* years ago, and it is now running to enormous audiences in New York.[1] Norman Marshall and one of the joint authors, Sewell Stokes (his collaborator was his brother Leslie Stokes), came here to see me two and a half years ago, having sent me a copy of the play. I allowed it to pass with a few slight alterations. If I had had any commercial sense I might have done very well out of it, as they offered me, as an inducement to get my permission to do the play (which they could not have produced otherwise), a percentage on the gross receipts. However I didn't like the idea of making money out of it (beyond the twenty-five pounds which I got for what I did to help the play), so I let it go. I think now this was rather stupid of me, as I am always frightfully hard up.

I think a better play could be made out of the whole story to which might be added the romantic runaway marriage of Olive and myself, which would bring in the feminine interest which the present play

[1] In the Gate Theatre production Oscar Wilde was played by Robert Morley, Lord Alfred Douglas by John Bryning and Frank Harris by Reginald Beckwith. At the Fulton Theatre in New York the respective parts were taken by Robert Morley, John Buckmaster and Harold Young. Martin Secker published the play in paper-back in 1937; Random House, New York, in hard-cover in 1938. Both volumes carried a preface by Douglas.

lacks. What do you think of this as an idea for a play? I wish you would do it with me. I couldn't write a play I fear. I am always being urged to try but I don't think I could. But of course *you* could do it brilliantly and I could collaborate out of my memory for real words and dialogue and actual scenes. I expect you will think it very cheeky of me to make such a proposal. It would be of course in any one else, but as you admit that I am the best poet of my age, and compare me to Shelley, I can suggest such a thing without impertinence.

I spent five days at Oxford feeling miserable all the time, (chiefly because I couldn't help remembering and regretting my mis-spent youth there!). I feel slightly more cheerful now, but I have a strong feeling that I shall not live much longer. Not that I mind that. Life is not very pleasant now. Your   CHILDE ALFRED

29 October 1938 [postcard]   1 St Ann's Court, Hove

Dear St Christopher, Many thanks for the stamps. Norma was thrilled by them (though neither she nor I know what country they come from!). Are they from Czechoslovakia, or where?

                                                    CHILDE ALFRED

7 November 1938   1 St Ann's Court, Hove

My dear St Christopher, I am in the most awful trouble, and sunk in the deepest depression. Norma has gone for good. I was suddenly informed by one of her schoolmates that she was leaving Hove for Birmingham. And on Saturday (an hour after I had heard the news) her parents left taking her with them. I saw them off, and her father told me that he had been suddenly 'transferred' to Birmingham (I have no idea what his profession or trade is) and that he was obliged to clear out at two or three days' notice. Norma herself did not know till the last minute anything about it. I don't know why I tell you all this, as most people would think that it is silly to feel so upset about it. But I have an idea that you will sympathize, and understand that it is really a tragedy for me. I don't suppose I shall ever see her again. As I told you before, Olive has also left Brighton. So I am desolate. What a life!

You haven't replied to my suggestion about a play, so I suppose it does not appeal to you.

Last night rummaging in a box of papers I unearthed the shorthand report (typewritten) of my examination and cross-examination in my libel action against Arthur Ransome in 1913. The cruelty and unfairness of the whole business and the wicked way in which Darling, throughout the trial,[1] used all his arts to destroy my case and prevent it from coming before the jury are almost unbelievable. All the same I would have won the case if I had stuck to 'le système Douglas'[2] and told the whole truth. The trouble was that in those days it was really almost *physically* impossible to tell the truth on certain subjects. All the same I *could* have done it, and with a fair judge I would have won the case even allowing for my not making admissions against myself as I did later on (with complete success). I have never really recovered from the effects of losing that case with the bankruptcy and complete material smash-up that it entailed, for though I subsequently turned the tables on Ross and Lewis and Lewis,[3] the result was very much the same as the result of 'winning' a war. Your   CHILDE ALFRED

12 November 1938   Ayot St Lawrence

Dear Childe Alfred, I have not seen the Wilde play. Anyhow it has knocked any possible successor on the head, however superior. So bang goes that notion.

The reason your Catholicism has ended in darkness of the soul is that becoming a Catholic (being born to it is quite a different thing) is only a sociable way of becoming an atheist. You put the church between you and God, and never mention God again. You never get any further,

[1] Mr Justice Darling permitted the defence's strategy of never letting the jury be clear about whether or not Ransome had libelled Douglas; he allowed counsel to concentrate instead on Douglas's past association with Wilde.

[2] See Douglas to Shaw, p. 41, n. 1.

[3] The solicitors for both Ross and Custance in their cases against Douglas.

and won't read Einstein, or Shaw on Creative Evolution. The miraculous world goes dead for you. You change your shoes once a year, but won't change your religion, which wears out faster, once in ten years.

This should have been posted thirteen days ago. I have just found it by accident as I often find my letters.

The stamps were Russian; but Norma is beyond that information now presumably. She will grow out of her present self and you will forget her.

No sonnet, please: what I want is an epitaph. Lady Kennet[1] of the Dene has sculpted a Shakespearean tomb; but she rejects my epitaph (on green paper enclosed) as 'nonsense verse'. G. B. S.

[*The enclosed epitaph*:]

> Weep not for old George Bernard: he is dead;
> And all his friends exclaim "A d——d good job"
> Yet classing George's celebrated head
> Among the more uncommon sorts of nob.
>
> Behold his image! On it Katheen plied
> Until one day the Lord said "No, my lass:
> Copy no more. Your spirit be your guide.
> Carve him *sub specie aeternitas*
>
> "So, when his works shall all forgotten be
> He yet shall share your immortality".

Turn this into poetry if you can.

---

14 November 1938   1 St Ann's Court, Hove

My dear St Christopher, Just got your letter which did me good because what *you* said about Catholicism was so silly. My dark night of the soul

---

[1] Lady Kennet (1878–1947, née Kathleen Bruce, widow of the explorer Robert Falcon Scott and subsequently married to Baron Kennet, P.C.), was a distinguished artist with public monuments to her credit. Her many statues and busts of important persons included King George V, H. H. Asquith, Neville Chamberlain, Lord Hailsham and Bernard Shaw.

The bust of Shaw by Lady Kennet

was no more the end of my Catholicism than it was in the case of St John of the Cross, quite the contrary of course and inevitably I passed through it and emerged into comparative light and cheerfulness. Only I was hurled back into deep depression by the departure of Norma. But even this grief has pretty well departed now . . . leaving only a sort of remembered dream which looks delightful in the distance but is recognized as being insubstantial and foolish. 'So find we profit by losing of our prayers'.[1]

I cannot see why that play now being performed, which you haven't seen, should knock out any other play. It superseded Rostand's play[2] on the same subject which was very bad, and another and much better one might be written.

Your 'epitaph' is skilfully done, but of course I won't hear of it as an epitaph of my beloved St Christopher. I now say a 'Hail Mary' for you every day at Mass, and I have for the last month resumed my old habit of going to Mass every morning at eight. I wouldn't be happy in Heaven if you weren't there. Your   CHILDE ALFRED

24 November 1938   1 St Ann's Court, Hove

My dear St Christopher, I went to the Wilde play last night. It's really quite good and very well acted. I dined as the guest of the producer and with Sullivan, who does Wilde, and the youth [Peter Osborn] who does me and others of the company in the restaurant of the Arts Club before the play. Olive is going to see it on Saturday at the matinée. They (the company I mean) asked me to persuade you to go and see the play. I told them I had *no influence* on you, but I promised to write to you about it. Hence this letter. Do go and see the play and tell me what you think about it. It could have been very much better of course. Your

CHILDE ALFRED

[1] *Antony and Cleopatra*, Act II, scene 1.
[2] *Le Procès d'Oscar Wilde*, by Maurice Rostand (1891–1968), produced in Paris in 1935. The London production was stopped by Douglas because the ending showed him abandoning Wilde after he came out of prison. See *Without Apology*, pp. 292–296.

P.S. If you go to the matinée on Saturday do look out for Olive, who is going with Peter Upcher.[1] I lunched with Olive today at her new flat, which is charming. I told her she ought to see the play.

15 December 1938   1 St Ann's Court, Hove

Dear St Christopher, I have just tracked down the original of that 'jingle' which you so unkindly applied to me, 'If boozy be bosie as some folks miscall it' et cet. I have been subconsciously trying to place it ever since you quoted it.[2] I have now discovered in the notes to one of my editions of Shakespeare that the original lines which you perverted to base uses are in a ballad about his enemy, Sir Thomas Lucy, supposed to have been written by Shakespeare.

> 'If lousie is Lucy as some volke miscall it
> Then Lucy is lousie whatever befall it.

Now, St Christopher, what have you got to say to this? You implied that you had written the lines yourself. At least that was how I took it, while all the time having a vague feeling that I heard them before. Please elucidate.

I am still horribly ill, but I think I have staved off pneumonia and I have come to the conclusion that this is not after all my last illness as I began to think it must be. I am glad to be able to tell you that I found myself not being at all frightened at death. On the contrary the whole situation suddenly cleared up and smiled at me in the most pleasing way. Your   CHILDE ALFRED

17 December 1938 [postcard]   4 Whitehall Court, London

Do you seriously mean to tell me that you have only just discovered 'If lousie is Lucy'? It never occurred to me that any literate person could

---

[1] Upcher, an eccentric young friend of Norfolk background, much interested in the theatre.

[2] See Shaw to Douglas, 4 July 1931.

not be as familiar with it as with 'Pop Goes the Weasel'. My parody of it must have seemed a senseless insult.

Adventures with death rob it of its terrors. I am exceptionally well today; but yesterday I flopped in the hall of Londonderry House on my way in to lunch,[1] and created a devil of a to-do for the rest of the day. In effect, I dropped down dead for the second time in my life. The third time will do the trick, probably.   G. B. S.

21 December 1938 [postcard]   Ayot St Lawrence

The play was very much better than it might easily have been.[2] Did you touch it up? At all events it was good enough to squash any possible return to the subject in the theatre for some years to come.

How did the parody come to your knowledge? I could not have published it, because the reply to 'If B—— be boozy as some folks miscall it' is simply 'They don't'. Quite apart from the bad manners of the thing, it didn't work. But some imp suggested it to me. That is what comes of having a ridiculously unsuitable nickname.

I am snowed up here for this week. Wonderful weather for writing. Twenty degrees of frost in my garden shelter at night, but very jolly in the forenoon, which is my professional working time.

The enclosed stamps are probably as common as dirt; but they look decent, which is the only merit a stamp can possibly have.   G. B. S.

19 February 1939   1 St Ann's Court, Hove

Dear St Christopher, You never answered my letter in which I asked your advice about the American lecture scheme.[3] I wish you would tell me what you think. I don't suppose anything will come of it, but I *would* like to know what you think. I am going to London tomorrow

[1] A lunch party too soon after a liver injection.

[2] *Oscar Wilde*, by Leslie and Sewell Stokes, at the Arts Club.

[3] A suggestion put forward by Douglas's nephew Cecil and by an American millionaire.

Shaw at work in his garden shelter

for two nights and on Tuesday I am going to *The Importance of Being Earnest* matinée with Francis Sullivan and his wife. He acted the part of Wilde in the play, as I dare say you know. I have been ill, on and off, for three months and am not well yet. Do please write. Your

CHILDE ALFRED

P.S. I am fated to make friends with my enemies. For the last three months I have been corresponding with a lady who wrote about my poetry and poetry in general. She expressed great admiration for me as a poet. She signed herself Marie Carmichael and wrote from a country house in Sussex, and is coming to see me next Saturday. I have only just discovered that she is *Marie Stopes*,[1] who has always been a sort of *bête noire* of mine. From her letters she must be charming and full of kindness. Do you know her?

20 February 1939   4 Whitehall Court, London

Dear Childe, I have known men—for instance Graham Wallas and Bertrand Russell—make, as I guess, round about fifteen hundred pounds a year by American lecture tours.[2] But it takes some toughness to stand the daily travelling to and from 'one-night stands'. The distances are sometimes pretty long. I have seen actors finish a tour in the condition of broken-down cab-horses. But their pockets were full; and you can of course limit the tour to what you can stand.

I should think an American tour, if it does not kill you, will do you good.

As a staunch R.C. you will have to keep off the subject of birth control with its prophetess. She is about fifty, a tremendous scientific swell,

[1] Dr Marie Carmichael Stopes (1880–1958), the celebrated crusader for birth control, agitator, lecturer, author of *Married Love* and many other books, had now fought her professional battles and was returning to an early enthusiasm, poetry. She asked Douglas how one might get poetry into print and sent a few of her poems for him to criticize.

[2] Graham Wallas (1858–1932), one of the witnesses at Shaw's marriage, a professor at the London School of Economics, made four lecture tours of the United States and found them exhausting. Bertrand Russell (1872–1970) made many more tours and found them exhilarating.

as litigious as you used to be, about as soothing as a bombardment and liable to drop into reckless poetry and drama at any moment. I have always got on very well with her. Her second husband is Humphrey Verdon Roe, pioneer aviator and veteran of the siege of Ladysmith.

I flopped again last Friday after an injection; and all the staff of our two residences are down with flu. Hence great haste and neglect of letters.   G. B. S.

14 April 1939   1 St Ann's Court, Hove

My dear St Christopher, I was pleased to see your remarks about Hitler quoted in today's *Daily Mail*.[1] It seems to me that everyone except you and me in this country, especially the newspaper people (Right as well as Left), has gone raving mad. Why should there be a war? What for? and what about? and why is Mussolini's occupation of Albania, which has practically been an adjunct of Italy for twenty years, be an awful outrage when our abominable proceedings in Palestine are accepted quite calmly by the Englishman in the street? It looks as if the papers were *determined* to force us into a war at all costs. The papers are perpetually telling us about the 'hysterical abuse' heaped on England in Germany and Italy, whereas they themselves howl themselves hoarse daily with violent abuse of Hitler and Mussolini. This is what is called Democracy I suppose! Any form of dictator, even a Nero or a Caligula, would be more reasonable.

How is your health now? I do hope you are better. I have recovered from my illness but feel very depressed owing to the prospect of being turned out of my flat next March, with which I am faced by my nephew Queensberry. Do you think there would be any chance of my getting a

---

[1] Shaw, as he strode along Great George Street, was interviewed by journalist Charles Graves. Asked what he thought about Germany's take-over of Czechoslovakia, Shaw repeated the thesis of his play, *Geneva*, that ' "the human animal has proved a complete political failure". The Almighty "may have to think again about us and invent something else to take our place" '. According to Graves, Shaw 'then went on to admit that few people realize what a marvellous job Hitler has done. But he doesn't seem to think there is going to be a war'.

civil list pension for 'services to literature'?[1] Even if it was only a hundred and fifty pounds a year that would just pay the rent of my flat and enable me to go on living here instead of having to eke out a miserable existence in lodgings deprived of all my pretty things, furniture, pictures et cet. I don't know how these things are worked, but I suppose strings can be pulled. I am in the good books of the Prime Minister,[2] from whom I received a very friendly letter a fortnight ago in reply to one I wrote him about the political situation. I don't think he would have answered my letter (as I don't know him personally) unless he had agreed with what I said. I believe he is an admirer of poetry. In my letter I said I felt sure that he was going on steadily with his policy of appeasement and that his bowing, or appearing to bow, to the storm was forced upon him against his will. If he hadn't 'bowed' he would have been swept out of office and we should have got Churchill and Eden and Duff Cooper in office, and war within a month. Seriously, please tell me if you think there might be a chance for me to get a small pension. I really haven't got enough to live on now if Francis carries out his intention to stop paying for my flat which he gave me, *as a present*, four years ago. After all I am the best living English poet. Or don't you agree? In any case I am your   CHILDE ALFRED

17 April 1939   Ayot St Lawrence

Dear Childe, The usual course is to send a letter to the P.M. with a string of well-known signatures, at least six, ten if possible, setting forth the literary achievements of So-and-so, and stating that he or she is 'in straitened circumstances' (this is indispensable) and is disabled by age or infirmity from earning a living, therefore is in need of and eligible for a civil list pension.

As your literary achievements include a criminal libel on a cabinet minister and six months' expiation thereof, I have some doubt as to the success of this course.

[1] Grants made by the Sovereign on the recommendation of the Prime Minister for needy persons distinguished in the fields of science and the arts.

[2] Neville Chamberlain (1869–November 1940), Prime Minister from May 1937 to May 1940.

The alternative is private wire-pulling. Some unaccountable pensions have been worked in that way.

But surely you can whitemail the Marquess into saving so near a relative from being put out into the street. You can urge that this possibility makes it impossible for you to get help elsewhere.

Of course the war scare is all nonsense. Now that the last page of the Versailles treaty has been torn up and flung in our faces (it being quite certain that we would not fight for it), and that we are frightened into a combination with Russia at last, there is no sane risk of war on the cards. Still, there are a good many fools about.   G. B. S.

19 April 1939   1 St Ann's Court, Hove

My dear St Christopher, It was kind of you to answer my letter so promptly. In spite of what you say I don't believe that my attack on Churchill and subsequent incarceration would now be counted against me. Hailsham (he was then Sir Douglas Hogg),[1] who was the prosecuting counsel at the Old Bailey when I was convicted, is very friendly to me. His stepson, Edward Marjoribanks, told me that he had expressed great sympathy with me, and some years later when I asked him (Hailsham) to help me to get the manuscript of *De Profundis* from the British Museum he wrote most kindly to me and told me to send my solicitor to see him at the War Office (he was by then Minister for War) and that he would advise him what steps to take. He told Marjoribanks that he considered that I had been very badly treated.

In spite of the fights I have had at various times it is the fact that I have a number of important people who are very well disposed to me. Anyhow I am going to consult various people and see if I can't work up a feeling that I *ought* to have a civil list pension. Unfortunately for what you say about 'whitemailing the Marquess' I hear that he really is very hard hit financially. The poor chap came into nothing when he suc-

---

[1] Hailsham (1872–1950), Attorney General at the time of the libel trial, became Viscount Hailsham in 1929. By his first marriage he was stepfather to Edward Marjoribanks (1900–1932), an Oxford man, and later M.P. for Eastbourne, who wrote the first volume of a *Life of Lord Carson*. Marjoribanks died by his own hand in 1932.

ceeded my brother . . . had only a few hundred a year when he succeeded to the title. He went into the City and joined a firm of stock-
brokers, Rowe, Swan and Company, and for about ten years, up till
two years ago, he was making over thirty thousand pounds a year. But
he is very extravagant, and as he had no capital and lived right up to his
income, when the slump began two years ago he was soon reduced to
comparative poverty. I had a letter two days ago from little Edythe
d'Erlanger,[1] who is a great friend of mine and of his, and she tells me
that he is giving up his house in Cheyne Walk and moving into a flat
and that he really is very hard hit. She promised to tackle him about my
flat, but said she feared it would be no good. So you see it really looks
as if he *could* not help me. I am still hoping that it may not be as bad as
that, but it looks pretty hopeless to me. I have written to his solicitor,
d'Arcy Hart, who does my income tax for me (by his instructions) and
I have asked him to see if he can induce him to go on paying the rent,
for which he is *morally* responsible as he *made* me take this flat and guaranteed to pay the rent—so I shall know the worst very soon. I am also
raising a certain amount of dust round the family in general. Everyone
is very sympathetic and says it's "really an awful shame" and so forth,
so I am not altogether without hope. What a life! 'From the beginning,
when was aught but stones / For English prophets?'[2] Your unfortunate

CHILDE ALFRED

P.S. William Watson[3] was given a pension of two hundred or two hundred and fifty pounds a year. He also had six thousand pounds raised by
private subscription and he was given a house. . . .

30 April 1939   1 St Ann's Court, Hove

My dear St Christopher, I have decided to chuck the idea of the pension.
A man who knows a lot about it and has actually worked one or two

---

[1] Edythe Baker, the petite American jazz pianist, who had been briefly married to
Sir Gerard d'Erlanger.

[2] Douglas is quoting the first two lines of his poem 'Rewards'; *Complete Poems of Lord
Alfred Douglas* (1928), p. 87.

[3] William Watson (1853–1935, knighted 1917), greatly admired in the 1890s, was a
poet in the Miltonic tradition, a champion of conservatism and bitterly critical of Oscar
Wilde and the aesthetes. Watson was twice a strong candidate for the post of Poet
Laureate.

told me that my four hundred pounds a year[1] would be considered a definite bar. No hope unless you are *really destitute*!! So I am resorting to prayer instead.

What do you think about Hitler's last speech? I think it's entirely logical and reasonable. I agree with what the Cardinal of Westminster said the other day, that if all our beastly (my word) papers were suppressed for a fortnight there would be complete peace at once. I get so annoyed when I read them that I am in danger of dying of rage as Flaubert did for (more or less) the same reasons. Your

CHILDE ALFRED

2 May 1939 [postcard]   Ayot St Lawrence

Four hundred?

Gosh!!
Of course, quite hopeless.
The technical phrase is 'straitened circumstances'.
In the present case it would probably be

OPULENCE.   G. B. S.

30 May 1939   1 St Ann's Court, Hove

My dear St Christopher, I ought to have explained to you that the celebrated 'four hundred pounds a year' is only a voluntary allowance which *might* cease, though I don't suppose it will. Actually I have *nothing at all* and my literary earnings *average* about fifty pounds a year! Or even less. Mrs Stopes tells me that Lord Hailsham wrote *most* sympathetically and regretted that his official position prevented him from signing, but he wished the idea every success. I have got dozens of other names, and I can get at least one archbishop (R.C.) or two if necessary, and an abbot (Hunter-Blair, *who is also a baronet*!), various ex-ambassadors and quite a good show of literary lights: Quiller-Couch, Blunden,

---

[1] From his wife.

de la Mare, Humbert Wolfe et cet. et cet.[1] But of course you would be the chief star of the galaxy. So please agree to sign. Mrs Stopes thinks it can be worked out all right.[2]

No news, except that I backed the winner of the Derby for the third time in the last four years. But perhaps this should be kept dark!

My rejected letter to *The Times* about the political situation was printed with great prominence in the *Deutsche Allgemeine Zeitung*[3] in Berlin and I got an official letter of thanks from the German Embassy and am snowed under with letters from Germans. But I have also had most friendly letters from Chamberlain and Halifax to save me from being considered too 'pro-German'. Why do I never see you? Your

CHILDE ALFRED

30 May 1939   1 St Ann's Court, Hove

My dear St Christopher, By a coincidence I wrote to you last night, but as it was late I did not post the letter. I merely stamped it and left it lying on a table for posting this morning. Now I get your letter with the stamps, so I write this letter rather than reopen the first. *Donc*, you will get two letters from me by the same post. It is most sweet of you

[1] Sir David Hunter-Blair (see Douglas to Shaw, 10 May 1938, note 1); Sir Arthur Quiller-Couch (1863–1944, knighted 1910), Professor of English Literature, Cambridge, editor of *The Oxford Book of English Verse* (in the 1939 edition of which three sonnets of Douglas appeared); the poets Edmund Blunden (1896–1974), Walter de la Mare (1873–1956) and Humbert Wolfe (1886–1940).

[2] She was oiling the wheels behind the scenes, bringing distinguished friends to her house, Norbury Park, to discuss strategy, among them Rose Macaulay, who drafted the petition to the Prime Minister.

[3] 21 May 1939:

To the Chief Editor of *The Times*

Sir: Mr Roosevelt's telegram to the dictators is excessively childish. The only effect it can have is to embitter the dictators or charm them to laughter. If we get entangled in a war on the side of Russia and France, of the Popular Front against Christian nations like Italy, Germany and Spain, would we not be fighting a war to make the world safe for Bolshevism? As far as I am concerned I can say only that in such a war I would not stand at England's side. Your obedient servant

Lord Alfred Douglas

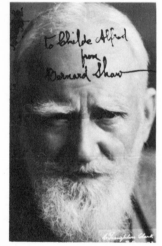

With Bernard Shaw's compliments

You will have to squint at them sideways to see the prismatic signature

4 Whitehall Court, London, S.W.1.
30/1/88

The five Shaw photographs
which Douglas framed

to send those stamps. I will post them on to the beloved Norma, who will be delighted. I had a rather tragic letter from her mother about a week ago. The letter was to thank me for giving Norma a bicycle on her birthday and to say that it was the pride and joy of her life and that she would like to take it to bed with her at night if her mother hadn't forbidden it! But it appears that the reason for the family's departure from Hove is that they have had heavy financial misfortunes and were obliged to clear out of their nice flat here and go to Birmingham, which naturally is a blow to poor little Norma, though her mother has concealed from her the reason for the move.

Talking of financial misfortunes, I really think you are mistaken about that four hundred pounds. It appears that I *may* get a civil list pension just for my 'services to poetry and letters'. It has been done in other cases. Mrs Stopes had consulted numerous people, including two cabinet ministers. . . . So please be angelic (you are that already) and sign the 'petition'. If it does not succeed at least no harm will be done. It is a nightmare to contemplate having to clear out of this flat where I have all my books and papers and some really good furniture. I would have to store the furniture and go to live in lodgings, and would probably never see my furniture again. So please don't refuse to perform once more your destined St Christopherian office across this river. I am taking your five photographs this morning to Pannell the photographer here to have a special frame made for them. I have been meaning to do so for months. Your   CHILDE ALFRED

2 June 1939   4 Whitehall Court, London

Dear Childe, Official people are so fond of a job and eminent people are so fond of a lord that, as I said, it is not impossible that a pension may be wangled for you if you select the names of your supporters judiciously, avoiding those of notorious celebrities whose mention rouses furious resentments among the jobbers and snobbers. Foremost among such fatal names I should blacklist Marie Stopes and G. B. S.

The main difficulty is that you are yourself notorious enough to be in that list.

Have you considered that if the four hundred pounds is really voluntary the donor may reduce it by the amount of any pension you may obtain?

The money available for civil list pensions, though it has been increased lately, is still disgracefully small. The grant of a single farthing to anyone rolling in such riches as four hundred pounds a year would be a scandal, if it attracted attention. It used to be impossible to extract more than eighty pounds a year on the case's merits. Now they give a hundred pounds, but are keen on genuine straits. My last attempt to get a pension for the destitute widow[1] of a man whose services to art in Manchester gave her overwhelming claims was turned down without apology. So much for the value of my urgent recommendation!

Since writing the foregoing I have had a talk with Marie. She has a fine list of names, but thinks that she had better risk her own rather than not have a woman's signature. She may be right. Anyhow her name is not as dangerous as mine. G. B. S.

16 June 1939 [postcard]   Ayot St Lawrence

The public will know nothing about it; if they did there wouldn't be half a chance. But three or four almighty people (and perhaps their wives) will. Lucky that the P.M. and Churchill are not, presumably, on chatting terms. Anyhow, when there is a highly respectable and harmless list available it is a mistake to add swanky names like M's and mine out of pure vanity. They can do no good, and may do irreparable harm.[2]

Watson, who was horribly poor, was a very good rhetorical poet; but nothing is more absurd than a price list of poets. G. B. S.

[1] Widow of Charles Rowley (1840–1933); he founded the Ancoats Brotherhood in Manchester, a working-men's arts organization.

[2] Marie Stopes presented her petition to Prime Minister Neville Chamberlain on 21 June. The signatures, besides her own, were: James Agate, Edmund Blunden, the Reverend Lord Clonmore, St John Ervine, John Gielgud, Christopher Hassall, Harold Nicolson, Arthur Quiller-Couch, Marie Stopes, J. C. Squire, Hugh Walpole, Evelyn Waugh, Humbert Wolfe and a second 'woman's signature', Virginia Woolf.

20 June 1939 [postcard]   Ayot St Lawrence

Yes, of course: why leave them there doing no good to anybody?[1]
But the slump is a fact. A lot went at Sotheby's for four shillings
apiece as well as I recollect. Not a very interesting one, however; not
double barrelled (A. D. and G. B. S.) like this one.

Possibly a good private contract would be better than risking Sotheby's.
As for Duckworth,[2] a job's a job. Have you anything better to do?
At least you can make fun of poor Sherard. That is, if the price ———— ??
How goes the scandal?[3]   G. B. S.

29 June 1939 [postcard]   4 Whitehall Court, London

You have a statutory right of fair quotation: No legal need to ask
leave. You are welcome as far as I am concerned.[4]

Sherard's contention that Frank's book is stolen from his, and that it
is a tissue of lies from beginning to end, is perfect Sherard.

Whatever you do don't start the old solemn recriminations; and get
as much detergent fun into the case as you can.   G. B. S.

27 July 1939   1 St Ann's Court, Hove

My dear St Christopher, I saw in the papers that yesterday was your
birthday, so many happy returns, and a candle to St Anthony will be
lit today for you. I saw a picture of you looking extraordinarily well
and vigorous. I hope you really are well.

I have been going through perfect hell, because I have been writing
this book for Duckworth about Wilde. . . . I very nearly wrote to
Duckworth returning his advance and saying I couldn't possibly do it.

[1] Pressed for money, Douglas was considering the sale of Shaw's correspondence. See
Shaw to Douglas, 23 June 1942.

[2] Duckworth, the publishers, had asked Douglas to write a book for them.

[3] The civil list project. Marie Stopes received an answer from Chamberlain's secretary
on 22 June, saying that March was the time the list was considered; any petition for Douglas would have to be presented in March 1940.

[4] Permission to quote from Shaw's preface to Harris's life of Wilde. There is no statutory right of fair quotation in Great Britain, but it is generally considered to be roughly
five hundred words of prose and less of poetry.

However now I have written twenty-two thousand words (all written in a week). The book is only to be thirty thousand and I am going tomorrow to stay with A. J. A. Symons at Brick House, Finchingfield, Essex, till Monday. He can help me with dates and facts and I hope to finish the book there. I came to the conclusion that in order to do the book in an original way (and to prevent it from being just a 'guide-book') I *must* deal with the whole question of homosexuality. So I start off with the first three chapters all on the subject. I would awfully like you to read what I have written, and I very nearly posted off the carbon typescript copy of what I have written (eight chapters) to you last night. But then it occurred to me that you would curse me and think me an awful bore if I did! I know what it is to have unsolicited manuscripts fired at me. So I refrained. I saw Symons in London yesterday (you know he is doing a full-length biography of Wilde) and he read what I had written. He told me he thought it quite excellent and that it "filled him with jealousy". This was an enormous relief (if he really meant it and was not just trying to 'buck me up'), as I really hadn't an idea whether what I had written was any good at all. I still feel nervous about it. For one thing I don't know whether Duckworth and the public will stand for my chapters about homosexuality. Of course I do not defend it, but my argument is that it is a moral offence (a sin) and not a crime and that therefore the law ought not to take any cognizance of it (as is the case with the Code Napoléon in France). I have quoted what you say in your Harris preface about Wilde's attitude to it which is admirable and completely true. Also said some nice things about you. . . .
Your ever devoted   CHILDE ALFRED

P.S. I spent the week-end before last at a place called Wadhurst Park (a place that used to belong to the Murrietas) with Grant Maclean and his wife (very rich). They had a Hollywood film magnate to meet me (he controls Paramount) and he wants me to do a film scenario about Wilde. I don't know whether anything will come of it, but he seems very keen and has written to me twice since I met him. If it came off I would make a lot of money.[1]

---

[1] Wadhurst Park, in Sussex, was owned by Grant Maclean, a retired solicitor, who frequently advised Douglas on legal matters. The 'film magnate' was a Mr Piazza.

27 July 1939 [postcard]   4 Whitehall Court, London

I shall have to read it [*Oscar Wilde, A Summing-Up*] someday; so why not now?   G. B. S.

9 August 1939 [postcard]   Ayot St Lawrence

Splendid idea, that about the free-thinking! Go it for all you are worth.[1] But don't forget that it serves the church right for not clearing out its old rubbish. None the less, nineteenth-century freethinking was disastrous. My old cliché about it—that its leaders were not really pursuing science, as they thought, but smashing the Bible, abolishing God and marrying their deceased wives' sisters—is roughly true. There was no salvation in that for your father: it lifted him out of the Bastille only to throw him homeless on the streets.   G. B. S.

9 August 1939   Ayot St Lawrence

—In great haste—

You must not identify [Vyvyan] Holland unless with his consent and at his desire.

Wilde's court costume was quite becoming; and you should not ignore the genuine aestheticism of his motive in adopting it on the platform. I don't think he ever wore it in the street.

I did not dislike Wilde; and I don't think he disliked me, though it was of me that he said, "Shaw hasn't an enemy in the world; and none of his friends like him". This was true; and so good that he used it several times of different people. He always did.

He did not exaggerate his mother's social importance *in Dublin*. You don't understand Ireland and Irishmen. Ireland is *all* plantation; Macaulay's notion that the planted Irishman is English is as absurd as the notion that the planted Englishman is a Norman Frenchman.[2]

                                                   G. B. S.

[1] See *Oscar Wilde, A Summing-Up*, pp. 126–127.
[2] Douglas quoted almost all of this letter in *Oscar Wilde, A Summing-Up*, pp. 83–84.

11 August 1939   1 St Ann's Court, Hove

My dear St Christopher, Here is the typescript of the book. I hope you will not think it too bad, and I hope you will approve of the first three chapters, where I have dealt with the whole question of homosexuality. I am worried about what Duckworth will think. In the end, after going through frightful agonies during which I was on the point of writing to Duckworth and telling them that I couldn't do the book and returning the advance, I wrote the whole thing in about three weeks. . . . I have two other copies of the typescript, so you can keep this copy a reasonable time, though I would like to have it back at your convenience.
Your ever devoted   CHILDE ALFRED

15 August 1939   1 St Ann's Court, Hove

My dear St Christopher, I am delighted to see your Charles II play[1] has had such a big success. I wish I could have seen it. I sent the typescript of my book to Duckworth yesterday. I am rather apprehensive as to what they will think about those chapters on the homosexual question. If you approve of them do write to me and say so, so that if necessary, and if they object to them, I can quote you. I feel pretty sure that you will not disapprove of them, but till I hear from you I shall be nervous about it.
Your devoted   CHILDE ALFRED

P.S. Are you publishing the text of your new play, so that I can get it?

15 August 1939   1 St Ann's Court, Hove

My dear St Christopher, The 'reader's report' is a brilliant skit. It is *exactly* the sort of drivelling idiocy that the average reader to a publisher (who nine times out of ten is a bloody fool) does write about a good book. Why have we not got the original reader's report of the man who

[1] *In Good King Charles's Golden Days* was a Malvern Festival play in 1939, published by Constable's the same year.

turned down Charlotte Brontë and Jane Austen? All the same, I wish you had written something serious. I was rather disappointed when I opened the envelope and read what at first I took for serious complaints that 'the scarlet Marquess' was 'confused' with my father, considering that I carefully explain that 'the screaming scarlet Marquess' was Wilde's nickname for my father (paraphrasing a phrase in his poem, *The Sphinx*, about the 'screaming scarlet ibis'). At first I thought you had suddenly lost your wits! But it is of course exactly the sort of rot that a publisher's reader writes. You have hit it off miraculously. My *Autobiography* was turned down by nearly every publisher in London (no doubt on the strength of similar reports) and yet it was a big success and had a large sale in English, French and German and completely revolutionized the Wilde story as accepted before I wrote it.

You might have told me what you really thought about the first three chapters and the homosexual question. . . . Why couldn't you write reasonably instead of making Irish jokes (I suppose they must be Irish because you say I don't understand Irishmen!)?

I have just had a man here from the *Sunday Pictorial* to interview me. He wanted to know whether it was true that I was pro-German and anti-British! And did I intend to fight for Germany in the war? This on the strength of the letter which I sent to Fitzrandolph[1] of the German Embassy who had it printed in the *Allgemeine Zeitung* in Berlin! I gave the reporter an interview, and his editor will probably distort it. If he does, I shall sue the *Pictorial* for libel! It's a foul rag anyway. Your devoted
CHILDE ALFRED

P.S. What about printing your 'reader's report' and my reply as a preface to my book?

P.P.S. I shall take your hint about Holland. Symons had already told me that he thought he would not like to be identified as Wilde's son. Your other (pencilled) points are also duly noted. I take them seriously, as distinct from the 'reader's report'.

---

[1] Sigismund Sizzo Fitzrandolph, press attaché at the German Embassy in London from 1933 to 1939. See p. 111.

Dear Childe, To come down to tin tacks.

You must rearrange that idiotic book as follows. You must begin with Wilde's birth and follow his history to his grave as matter-of-factly as the *Dictionary of National Biography*. Then, when the reader is in full possession of all that Wilde was and exactly what happened to him, you can moralize about him to your heart's content; for not until then will your alarums and excursions be intelligible.

You must explain why the new biography is needed in spite of the admirable work by Harris, revised by yourself and, considering its date, a model of what a biography should be (just as your manuscript is a model of what it shouldn't be).

You must explain that Harris and Sherard were hampered by the fact that in their time it was generally believed that homosexuality involved the most horrible depravity of character, and was unnatural and unmentionable. Since then the work done in England by Havelock Ellis and Edward Carpenter and abroad by Freud and the psychoanalysts has completely changed all that. Not only have sexual subjects become mentionable and discussable (compare Thackeray's novels with D. H. Lawrence's) but it is now known that a reversal of the sex instinct occurs naturally, and that the victim of it is greatly to be pitied and may be a person of the noblest character. Wilde's life must therefore be taken out of the old atmosphere in which Harris and Sherard wrote, and retold with a healthy objectivity which was impossible before the war.

In doing this you must clear your mind of Sodom and Gomorrah and the Catholic categories of sin-as-distinguished-from-crime and all the rest of it. You will have to explain that Wilde was prosecuted not for sodomy but for offences under the Criminal Law Amendment Act for the protection of boys, as to which he was guilty. It is not necessary to pester the reader with assurances that you are bound as a Catholic to proclaim Pickwickian opinions and values that are now obsolete, irrelevant and ridiculous.

You must cut out the sentimental rubbish about Mrs Wilde, which is just like Sherard. She was not a pretty woman, and never can have been; but she was not ugly: her appearance simply calls for no comment. As for its being her duty to stick to Wilde, did your mother think it *your* duty to stick to Wilde? You forget that Constance had two sons to bring up, much younger than the one son your mother felt responsible for. To combine your pious condemnation of Mrs Wilde with your disclosure of Holland's parentage is unspeakable.[1]

You are bound not only to narrate the trial with documentary calm, but to tell the important and indispensable truth that Wilde, like Edmund Kean, [Thomas] Robson and Dickens, died of an attempt to live on alcohol for the sake of the extraordinary power it gave to him as an actor.

You must make up your mind as to whether *De Profundis* is a forgery or not. If it is, you have no grounds for complaining that Wilde attacked you; and all that stuff must come out. If you accept it as genuine, which it obviously is, you have no ground for describing it as a fake. As nobody now remembers anything about Ross, your weakness for vulgar abuse really does him a resurrectional service.

Your spluttering letter needs no reply. My sketch of what any intelligent and not unfriendly publisher's reader would report was meant to open your eyes to the effect your book must make. Years have passed and oblivion has thickened since your autobiography was published. Symons was right in concluding that what you wanted was not criticism but adulation; and he laid it on accordingly. He ought to be ashamed of himself. Now go and rearrange your book exactly as I tell you, and be damned to you. I do not enjoy having my time wasted.   G. B. S.

P.S. As you have rashly sent the book to Duckworth without waiting for my instructions you had better send him my 'reader's report' also and ask him whether he agrees. You will thus get an independent opinion. Of course he will agree with every syllable of it.

You are an exceedingly troublesome Childe.

18 August 1939   1 St Ann's Court, Hove

My dear St Christopher, Why don't you write a life of Wilde yourself in thirty thousand words and see how you make out on it? Whatever

[1] They were not altered in the published book (*Oscar Wilde, A Summing-Up*, pp. 95–103).

you made of it, it could not be a greater failure or have a more devastating 'press' than your edition of Harris's imbecile work (redeemed of course by your brilliant preface) which you (absolutely alone as *Bernardus contra mundum*) persist in considering the best life of Wilde. Seriously why do you want to turn me into a sort of little Bernard Shaw? Nothing could be more absurd and more fatal than for me to write a life of Wilde on your lines, and from your point of view which is almost the exact opposite of mine. I write as a devout Catholic (although I have the advantage of having known all about the homosexual question long before your Havelock Ellises and Freuds turned their attention to it) and, as regards my friendship with Oscar, a sentimentalist. I am not going to change my views just to please you. It would take a twenty-page letter to answer all the absurdities of your 'reader's report' (which has gone into the waste-paper basket) or your letter received this morning. You are utterly unscrupulous in argument. You just say anything that comes into your head. In your utter inability to appreciate any point of view but your own you remind me forcibly of my father! e.g., on a quite minor point, you say that Mrs Wilde was not pretty. Well, which of the two, you or I, is more likely to be a judge of that point? I who spent weeks at a time in her house, played tennis with her, danced with her and saw her continually on and off for more than four years, or you who hardly knew her and cannot have seen her more than a few times, generally in the distance? However, I utterly decline to be lured into a slinging match with you. I don't suppose I should have a chance, because I hate hurting anyone's feelings and you thoroughly enjoy it. I remain quite devoted to you, and if you like me at all you must make up your mind, like the schoolboy, to 'know all about me and still go on liking me'. You can't have me on any other terms.

I sent in my book to Duckworth's three days ago and so far have only a formal acknowledgment. I don't intend to alter it at all except on minor points (e.g., I will, if you like, mention that you deny disliking Wilde and that Lady Wilde, from the Irish point of view, was a *grande dame*)[1] and if Duckworth's don't like it, *tant pis*. I know that Secker

[1] Both alterations were made by quoting from Shaw's letter of 9 August 1939 (*Oscar Wilde, A Summing-Up*, pp. 83–84).

would be delighted to publish it if they don't want it. Your devoted

CHILDE

P.S. It is characteristically unfair of you to say that you 'don't like having your time wasted'. I asked you if you would like to see my book and you replied by return of post saying you would. I then, at your request, sent it to you. So why am I *wasting your time*? What about *my* time, to say nothing about my nerves, and my self-esteem, which (although I have some of the virtue of humility, to which you are a complete stranger) is hurt by your vicious kicks?

18 August 1939   4 Whitehall Court, London

You BLASTED idiot, who has asked you to change your views?

Is a couple of days' work too much to give to providing your pronouns with antecedents and deferring your criticisms and moralizings until the reader knows what you are talking about? Three or four sentences omitted and perhaps half a dozen modified will get rid of the contradictions.

You will aspire in vain to be even a sixth-rate Bernard Shaw until you learn to forget yourself and, bearing your reader in mind all the time, hammer at him incessantly as a capable barrister hammers at the jury and the judge until nothing but his case—least of all himself—fills their minds. Then there will be no reason why you should not be a first-rate B.S.

At present you are a squalling baby. It is no use asking me to like you: I HATE a slovenly workman.

You are a monster of selfish ingratitude. Let me hear no more of your bungled book.   G. B. S.

27 August 1939   4 Whitehall Court, London

Here is your scenario. Very nice of your friends to butter you; but such butter is no good for parsnips.

Note that on Tuesday I go down (D.V.) to the Hotel Esplanade, Frinton-on-Sea, Essex, where I expect to be until the end of September. In haste—packing   G. B. S.

CHAPTER I	The Nativity in Seventeenth-Century Ireland.	CHAPTER XIII	Justice Wills Has Read the Bible but Not Havelock Ellis or Freud.
CHAPTER II	Protestant Portora in the Island of the Saints.	CHAPTER XIV	*De Profundis* and Clapham Junction.
CHAPTER III	Trinity College, Dublin, and Its Blackguard Students.	CHAPTER XV	Two Years without Drink. Oscar the Athlete.
CHAPTER IV	Oxford, Civilization, Mahaffy and Greece.	CHAPTER XVI	The Whelp, Grown Poet, Is Faithful in Friendship.
CHAPTER V	The Mad Marquess and His Parricidal Whelps.	CHAPTER XVII	The Swan Song of Reading Gaol.
CHAPTER VI	Aestheticism and Dublin Snobbery in London.	CHAPTER XVIII	Ink or Drink? Kean, Robson, Dickens.
CHAPTER VII	*Lady Windermere's Fan* and Lady Wilde's Immoralism and Acromegaly.	CHAPTER XIX	Immortality as a Talker on Alcohol.
CHAPTER VIII	Success. "I thought I could do anything".	CHAPTER XX	The Price: Death at Forty-six. Shaw Active at Eighty-three.
CHAPTER IX	The Super-Aesthete Is Seen in Low Company.	CHAPTER XXI	Asinine Obituaries. The *Encyclopaedia Britannica*.
CHAPTER X	The Mad Marquess Strikes at His Whelp through Oscar.	CHAPTER XXII	The Aftermath of Litigation and Biography.
CHAPTER XI	The Whelp Counters, also through Oscar.	CHAPTER XXIII	Necessary Revision of Valuation. Oscar a Great Man.
CHAPTER XII	Oscar 'between the fell incenséd points of mighty opposites'. [*Hamlet*, Act V, scene 2]	ENVOI	The Whelp's Amends.

10 September 1939   Hotel Esplanade,
                                                    Frinton-on-Sea, Essex

Childe, Childe, My scenario was an arrangement of *your* manuscript, not of anything that I have any intention of writing. Anyhow, what does it matter whether it is mine or yours if it does the trick? When Shakespeare lifted the moralizings of Gonzalo out of Montaigne just as they stood, he was not jealous of his 'originality' like a nineteenth-century gentleman amateur scribbler. When Handel copied 'The Lord is a Man of War' into the score of *Israel in Egypt* he was glad to be saved the time it would have taken to compose it. When I appropriated Mrs Clennam and Jaggers from Dickens and the brigand-poetaster from Conan Doyle, I had no scruples and have none.

But you are such a d——d fool!

It is waste of time trying to help you.

Four pounds a week is about the salary of a Japanese general. You can live on it. Many a large family would be proud to take you on for fifteen shillings a week. An Irish monastery could make a profit out of you. Any hotel in Yugoslavia would take you *en pension* for ten shillings a day. If you can't afford St Ann's Court you must live in St Ann's Alley. And you can always threaten to starve on Francis's doorstep.

I don't see how we can blockade Hitler now that he has Russia to buy his supplies in. And victory nowadays means blockade.

My wife has been bedridden and in great pain (lumbago) for days. The closing of the theatres and the blackout are exasperating extremities of blue funk. I am in the worst of tempers. Do not tempt me to vent it on you. What do I care about your flat? Shoot the moon if you must. This hotel closes on the 30th, when I must return to Ayot.

G. BERNARD SHAW

18 September 1939   Hotel Esplanade, Frinton-on-Sea

No, dear Childe, we are not like Higgins and Eliza; we are like the fighting mate and the true British sailor. Thus.

LOOK OUT FOR SQUALLS : A NAUTICAL MELODRAMA

F. M.   Stand by to ease off that sheet there.

T. B. S.   (*day-dreaming*) ????? (*A minute elapses.*)

F. M.   (*thinking he did not give the order*) Stand by, etc. . . . (*Another minute elapses.*)

         (*ominously*) Did you hear me tell you to stand by, etc?

T. B. S.   (*apprehensively*) Yes, sir.

F. M.   Then why the b—— h—— didn't you obey your orders, you —— you —— you —— —— —— (*punctuating the foulest epithets with violent kicks*).

T. B. S. (*ruefully rubbing his contusions*) I didn't think you meant it. (*The Mate executes the order himself.*) *Curtain.*

I wish I could find any extremity of vituperation that would induce you to attend to what I write. For instance, you make the usual low-spirited noises about having to leave out your remarks on homosexuality. I give you a scenario in which I provide you with a chapter—that on Justice Wills—which is the right place for these remarks. And all I get out of you is more noises and a claim—always a claim—that you read Ebbing (meaning Ebing)[1] long before Havelock Ellis and Freud knocked some sense into ordinary Bible students like Wills. I dare say you did; but was it you that sentenced Wilde or was it Wills? Can you never cease thinking of yourself, damn you?

I knew, of course, that Francis couldn't afford to have you sitting against his railings, earning coppers as a screever. St Jude always sends some soft-hearted idiot like Mrs Denham[2] to the rescue of incorrigibly lazy worshippers. These saints love flattery. . . .

I have just written to *The Times* about the blessed intervention of Russia,[3] and have no time for more.   G. B. S.

12 October 1939 [postcard]   4 Whitehall Court, London

I don't know [Vyvyan Holland].

Why not offer to withdraw your objection to *De Profundis*?[4] My recollection of the suppressed sequel is that it was so belittling to Wilde that Ross was quite right to suppress it, though wrong to suggest that it was of any importance.

---

[1] Baron Richard von Krafft-Ebing (1840–1902), German author of *Psychopathia Sexualis* (1886).

[2] Mrs J. D. Denham-Smith of Hove, a recent widow, offered to give Douglas financial assistance in March 1940, when Queensberry's lease on the St Ann's Court flat was due to expire. She and her husband, a barrister who wrote light verse (*Love, Laughter and After*, published in 1934), were old friends of his.

[3] 'Poland and Russia', 20 September 1939.

[4] For a number of years Wilde's son had wanted to publish the full text of *De Profundis* but, though he owned the copyright, Douglas's threat of a libel suit continued to block the venture.

It is also in the same way belittling to you, though not exactly libellous. Who on earth cares now whether you visited him when he had influenza, or which of you paid for the grapes—or whatever his petty injuries were? Pitiful, all that!   G. B. S.

3 January 1940 [postcard]   4 Whitehall Court, London

The Gregynog Press is a private affair run by a rich Welsh family. The alleged autobiography is only a collection of old prefaces, interviews and bits and scraps that I have written about myself and my family at odd times. Nothing new.[1]

The Christopher ring[2] is too small for my lifelong accumulation of keys; so I shall stick to my old ring which I bought sixty-eight years ago in Dawson Street, Dublin, for fourpence. It is in better preservation than I.

When I get a really nice present I pass it on to the first really nice comer. This practice infuriates the original donors, but adds the gratification of the final recipient to my own.   G. B. S.

9 February 1940 [postcard]   4 Whitehall Court, London

I have written to the *Literary Supplement* about that review.

The book[3] is very readable to anyone over sixty and, I hope, to younger people, but naturally I cannot feel so sure of them.

You must drop this cackle about *The Importance of Being Earnest*, a

---

[1] *Shaw Gives Himself Away: An Autobiographical Miscellany* (Gregynog Press, 1939), an edition limited to two hundred seventy-five copies. The Gregynog Press, devoted to fine printing, was founded in 1922 by Gwendoline and Margaret Davies at Gregynog, near Newtown, Montgomeryshire.

[2] A Christmas present from Douglas.

[3] *Oscar Wilde, A Summing-Up*, published by Duckworth. The *Times Literary Supplement* (3 February 1940) gave the book a prominent and favourable review. It stated, however, that Douglas had been misled by Bernard Shaw, confusing crime with vice: Wilde was not right in pleading not guilty. The next issue carried Shaw's strong rebuttal: the 'leading case in British history is the acquittal of the seven bishops in 1688, where there was no dispute about the facts'.

soulless farce without a single human being or human moment in it. *The School for Scandal* has three or four quite Shakespearean characters in it; and this, in spite of its utterly thoughtless morals, makes a genuine comedy of it.   G. B. S.

15 February 1940   4 Whitehall Court, London

Dear Childe, There may be a job for you in this. Why not persuade your publisher, or some publisher, to bring out a volume entitled *The Famous Comedies of Oscar Wilde*, edited by you, with a long preface by you. I believe it would sell; and anyhow the publisher would not lose by it and would gain prestige.

It is so long since I have seen or read a play of Wilde's that I shall not commit myself until I have refreshed my memory. Only the other day a manager who was looking out for revivals (tempted by the success of *The Importance*) told me that he had looked up *A Woman of No Importance* and found it utterly impossible and obsolete. My own recollection of them from their first production is that they were of a godlike brilliancy compared to the fashionable pieces of that day: they were not only witty but literature with a large 'L'. If Wilde had not been up against Ibsen, who reduced even Shakespeare to flapdoodle, they would have been epoch making. I must read them again: Oscar sent me copies; and I must have them somewhere.

Oscar's superiority to Sheridan and Congreve lies in the fact that he was an original moralist, whereas, though Sheridan could create characters like Sir Peter Teazle, Joseph Surface, Bob Acres, Sir Anthony Absolute, Mrs Candour, Mrs Malaprop, etc., etc., Oscar couldn't or at any rate didn't, Sheridan's morality being of the most barren conventionality, with the result that his virtuous heroine, Lady Teazle, is now a dirty little cad, and his hero, Charles Surface, a vaurien feebly redeemed by the touch of feeling that made him refuse to sell his uncle's portrait. Sheridan, it is true, named him Surface, but that was meant not for him but for Joseph.

As to Congreve, he had literary and dramatic talent; but how are you to class a playwright whose notion of humour was to ridicule cuckolds and lecherous old women, and to make a laughing matter of syphilis?

Wilde was heavens high above that. There is plenty of writing-up for you to do here.

Goldsmith, who in *The Deserted Village* and *The Vicar of Wakefield* anticipated Karl Marx, was by far the biggest of the Irish bunch, the only one who cuts a noble figure. In *The Goodnatured Man*, the failure of which crushed him as a playwright, he made the first move in the direction of Ibsen and Wilde by challenging the moral valuations of the bourgeoisie, but unfortunately accepted the convention that a play must have a plot, and killed his play with it.

When next you explode on the subject of the Irish plantations, remember that *all* the Irish are planted. The extreme type, which used to be caricatured in the English papers with long upper lip, is as obviously a Spanish muleteer as the Duke of Wellington was a gentleman of the garrison. Both are planted on Irish soil; and the climate makes both of them as completely Irish as I am, though I have lived for sixty-three years in England and only twenty in Ireland. The odd thing is that two years spent in Ireland will change an Englishman into a different person; but a century will not rub the Irish mark off an Irishman. Therefore be careful not to be led away into Hitleresque nonsense about race.

However, that is not to the present point, which is to emulate Heming and Condell by producing a first folio Wilde. I presume you have all the quartos.   G. BERNARD SHAW

17 February 1940 [small card]   4 Whitehall Court, London

My secretary[1] is ill; and I haven't a moment. That passage of mine about Oscar Wilde being the champion playboy is worth considering. I meant it as a high compliment to Oscar; but it explains why, up against the terrible Ibsen, Oscar became the Supertrifler.   G. B. S.

20 March 1940 [postcard]   4 Whitehall Court, London

I have just discovered that the four comedies are published in one volume by Nelson and Sons, 'The Nelson Classics', half a crown.
                                                            G. B. S.

[1] The efficient Blanche Patch (1879–1966), who had been with Shaw since 1920.

25 June 1940 [postcard]   Ayot St Lawrence

Have you seen *The Story of Anne Whateley and William Shaxpere*, by
William Ross?[1] It is amusing to find how well a lot of the sonnets fit
into his discovery that the real Shakespeare was a woman and that Mr
W. H. was Shaxpear. Quite amusing enough anyhow to take one's
mind off the war for a moment. I have asked Ross to send you a copy:
if he won't I will send you mine.

I want Churchill to declare war on France *pro forma* and Copenhagen[2]
the French fleet before Jerry has time to breathe. But, as usual, all parties
dread me as Enemy Number One; and I am not let broadcast nor write.

I like being prayed for.   G. B. S.

15 July 1940 [small card]   Ayot St Lawrence

Childe, Childe, Damn your Noodle's Oration about Russia![3] What do
you mean by sending such stuff to ME?   G. B. S.

26 July 1940   4 Whitehall Court, London

Dear Childe, St James be blowed; he was a day too soon: I was born on
the *26th* of July 1856.

A relative of mine[4] acquired a duodenal ulcer lately. I sent her to
University College Hospital, where they are up to date and don't operate. Also their private wards are comfortable and quite the thing for
paying patients. They cured my relative in five weeks by the simple and
inexpensive method of giving her nothing to eat.

Nursing-homes are out of date; keep Olive[5] out of them at all haz-

---

[1] Published by W. and R. Holmes, Glasgow, 1939.

[2] At the battle of Copenhagen in 1801, a naval expedition under Vice-Admiral Nelson
and Admiral Sir Hyde Parker destroyed the Danish fleet in its own harbour.

[3] The broadsheet Douglas circulated in both houses of Parliament and elsewhere,
claiming that the Left-Wing and Communist element were getting control of the Government, and that there was no Conservative paper left; even *The Times* was pink.

[4] Mary Ethel Shaw Davis Walters, a daughter of Shaw's first cousin James Cockaigne
Shaw. Throughout her life she depended upon Shaw for financial help.

[5] Her doctors suspected an ulcer and advised her to go to hospital.

ards. The new private wards at the Westminster are the latest and said to be the best; but I know nothing as to whether they are up to date in duodenal ulcer [treatment]. In great haste (I am making my will).

G. BERNARD SHAW

28 August 1940   4 Whitehall Court, London

Importunate Childe, Those rhymes[1] should be made into a Christmas book for children, with pictures of the animals. As Bewick[2] is dead, and it is very difficult to find photographs that do not make the animals hateful or terrifying, I recommend a certain Agnes Miller Parker,[3] who has illustrated Aesop's fables with wood engravings so good that you can almost feel the animals' fur. No other sort of publication would be of the slightest use. Propose it to your favourite publisher and call the book *Bosie's Fables* if you like, or, for alliteration's sake, *Bosie's Bestiary*, though I doubt if the children would like that. *Alfred's Animal Book* would be better. They may as well have verses by a master hand as doggerel.

We also sleep through the raids. My wife does not give a damn for bombs, but dreads shelters and prefers death to getting up and dressing. After all, bed is the proper place to die in.

Why do you recommend me to go to Russia? I've been there. It is a paradise: no ladies and gentlemen there.

The Catholic church is like Democracy, an eternal ideal, noble and beneficent as such; but all attempts to manufacture it in the concrete reduce it to absurdity. Read my old play *John Bull's Other Island*. Father Keegan is an ideal Catholic; and he is 'silenced' for his pains. Father Dempsey is the very parochial reality. Democracy was great in the nineteenth century, when Gladstone and Bright and Disraeli and your

---

[1] Douglas had sent some light verse for criticism.

[2] Thomas Bewick (1753–1828), wood engraver, illustrated *Gay's Fables* (1779) and *Select Fables* (1784).

[3] Agnes Miller Parker, artist and wood engraver. Her illustrations for *Aesop's Fables* were published in 1931. She was the wood engraver for the Gregynog Press from 1930 to 1933.

father believed in it. What is it now, when every fool and every flapper has a vote? Government by the unqualified, chosen by the—if possible —less qualified. Russia shoots such impostors. Can you blame her?

I made surprise visits to churches in Russia and found priests in gorgeous vestments blazing away, with congregations genuflecting, prostrating, smiting the ground with their foreheads as if the Vatican had annexed the Kremlin; but there were only about fifteen worshippers, including myself; and I left before the collection.

Miss Patch has made a frightful mess of this letter. She must be out of sorts. Forgive her.   G. BERNARD SHAW

31 August 1940 [postcard]   4 Whitehall Court, London

Note that copyright cannot pass 'without a consideration'. A verbal consent to a casual production does not affect it. Unless there is a specific assignment in black and white with an acknowledgment of a payment therefor (Arnold's[1] fifty pounds for example) your rights are unaffected.

Note also, however, that additions made to a play during rehearsal *by the producer* become the copyright of the author automatically unless there is a written agreement to collaborate. As to collaboration, see below.

Never, on your life, part with a copyright. Always hold on to it, and *license* publication or performance.

Never collaborate; and beware of accepting any suggestion on which a claim for collaboration could be set up. I have known a case in which a cad claimed half royalties for suggesting a name.   G. B. S.

P.S. I could do nothing for [Giuseppi] Catalani.[2] London is full of refugees in his predicament. My translators, and people who have written books on Shaw or backed me up as critics, are destitute and appeal to me in vain. I have either to acquire complete callousness or share their ruin.

[1] Edward Arnold had published Douglas's animal verses, *Tails with a Twist*, many years earlier.

[2] Catalani, a retired Italian diplomat (at Harrow as a boy) who refused to leave England when war was declared. He was saved from internment by Douglas and Harold Nicolson. Deprived of his property in Italy by the Fascists, Catalani was now in Hove, destitute.

29 September 1940 [postcard]   Ayot St Lawrence

We are like the Poles: geniuses and cretins, lacking in mediocrity. Nature maintains that sort of balance. The most horrifying of sub-humans I have seen only in two places: 1. the charcoal people in the forests of Luxembourg; 2. the waterside people of Ringsend, the Dublin Isle of Dogs. Curious that Norway should produce in extremes, and Sweden, so contiguous as to be geographically identical, surpass the Swiss in mediocrity, though on a very high level. Your fatherland also produces Rob Roys and Dougal creatures, mad Marquesses and poets.

I await the book[1] with lively interest.

Meanwhile I embusk myself here in Ayot, where I can see and distantly hear the London fireworks, with only an occasional stray bomb to add a twist of funk to the enjoyment. Hove must be distinctly hotter; but one sleeps.   G. B. S.

27 October 1940   Ayot St Lawrence

A threepenny pamphlet marked two shillings, *new*.

Hm!

The Richards Press.

Hmm!!

The Black and Tans all Galahads and the Shinners all blackguards.

Hmmm!!!

These things are not done for nothing.

Where did the money come from?

And that incorrigible Childe giving his name and title to a page and a half of reminders of *Plain English* just when he had succeeded in living it down.

Apparently he expects me to congratulate him on this achievement.

I renounce him and all his works. The man is a blasted idiot. Given under my hand this Sunday as ever was   G. B. S.

---

[1] *Ireland and the War Against Hitler* (Richards Press), a thirty-seven-page pamphlet containing an introduction by Douglas, followed by a reprint of the chapter on the Sinn Fein rebellion from Major Montmorency's *Sword and Stirrup*.

Impossible Childe, It is a relief to learn that the pamphlet is not an out-of-date attempt at Orange propaganda paid for with more or less secret service money, but an act of pure folly on your own private part. You certainly are a jumping sillybilly.

Now listen to me. At present it does not matter the millionth fraction of a tuppenny damn what the Shinners and the Black and Tans did before the treaty. They are done with and mostly dead. Collins burnt the châteaux (including the one in which my wife was born) and the police stations. The Tans burnt the creameries and shops: I saw a champion sample of their work in Mallow. Collins, with the people on his side, had the better of the burning: the gentry dared not prosecute, and could only write privately to say that they were done. Collins won, and was immediately shot by his countrymen for it.[1] I made his acquaintance a few days before his end. His nerves were in rags: his hand kept slapping his revolver all the time he was talking pleasantly enough. But all that is now ancient history: nobody with the least grip of the present situation has any time for it.

De Valera[2] is in a frightfully difficult situation. The last thing he desires is a conquest of Ireland by Nazi Protestant-Atheists. But if he calls on England to fulfill her treaty obligation and reoccupy the Irish ports with British troops and British ships, he annuls Ireland's neutrality and not only infuriates the I.R.A., which he might in extremity dare to defy, but provokes Hitler to make Ireland the cockpit of the war, which would suit England down to the ground but which no Irishman could justify himself in doing. He must do just what he *is* doing: that is, stick to Ireland's neutrality and take his chance of an invasion. Fortunately invasion seems off just now; and Dev may win through; but if it happens, then Churchill must reoccupy Ireland. It will be willy-nilly for him, for Dev and for the I.R.A. If Dev fought he would have to fight on four fronts, against Hitler on the west, Churchill on the east, Belfast

[1] Michael Collins (1890–1922), Irish revolutionary leader and chairman of the Provisional Government. On 22 August, returning to Cork with members of his staff, he was ambushed by a band of irregulars and killed.

[2] Eamon de Valera (1882–1975), since 1932 both Prime Minister and Foreign Minister of the Irish Free State.

on the north and the British navy on the south, and to forfeit all the American support and sympathy, which is still as important to Eire as when it helped with the treaty. What can he do but sit tight and let events take their course.

The situation is dangerous, but has the advantage that it offers an opportunity for the first time to unite Ireland, not in support of England, but against Hitler, which comes to the same thing.

And this is the moment you choose to dig up the rotten apple of discord and throw it in again to revive the strife of Shinner and Black and Tan! Can you imagine anything more thoughtlessly stupid and wicked?

And to put it all on poor innocent St Jude!

If you go on I shall be tempted to use strong language. Burn that mischievous trash, and never mention Ireland to me again. G. B. S.

14 November 1940   4 Whitehall Court, London

Childe, Childe, Politically you have the brains of a grasshopper; and you have far too much courage. If the Douglases had had less courage and more common sense they would now be the royal house of Scotland. Providence, knowing how valuable my life was going to be, took care that I should be born a devout coward. As a boy I was horribly ashamed of my poltroonery; now I am thankful for it. Samuel Butler wrote a book called *Luck or Cunning*. Some day I shall write one called *Pluck or Cunning*.

The Irish question is going to be a very vital one. If the submarine campaign on the west coast of Ireland continues to be successful and we come, as we did before, within five weeks of being starved out, we *must* seize the Irish ports or surrender. Obviously we will not surrender for the sake of the I.R.A.'s beautiful eyes. We will exterminate the whole four millions of Irish in Ireland first.

Your notion of dealing with this situation is to rake up old dirt to set the Irish by the ears again, and to call de Valera a skunk and declare that you do not care two damns about his difficulties. How much farther will that get you or anyone else, do you think?

De Valera is not, as a matter of dispassionate fact, a skunk. He is an ex-schoolmaster of unblemished character who, when, like you, he had more courage than common sense, risked his life in the Easter Rising and escaped hanging by the skin of his teeth. He is where he is because Ireland needed a schoolmaster very badly and had enough of hanged heroes. His difficulties, about which you do not care two damns, happen to be England's difficulties as well. If I were in his place I should probably write a very private letter to the P.M. as follows; 'Dear Churchill: I cannot give you the ports because I should provoke an I.R.A. rising and lose such power for good as I have. I cannot prevent you from taking the ports, as I have only four millions to your forty, and you have America at your back this time. So for God's sake *take* the ports as nicely as you can as a temporary forced loan, promising to give them back when our common enemy the atheist Hun is disposed of. Faithfully, Eamon de Valera'.

What have you to say to that, courageous but idiotic Douglas? Which cat, by the way, are you going to bell?   G. B. S.

15 November 1940 [postcard]   Ayot St Lawrence

I have just given an interview (in writing) to the *Sunday Graphic* which will interest your friend, the Beamish Boy.[1]

Look out for it on Sunday.   G. B. S.

24 February 1941   Ayot St Lawrence
[*pasted on a sheet of the*
Weekly Review *of 13 February*]

Dear Childe, You really must not be *insolent*. It gives away your class. Your letter[2] is a good one except for the eight words I have underlined.

---

[1] Shaw's interview with W. R. Titterton, 'Call in Britain', appeared in the *Sunday Graphic* on 17 November; the points made were precisely those Shaw had written to Douglas. The 'Beamish Boy' was Rear-Admiral T. P. H. Beamish, M.P. for Lewes, a Unionist, who was pressing for the occupation of the ports, by force if necessary. See his letter to the *Weekly Review*, 16 January 1941.

[2] Douglas's letter (Shaw's italics):

Sir, 'Ex-Officer of Irish Guards' calls me a 'doughty seeker of free advertisement' be-

Look at the letter signed M. Evans.[1] It is more effective than yours because yours not only makes your point but implies that your attitude is that of a noble lord (by courtesy) dealing with a dirty cad.

Forgive the lecture; but I must educate you.   G. B. S.

26 March 1941   Ayot St Lawrence

Dear Childe, I have more compulsory writing than I have time for; for long intervals I have to let private letters lie until I am forced to take a few days relaxation and answer them all in a heap.

Marie [Stopes], who is a pertinacious devil, is on the war-path again for the pension[2] and has called in Lady Diana Cooper, who has written

---

cause, in reply to an attack on me by another of your correspondents I mentioned the name of my recent pamphlet! This is a priceless specimen of the 'arguments' and the 'logic' used by the supporters of de Valera *and his gang*. I have no cause to advertise my pamphlet (which was published purely out of patriotism and at a price which made it impossible for me to make a profit on it) because, as it happens, the whole edition of five hundred copies is exhausted. On the same level are his ravings about 'Douglas chieftains' and 'battle tartans'. The Douglases being a Lowland family, have not, properly speaking, got a tartan. The 'Douglas tartan' as sold in the shops was invented by an Edinburgh tailor in the eighteenth century, though my branch and other branches of the family are entitled to wear the Hunting Stewart. But all this seems to have very little to do with the question of the Irish ports on which the safety of our country largely depends. It shows how little the admirers of 'Kathleen' [ni Houlihan, the personification of Erin] have got to say for their cause when they indulge in ignorant and pointless abuse *and similar exhibitions of ill-breeding*.

                                                        ALFRED DOUGLAS

[1] M. Evans's letter read, in part:
Mr de Valera has made it perfectly clear that if Northern Ireland wants to join Eire, she must become neutral. That is to say, our British troops, the Navy and the Royal Air Force, must clear out, lock, stock and barrel, and the Nazis given more scope to deal with our vital shipping around the Emerald Isle.
Personally, I cannot imagine anything more suicidal.

[2] Marie Stopes presented a second petition for Douglas's pension on 28 February 1940. On 12 March, Anthony Bevin, for Chamberlain, declined the recommendation, writing that 'while Mr Chamberlain has great sympathy [for Douglas] he has not felt able to submit his name to the King for the award of a pension'.

Renewal of the request in 1941 was an even greater challenge, for the sympathetic Chamberlain had resigned as Prime Minister on 10 May 1940. Winston Churchill now headed the Government. Some of the previous petitioners thought there was no chance,

to me to say that you are 'grievously poor' and that something must be done. I told her that from the civil list point of view you were opulent on four hundred pounds a year, and that even if Winston bears no malice, the Treasury will not count four hundred pounds or three hundred pounds, or even two hundred and fifty pounds as 'straitened circumstances'. If only you had four thousand pounds a year, you could have another thousand for the asking. To him that hath shall be given.

But Lady Diana has some notion of getting a group of people to guarantee something. If only you could get your rent covered it would save you the horror of moving. I had to pay two thousand pounds more than its market value for this house because finding another house and moving would have taken more of my time and attention than two thousand pounds' worth of writing. But can you not whitemail your people? For years I have had to support my mother's half-sisters, my paternal first cousins and even second cousins to keep them out of the workhouse. The Marquess surely cannot afford to have you interviewed in the workhouse or sitting on the pavement with coloured chalks doing pictures on the flags, with your cap beside you for the pennies.

If you must submerge, go deep enough: be a glorious lord among proletarians and avoid your own class—the impecunious younger sons —and mine—the snobbish impecunious bourgeoisie who call a lodger a paying guest.

I have never been insolent to you. I may heap vulgar abuse on you: but I regard you as a fellow-creature.

Politeness is a deadly weapon against rudeness; and brutal rudeness is perhaps the best counter for it. Exchanging punches is all very well if you are the harder hitter and great fun for the spectator. I know all that; but it has nothing to do with insolence. De Valera made a mistake when he said I was contemptible. That was because he regarded me as

---

others felt that Churchill's generosity would prejudice him in Douglas's favour on account of the old libel attack rather than against him. Marie was uncertain what to do.

Lady Diana Cooper offered an alternative: to raise the hundred and thirty pounds needed for the annual rent of Douglas's flat by soliciting yearly pledges by covenant from a few friends. Lady Diana and Duff Cooper, currently Minister of Information, had met Douglas in January of this year.

being of a different class and religion, and supposed I thought myself better than he. He retorted in imaginary contempt. You must not make the same mistake in political controversy, especially when you have a good case.

I must stop: I am quite incapable of writing a decent human letter: I suppose I am tired.

I forgot to say that Lady Diana was afraid of wounding your delicacy. I told her not to worry—that your mouth was wide open and that you would swallow a dozen pensions with avidity. There is nothing so embarrassing and sometimes so cruel as delicacy in money matters. Sempre

G. BERNARD SHAW

26 May 1941   Ayot St Lawrence

[*on a form card, regretting
all invitations to speak*]

I hope it did not worry you (I forgot all about it)[1] and that the eased situation puts off the question of *déménagement* sine die.   G. B. S.

28 May 1941   1 St Ann's Court, Hove

Dear St Christopher, All that has happened is that I got a couple of hundreds in settlement of an action against the publishers of an outrageously libellous book, American but represented in London by Hamish Hamilton. *I devoted a hundred pounds of the booty to paying off the overdraft.* What is left will enable me to hang on here for a little longer. So please don't now tell everyone that I am rolling in money! The overdraft has been a nightmare to me, because, consciously and subconsciously, I have been imagining for the last twelve months or more that you were feeling disgusted with me and disliking me for not settling it up long ago. I wish I had known that my fears were groundless as you now tell me.

I lunched with Francis Queensberry yesterday when in London and

---

[1] The overdraft of one hundred pounds which Shaw had guaranteed in May 1938.

he told me that "a few of us" were going to "see what could be done" about my affairs, so I beg that you won't do or say anything to 'queer' me in this matter. Of course I would never have dreamed of such a possibility if Marie Stopes had not told me that you were doing something of the kind. I did not believe it because I felt sure she must have misunderstood you. So don't feel it necessary to deny it.

One of the terms of the settlement with the publisher of the libellous book (Harper and Brothers, New York and London) is that I have undertaken to write a preface or foreword to further issues of the book, which is meanwhile held up. I expect of course to be decently paid for this, but I hate having to do it and to be obliged to go all over the ground again and defend myself for the five-hundredth time against imbecile accusations which no reasonable person would believe. But of course I *must* do it. I wish you had read the book and could advise me. If I can get you a copy (it is not on sale in England) will you read it? It is called *Oscar Wilde and the Yellow Nineties*, by Frances Winwar. Most of the libels are already answered by your preface to the reissue of Harris's book. I have to see Hamish Hamilton about it. He is very friendly and declares that he violently protested against the publication. Your devoted

CHILDE

7 July 1941   1 St Ann's Court, Hove

Dear St Christopher, On the rash assumption that you are still mildly interested in my affairs, I give you the news from the home front. A group of friends, including my nephew Francis Queensberry, Marie Stopes, Lord Tredegar and Lady Diana Cooper, have with the greatest kindness and generosity made up for me the equivalent of the civil list pension which I was assured I was to have, when Chamberlain was Prime Minister.[1] This means that I am now securely embedded in my

[1] A dream only; no assurance was ever given by Chamberlain. Lady Diana's plan was the one adopted. Contributions from the four donors were sent to Albert Oppenheimer, Lord Tredegar's solicitor, who handled the payments.

Viscount Tredegar (Evan Frederic Morgan, 1893–1949) had been a close friend of Douglas for many years. He was a large landowner in Monmouthshire, a generous host and keen sportsman, a devout Roman Catholic and a poet.

Douglas at 1 St Ann's Court

flat and that the nightmare of forcible evacuation has been dissipated. My rent is guaranteed and paid direct to the landlord. I had actually given my landlord three months' notice that I was leaving here at the end of the current quarter, and the news of my salvation came as a sudden surprise. All due to St Jude of course. Harold Nicolson told me that he had done "a lot of lobbying" for my pension but that success was made impossible by "the violent hostility of the Labour Party". It gives me considerable satisfaction to hear that they dislike me so much because I have always had the most profound contempt for them, and they wouldn't be so virulent if my various attacks on them had not hit them pretty hard!

I quite expect to get a sermon or moral lecture from you about this because, although I never really profess to understand your point of view, I suppose you admire them—or don't you? . . .

I suppose you don't read the *Daily Mail*? So you probably did not see my sonnet on Winston Churchill ('starred' on the leader page) last Friday July 4th.[1] I wrote this sonnet, which is the first I have written since 1934, at the urgent request of and egged on by my nephew Francis Queensberry, who is now very thick with Winston and is quite devoted to him. I sent it to the *Mail*, who received it with enthusiasm and were eager to print it but said they must first have an assurance that Churchill did not object. This caused the sonnet to be held up for a week or more, but meanwhile Francis sent it to him and a few days ago wired to me, 'Winston is delighted certainly publish sonnet'. I passed this on to the *Mail*, who thereupon published it, marred unfortunately by a vile misprint in the thirteenth line.

How are you, dear St Christopher? Do send me a line. Your devoted

CHILDE

[1] Douglas's sonnet in the *Daily Mail*, 4 July 1941:

'Winston Churchill'

by

Lord Alfred Douglas

Not that of old I loved you over-much
Or followed your quick changes with great glee,
While through grim paths of harsh hostility
You fought your way, using the sword or crutch
To serve occasion. Yours it was to clutch

Importunate Childe, My correspondence has quite beaten me for the moment; my silence means only that I have no leisure to write anything that can wait without disaster.

The news of the Francis-Marie-Diana syndicate is good, *pourvu que ça dure*, as Napoleon's mother used to say. When Marie started the pension project knowing nothing about pensions, I had to warn her that there was practically no chance; but of course I did nothing to defeat the forlorn hope. You suspect me of susceptibilities which have been extinct in me for three quarters of a century. I know your politics as a doctor knows measles. In your case they are incongruous, because a poet, however pedigreed, should in this wicked world be a revolutionist like Shelley and Byron. I wish you would send me a copy of the sonnet to Churchill, as such a thing appeals to me as a unique curiosity.

But I have had to write a prose sonnet to Russia. Verse would have been wasted on the Kremlin; but the material for a sonnet is there. I enclose a copy.[1] Churchill knows how to play to the British gallery but not to the Russian.

I write in great haste and must break off abruptly. This is just to reassure you: I am quite unperturbed and very glad that your rent is guaranteed.   G. B. S.

And lose again. Lacking the charity
Which looks behind the mask, I did not see
The immanent shadow of 'the Winston touch'.

Axe for embedded Evil's cancerous roots,
When the whole world was one vast funeral pyre,
Like genie smoke you rose, a giant form
Clothed with the Addisonian attributes
Of God-directe[d] angel. Like your Sire
You rode the whirlwind and out-stormed the storm.

[1] Shaw's requested 'prose sonnet', cabled to Alexander Fadeyev, Chairman of the Union of Soviet Writers:

Never mind the barbarism: all war is barbarous; and to squeal is childish. Let us rather apologize for the terrible thing we must do to our German comrades before their Führer loses his glamour for them. When two mighty ideas clash millions of lives count for nothing.

It is as the champion of an idea that Adolf Hitler has flung down his glove to

My dear St Christopher, I'm very glad to get your letter. You must remember that Marie Stopes definitely told me that you were doing your best to 'queer' my chances of a pension. I didn't believe it, but when you received my (to me exciting) news that I had actually got the pension[1] with a stony and fish-like silence, I began to think that perhaps she had been right after all, and this upset me very much. At any rate it appeared that you had ceased taking any interest in your tiresome Childe!

I am indeed pleased to know that this is not so. Your silence is explained by your preoccupation with propaganda for the Soviet. I don't think things will work out in that direction as you imagine they will, but *nous verrons*. I think St Jude will take a hand in the game. Why should a poet be a revolutionary? I grant you Shelley (who would have probably got over his youthful follies if he had lived longer) and Byron, but what about a far greater poet, Shakespeare, who practically has always been my god and (from the point of view of form and technique) my master? And I could give you a dozen more examples. However, as Lady Bracknell would say, these speculations are fruitless.

I enclose a cutting from the *Border Standard* which contains a reproduction of my sonnet on Winston in the *Daily Mail*. Luckily the editor of the *Border Standard* (local journal of 'the Douglas country' in Scotland) sent me twelve copies of this paper and I can now send a few copies to friends. I hadn't a single copy of the *Mail* left.

I expect you saw my 'Blimp' sonnet, 'The Old Soldier', in yesterday's *Evening Standard*, but in case you missed it, I send it along as well

---

Russia. Russia picks it up as the champion of a far mightier idea. When she strikes down Adolf's idea she will become the spiritual centre of the world. And with that task before her she may not heed the cries of the wounded or the tears of the bereaved.

The combat is between Lohengrin and Telramund; and it has fallen to the lot of Russia to show the world which is Lohengrin and which Telramund.

Remember: we are at a corner that civilization has never yet got round. Russia is pledged to get us round it this time or perish; SO ONWARD RUSSIA FOR THE LEADERSHIP OF THE WORLD, FOR THE SICKLE, THE HAMMER AND THE SWORD OF JUSTICE.

[1] No pension. Contributions from four donors. See Douglas's letter of 7 July 1941, note 1.

as the Winston one. I sent the 'Blimp' sonnet to Frank Owen simply to annoy him and my bête noire, Low the cartoonist, and I was amazed to find that he had printed it; he must have sent it over to the printers within half an hour of receiving it. I must say I thought this was rather sporting on his part. I also have a very friendly and flattering note this morning about my 'brilliant little piece' from Tudor Jenkins (if I read his signature right), the editor of 'Londoner's Diary' in the *Evening Standard*. I am now meditating a sonnet on Hitler. But so far it seems impossible to get it. Mere abuse or invective won't be good enough, and I must endeavour to get an original idea. I have invoked St Jude and shall leave it to my subconscious mind to work it out. Your prose about Russia and Germany is admirable but *I* couldn't make a sonnet out of it for obvious reasons. Your ever devoted CHILDE

31 July 1941 Ayot St Lawrence

Dear Childe, You have certainly performed an extraordinary feat. I tried to imagine how you could possibly make Churchill the addressee of a sonnet. Ridiculous rhymes jingled in my head.

> Churchill: both blessed Jude and Christian God,
> Bid me forgive your putting me in quod

and

> Just one last thing I hardly like to mention
> But it must out. Say: what about that pension?

However, you seem to have solved the problem quite easily; and it was really a delicate one.

The war situation is amusing though horrible. We have lied to one another about Russia so frantically for twenty years that we have persuaded ourselves that the Bolsheviks, far more than the Nazis, are a gang of thieves and murderers who must be scattered like chaff the moment they come up against a civilized army led by gentlemen. In 1918–20, in Mongolia, in Poland, in the Baltic provinces, in Finland, there was plenty of evidence that the Red Army was the most formidable in Europe, just as there was an utter lack of evidence that the French Army was the wonderful fighting force that we insisted on assuming it to be. And now that the French Army has cracked up worse than in 1870, and Hitler is fighting like a rat in a corner without a dog's chance of getting even as far as Napoleon did, we are still wishing that Russia will be smashed and partitioned whilst hoping that Hitler will presently be in St Helena.

It seems impossible that the enormous economic and moral superiority of Communism will not prove its ruin in the midst of a world of robber-barons and their money-lenders; but it has not weakened Stalin, who has shot the right people whilst we have given them peerages.

My machine having messed up these lines I forbear.   G. B. S.

27 December 1941   Ayot St Lawrence

Dear Childe Alfred, Swift was not born in Surrey. He came of British stock (York and Leicester) and was related through his two grandfathers to Dryden and Herrick; but he was born in Dublin, schooled in Kilkenny, graduated at Trinity College, Dublin, did not set foot in England until he was twenty-two and of the seventy-eight years of his life spent ten in London, ten back and forward between London and his benefice in Trim and fifty-eight in Ireland.

Of my eighty-five years, twenty have been spent in Ireland and sixty-five in England; and yet what mortal power could make an Englishman of me? The climate of Ireland and its society will stamp an Englishman for life; but nothing will erase the native stamp on an Irishman.

I learn from a letter in the *Irish Times* that Eire is a Gaelic translation of Ireland, which is still the correct name of the island in the English language.

Russia is rather in a fix about Japan. When she offered us the same non-aggression trading pact that she made with Hitler, we contemptuously refused, and made no secret of our hope that some day we should be able to rally Germany and Japan to the sacred task of smashing the Bolsheviks and making a new partition of Russia among the western Capitalist powers. Japan had more sense, and made the offered pact. And as she has not attacked Russia, Stalin has no excuse for a breach of neutrality. And we can hardly ask him to take on another front when we have taken no notice of his suggestion that we should do this ourselves. Nobody but Strabolgi has said we ought to. So for the moment Stalin can do nothing but help China all he can without declaring war, as we did in Spain when we made the horrible mistake of securing victory for Franco, with the result that Franco will probably sell Spain to Hitler for Portugal, and give us a fearful job in the Atlantic.

When you say that I will become a Catholic you miss the point that I am already an ultra-Catholic, being a Communist of sixty years' standing. Rome is behind me, not before me. Am I an Aztec that I should eat the god, or a child that I should believe the Apostles' Creed, or a tribal savage that I should worship an idol like Jehovah and offer blood sacrifices to appease him? As to becoming a Christian and letting Jesus suffer for my sins, damn it, Childe, I have still some instincts of a gentleman left. I have never said these things to you before because you had better have the Roman faith than none, and Jesus was right when he refused to attack the established religion of the Jews on the ground that if you tried to rid a field of wheat of its tares you would pull up too much of the wheat with them. Still I am showing you my background just for a moment so that you may understand that you are up against a modern Catholicism compared to which the Vatican is only a little meeting-house in a village, preaching an impossible Protestantism.

My book,[1] which I thought would be finished this year, is a mass of senile ramblings and repetitions. I shall never get it into any very orderly sequence. But perhaps my second childhood may go down with the mob better than my maturity did.

Time for me to die, Childe, time for me to die. But I can still saw logs. I am really proud of the pile of them in the garden, though nobody will ever call them immortal works.

Lady Keeble (Lillah McCarthy)[2] is a nailer at reciting sonnets: the BBC should have found that out. Instead of boring me with small talk she declaims them at me by the dozen—knows them all by heart. Enough.

G. B. S.

[1] *Everybody's Political What's What?* was not published until 1944.

[2] McCarthy (1876–1960), the actress, wife of Harley Granville Barker (1877–1946), was a mainstay of Shaw's 1906 Court Theatre productions. In 1920, after divorce from Barker, she married Sir William Keeble, Professor of Botany and Fellow of Magdalen College, Oxford.

1 January 1942   Ayot St Lawrence
[*on a War Economy postcard from*
the reign of Edward VII]

I think the lady [Keeble] attaches profound importance to the word
SHAKESPEARE and none whatever to the word sonnet. But she likes
learning sonnets and declaiming them.

The gentleman [Sir William] is not by nature rude. But he did not
love his varsity pupils, as they took not the least interest in his subject
and wanted to know only how to answer examination questions.

                                                                    G. B. S.

6 January 1942   Ayot St Lawrence

Dear Childe Alfred, The preface is all right.[1] It has your extraordinary
quality of being what Shakespeare called unpoliced. Every sentence I
write is policied to the last comma; but what you write is the cry of a
living soul, with the result that people wonder what is behind my writing and must sometimes doubt—I do myself occasionally—whether
there is anything behind it. They know you and love or hate you as the
case may be; but they cannot make me out clearly enough for that. I
am an invented, histrionic figure, mostly quite impossible; but you are
a human being for them. We both get round them by our literary
power, reinforced in your case by attractive good looks.

If I had written that preface I should have introduced Harris as a
comic personage: a Captain Matamore,[2] and not quoted his entirely
venal eulogy. Sherard, with his absurd contradictions and his ridiculous
worship of Wilde (they finally cut one another) as a Sir Galahad, I
should have ignored or made ridiculous. This is in fact what I did in the
preface I wrote for poor Nellie.

By the way, I wonder what has become of her. The last I heard was
an S.O.S. sent from Nice, to which I was about to respond by sending
her a little money to save her from starvation when I happened to look

[1] Douglas's 'Foreword' appeared in the Garden City, N.Y. edition of Frances Winwar's *Oscar Wilde and the Yellow Nineties*.

[2] *Le Véritable Capitan Matamore* is a seventeenth-century play by Antoine Marechal.
The Captain is closely modelled on the braggart captain in Plautus's *Miles Gloriosus*.

at the date of her letter, and found that it had taken three months to reach me thanks to the war. So as she was either dead or had found a way out of her desperate need I did nothing.

The Constable edition of Harris's book was really edited by you. I found all my work done for me on the copy you corrected for Harris. Your preface reads as if the pages afterwards withdrawn were objectionable as being untrue; but they were only too true, but so hard on Wilde (the 'old prostitute' passage) that I suddenly remembered that his son would read it; and we agreed to suppress it.

However, the preface is all right: there was no reason to suppose that I should be opprobrious. It will spike the lady's [Frances Winwar's] gun pretty effectually. I return it, as you may want a spare copy.

G. B. S.

21 January 1942   Ayot St Lawrence

Dear Childe, I return Harris's letter.[1] I thought (through a mislay) that you had forgotten to enclose it. When I said that it was venal, that is, written only to obtain your leave to reprint his book from the old plates and withdrawn when you insisted on a new set-up, I did not mean that it was either ill written or insincere. It was neither. But he wrote it to serve its turn; and when it failed—well, I discussed it with him in Nice and will not attempt to reproduce his language.

The point I am trying to make is that it is a bit too unpoliced on your part to quote him as an authority and in the same breath revile him as a corrupt scoundrel whose every word was a lie.

The truth is that Harris had the supreme virtue of knowing good literary work from bad and preferring the good. For that I forgave him all his sins, and have always defended him as far as he could be defended. He was hated because he frightened people with his voice and his trenchant articulation, acquired chiefly to recite Poe's 'Raven' effectively, but also to pass as a gentleman and a scholar in London. I was a public speaker, able to articulate his head off; and I was not afraid of him. And

[1] Of 20 August 1925: 'Your character is vindicated so far as I can do it and no offence is given to anyone. The defence too is short and reasonable. If there is anything you wish altered or elaborated please let me know: if I can do what you wish, I will'.

Frank Harris

I found out the truth of Mrs Frankau's[1] remonstrance with me for bullying him: that outside literature he was a sensitive child who understood London society as a bush-ranger would understand it. He was genuinely puzzled at my calling him a buccaneer; for he thought he resembled Jesus Christ, and died broken-hearted when he proposed to write a book on him, and the publishers said, "No: we want a book on Shaw".

Look at the poor fellow's handwriting!   G. B. S.

23 June 1942   Ayot St Lawrence

Dear Childe, I am so overwhelmed with American film business and tax business that if I attempt to write a private letter my book, which I am feeding to the printer chapter by chapter, stops dead.[2] Unless I tackle it first thing in the morning and let everything else go hang it will never be finished. It leaves only the afternoon for imperative business and not enough for that.

Last week I had to go up to London and tackle a conference with the County Council about the National Theatre project. The effect of my revisit as a gibbering ghost to the scene where I was once a star tub-thumper was so ghastly that I stupefied the meeting; and the leader of the opposition rose chuckling and said that his presence was superfluous, as the opposition was safe in the hands of that fine old Tory, Mr Bernard Shaw. Fortunately my teeth did not drop out; and I got through without forgetting what I was talking about and who I was talking to: a great triumph at eighty-six. But it was positively my last appearance: I daren't try it again.

All this is to explain why I have not been able to write to you, though I am always glad to have a hail from Hove.

[1] Julia Frankau (1865–1916) was a novelist who wrote under the name of Frank Danby. Shaw in his preface to the Harris biography, said, 'Mrs Frankau was quite right. I did deal with [Harris] as if he was a buccaneer, not then realizing what a daisy he really was' (p. xix).

[2] Still *Everybody's Political What's What*? and Shaw was also deeply involved with the Hungarian film director Gabriel Pascal and with scheduled United Artists productions in Hollywood. Pascal was the first producer to whom Shaw entrusted his plays, and he was taking an active part in the filming operations.

Never collaborate.[1] There is not room on any literary job for more than one. Also the law on the subject is terrible: I have known a case in which a man took half the royalties on a play because the other adopted a suggestion of his for the name of one of the characters, all the rest of his suggestions being too imbecile to be entertained. As it happened there were no royalties; but there might be in your case.

A man wrote to me the other day enclosing an old postcard of mine, of no interest whatever, for which he had paid a guinea at Hatchard's. If such prices can be obtained it seems to me a thriftless waste of money to keep such things instead of selling them. If people want to read them they can keep copies. My Irish Protestant stock revolts against relics, which is what autographs essentially are. So if the sale of your postcard realizes an encouraging figure, send the entire collection to Sotheby's (no taxation on the proceeds) and have a good spree before the war leaves us destitute on the streets.[2] I cannot practise what I preach in this matter, as I agree with Dickens that keeping letters is a mischief-making habit (he burnt all his solemnly at Gadshill) and I don't keep mine.

I did not say that the church forbade dancing; but I may have described the rabid kill-joy Puritanism with which some Irish priests forbid dancing and will not let boys and girls walk together. Read *John Bull's Other Island*; and you will realize that 'the church' means sometimes Father Dempsey and sometimes Father Keegan. And Dempsey is quite a favourable specimen of the sort of priest Maynooth[3] turns out.

G. B. S.

[1] Poppoea Vanda, an agent for the Anton Dolin dance company, had suggested that Douglas write a ballet scenario, and Douglas asked Shaw to collaborate. Shaw refused and Douglas wrote the scenario himself, based on Thackeray's *Vanity Fair*. Dolin liked it and interested Sir Thomas Beecham and Sir Edward Elgar, but nothing came of the venture.

[2] Douglas had sent his postcard from Shaw, 28 May 1938, to Sotheby's Red Cross sale (13–15 October 1942). His comment sheet describing the card: 'I had put up a candle to St Anthony of Padua for him and had had a Mass said for his recovery from his illness'. Sotheby's catalogue description read: 'An amusing note about finishing a play, the uselessness of interceding for him and his old friendship with St Anthony of Padua'.

[3] St Patrick's College, Maynooth, Kildare, founded in 1795 as a seminary for the training of Roman Catholic priests and recognized as a College of the National University in 1910. Its first lay students, men and women, were admitted in 1967.

23 January 1943   Ayot St Lawrence
[added to the following letter from Otto Kyllmann,
20 January 1943]

My dear Shaw, I think the following paragraph from the *Publishers Weekly* of New York, dated 25 November, may interest you:

> Authors and producers of the play *Oscar Wilde*, which had wide success a few years ago, will have to pay $57,767 damages for copyright infringement to Nellie Harris as assignee of the biography of *Oscar Wilde* written by Frank Harris, her late husband. This sum was recommended on November 12th as Mrs Harris's award by Joseph McGovern, who conducted a hearing to determine the sum due to her. Defendants in the infringement case were Leslie and Sewell Stokes, authors, and Gilbert Miller, Norman Marshall and Heron Publications, producers.[1]

Ever yours   O. K.

Somebody must have impersonated you in this film.

Now they want to film Hesketh Pearson's book and put a pseudo-Shaw on the screen.

I am trying to find out the legal position. Have we a copyright in our own persons and style of dressing—a common-law right? Can we prosecute for impersonation?

Have you any lawyer friend from whom you can get an obiter dictum on the point?   G. B. S.

1 March 1943   Ayot St Lawrence

Dear Childe Alfred, The two secretaries of the Society of Authors, both of them lawyers, agree that there is no such thing in English law as a right of privacy.[2] Apparently anyone may write your private life, paint pictures of you, draw and publish caricatures of you, impersonate you

---

1 The awarded damages did not solve Nellie Harris's problems. She continued to be in serious financial straits until her death, 25 March 1955, in Nice.

2 Kilham Roberts, secretary; M. Elizabeth Barber, assistant secretary.

on the stage or screen, copy your style of dress and cut of beard, and you have no remedy unless you can prove pecuniary loss or malicious hatred, ridicule and contempt, in which case I presume you can sue for damages or initiate a criminal prosecution for libel. In practice this means that unless you have been done out of your job, in which case you can always count on a British jury to find for you, the verdict will be against the artist and for the tradesman.

Religion is so utterly thoughtless with most people that it is, as you say, quite common for the dogma of the Immaculate Conception to be confused with the Virgin Birth. You will find Protestants, to whom the two are the same, denouncing the one as a folly of Pope Pius IX and accepting the other as part of the Apostles' Creed. That was my view when I first heard it talked about; but I was enlightened by the Belfast contention that Pope Pius's logic leads to the conclusion that not only the Blessed Virgin, but her mother, her grandmother, her great-grandmother and so on back to Eve (conceived parthenogenetically whilst still in her primal state of innocence) must have been equally free from original sin.

One day years ago I was lunching at the Cliffords.[1] Lady Clifford was a devout Catholic who retired to her oratory many times a day to make her soul. I was sitting next her; and on her left was a very Prussianized Teuton. Suddenly a fragment of his conversation rang out. "Why, they imprisoned a friend of mine for saying that the Immaculate Conception is all rot!" There was a terrible silence. It was exactly as if he had struck the dear lady in the face. No one knew what to say. I saved the situation by saying quietly but pontifically, "Quite right, too. All conceptions are immaculate". The Teuton, who had expected me to support him, and who felt that something was wrong, could find nothing to say. Lady Clifford was grateful to me for my apparently deadly riposte, and yet a bit puzzled, as it was not exactly what her confessor would have said.

However, enough of the subject. I know all about it; but as I regard the Blessed One and her Son as my fellow creatures and don't believe either of them was born parthenogenetically, I should jar on you if I

[1] Sir Hugh and Lady Clifford. Under her first married name, Mrs Henry de la Pasture, she was the author of a number of popular novels and plays.

discussed it. I will only say that I consider your church has a great advantage over its Protestant rival in adding a Mother God to the Trinity. It is always so in the Hindu religions. But my friend the Benedictine Abbess[1] was deeply shocked when I attributed divinity to the Blessed Virgin Mary. She forgave me, or perhaps even thought better of it, on reflection.

As to my politics, they are those of Shelley and Keats, Ruskin and Morris, plus Karl Marx and myself. Yours are those of a Culloden Jacobite. Our centuries are different. Still, you contrive to be a sufficiently modern poet; so the correspondence can continue very pleasantly.

G. B. S.

25 August 1943 [postcard]   4 Whitehall Court, London

I am a Fellow of the Royal Society of Literature, and don't need any ticket.[2] It is doubtful whether I can attend (I never do); but it is possible, as we have had to come up to town. We have been here since the 26th July and may have to spend September here through a break-up of our Ayot staff.

My poor wife is a crippled invalid[3] and cannot even go out of doors in London, much less go to lectures. I am myself a deplorable spectacle (eighty-seven) and much too old for London. On Saturday last I was robbed by a confidence-trick crook whose technique was new to me. I fell for it like the veriest greenhorn. The fellow squirted some shiny

[1] Dame Laurentia McLachlan (1866–1953), Abbess of Stanbrook, the cloistered Benedictine Convent in Worcestershire. For this remarkable friendship and test of Shaw's belief in Creative Evolution, see *In a Great Tradition* by the Benedictines of Stanbrook (1956).

[2] In February Douglas had been asked to give the Tredegar Memorial lecture on 'The Principles of Poetry', scheduled for 2 September. It was to be an attack on Eliot, Auden, Pound and other anti-formalists. Douglas was so disturbed by personal and financial problems that he was unable to put the talk together and called upon a young friend, Richard Jones, to help him. Much material was taken from Douglas's 'Note' to his *Collected Poems* and from the 'Preface' to his *Complete Poems*, but the text beginning with the passage of Plato (p. 9 in the pamphlet) to the end, p. 26, was largely written by Jones (see Douglas to Marie Stopes, 29 September 1944, British Library Add. Mss. 58495).

[3] She had osteitis deformans, misdiagnosed as lumbago in 1939.

stuff on my back, and stopped me to point it out. He took me to an underground railway lavatory and helped most kindly to clean me up [and] cleaned out my pocket. G. B. S.

15 September 1943 [postcard]   4 Whitehall Court, London

A Mass does nobody any harm; and I may for all I know have been living on prayers for years past. But my wife's orders in her will were 'no flowers; no black clothes; no service'. So this morning at Golders Green not a word was spoken; but Handel gave the music he set to 'nor didst Thou suffer thy Holy One to see corruption' for the committal, and *Ombra mai fu* (vulgarly known as Handel's *Largo*) for the voluntary. Who could ask for more?[1]

Handel was her favourite composer.

Miracles of rejuvenation occurred and made the end touchingly happy, making grief and sorrow impossible. Envy me; but don't condole. I am exaltedly serene and vigorous. G. B. S.

17 September 1943 [postcard]   4 Whitehall Court, London

This is all poppycock. The Royal Society of Literature has no magazine: it prints annually a volume of *Transactions* containing the lectures read at its tea parties; that is all. Even if this could pass technically as a magazine, the old hold of a magazine editor over a contribution was extinguished by the Copyright Act of 1911; and in the absence of a written agreement to the contrary the author can do what he likes with his work, even before the usual month has elapsed during which the magazine is current and on sale, though a decent author will not take advantage of this. The R.S.L. [volume] appears only once a year; and

[1] Charlotte Shaw had died at Whitehall Court on 13 September. She was cremated at Golders Green in the presence of only Shaw, Blanche Patch and Lady Astor. The wish that her ashes be scattered on Three Rock Mountain, near Dublin, was not possible to fulfil in wartime.

its distribution to the members is not a real publication. You are, I should say, quite free in the matter.[1]

I meant to come, but mistook the day. I am always making these senile blunders.   G. B. S.

29 October 1943   1 St Ann's Court, Hove

My dear St Christopher, I sent your card about my publishing rights in the lecture to the secretary of the Royal Society of Literature, with the result that the Society completely climbed down and withdrew its objection to my bringing out the lecture as a pamphlet.[2] Secker is now bringing it out and I corrected the proof yesterday. So it should be out in a few days and I will send you a copy. The Society gave me twenty-five pounds for my lecture (Tredegar told me it would be forty but I only got twenty-five!) and they had the gall to claim that this fee included their exclusive right to publish the lecture in their *Essays by Various Hands*. I had no agreement and no hint about this. Not a word was said about publishing rights, and while I would have been pleased to let them publish the lecture in their magazine I didn't see any reason why I should not also publish it as a pamphlet. Thanks chiefly to you this was conceded, but they say that they now will not print it in *Essays by Various Hands*, which leaves my withers entirely unwrung. I think sufficiently well of my lecture (which they professed to admire enormously) to think that the loss is theirs and not mine. I really couldn't see why they should get a ten-thousand-word essay for nothing, which is what it amounted to, and then claim that I was debarred from publishing it elsewhere.

I hope you are well, dear St Christopher. Your devoted   CHILDE

[1] Martin Secker had agreed to publish the lecture as a pamphlet. He had been urged to do this by a young man whom Douglas had met the year before, Adrian Earle, twenty-one, once at Winchester and with hopes of going to Oxford, a book collector and aspiring poet. Earle had ingratiated himself with Douglas and become a strong influence in his life. In May of this year Douglas had written a will designating Earle as his literary executor and chief beneficiary (Douglas to Earle, 30 May 1943, Clark Memorial Library).

Earle's letter to the Royal Society of Literature, asking if there would be any objection to Secker's booklet, received an immediate and stern reply: request denied; the Society had the exclusive right of publication.

[2] Secker published *The Principles of Poetry* (Richards Press) in November, a pamphlet in pale grey wrappers, limited to a thousand copies.

[early November 1943]   4 Whitehall Court, London

Dear Childe Alfred, Keeping letters is a mischievous practice which I avoid on principle when they are really private and not documentary. . . . I could have sworn that your letters, recklessly outspoken as they are, had all been conscientiously destroyed.

Yet in the course of a tidying-up into which my wife's death and the daily possibility of my own has driven me, I find the enclosed. I cannot account for it. I dare not destroy them: I leave them to you.

I shouldn't bother about the Royal Society of Literature. When the time comes to publish their annual budget of lectures they will think better of omitting yours. If not, it will make no difference to you, and get them into trouble with the members who don't attend the meetings.

Englishmen must have their quarrel, preferably about nothing.

G. B. S.

27 November 1943   1 St Ann's Court, Hove

My dear St Christopher, I was delighted with your answers to the idiot interviewer about Mosley[1] in yesterday's *Express*. Every single answer you gave is exactly what I would have said myself (except of course about being a Communist, which seems to imply that you don't realize that it is just exactly Communists and Socialists or at any rate Left-

[1] Herbert Morrison had just released Sir Oswald Mosley, leader of the British Union of Fascists, from prison, where he had been interned (without trial) since May 1940. Miss Wheeler Ryan, a newspaper woman who strongly opposed the release, questioned Bernard Shaw for the *Daily Express* (26 November 1943).

Miss Ryan asked if "anything short of the resignation" of Mr Morrison would "pacify those who are risking life and limb" to defeat Fascism. Shaw replied:

Those who are risking life and limb . . . are soldiers, sailors, and miners chiefly. You are asking me whether I think that the soldiers and sailors will run away and the miners go on strike unless Mr Morrison resigns. To put it more briefly, you are asking me whether I am a damned fool or not.

Asked if Morrison's decision would not cause alarm and despondence among the masses:

SHAW: It makes me suspect that you are mentally defective. I think this Mosley panic shameful.
MISS RYAN: Are you a Fascist, Mr Shaw?
SHAW: No, I am a Communist.

Wingers who hold the very views of which you make hay in your answers). But your brand of Communism is not the least like that which appeals to the average Communist or Socialist. If you are a Communist then the word requires a new definition.

I think it is rather unkind that you did not write to me about my lecture. But I suppose you are as usual overwhelmed with correspondence. I have been inundated with letters about it (the lecture I mean). So far nobody has a word to say in defence of Eliot. The only thing that worries me is, if they all dislike Eliot so much and have a complete contempt for his alleged poetry, why has none of them ever said so before?

I am going to spend the week-end with a farmer[1] and am looking forward to good food. I'm half starved here. Your devoted   CHILDE

2 December 1943   4 Whitehall Court, London

Dear Childe Alfred, You are so clever and quick-witted, and so unerring a judge of poetry that you are always right in your selected cases; but then you are such a thoughtless devil that you are as often as not wrong in your law. Of course you can play skittles with these silly people who think they are writing poetry when it is not even prose in any artistic sense: it is twaddle. But you leave yourself in the position of contending that everything that rhymes and scans correctly is poetry and everything that doesn't isn't. T. S. Eliot has only to reply that he declines to discuss poetry with a man who thinks that Hoole's translation of Tasso is poetry; that there is no poetry in the authorized version of the Bible; that a child's recitation piece like the 'seven ages of man', or an argument in basic English like 'to be or not to be', is poetry and not 'What a piece of work is a man!'; that Macaulay's *Lays of Ancient Rome* and Walter Scott's 'Lochinvar' place their authors above William Blake and Whitman as poets; and that the only scraps of poetry in my plays are the four lines in *Heartbreak House* which scan and rhyme. Your definition of poetry is a definition of verse, which is quite a different

[1] Douglas had been introduced to Edward Colman and his wife, Sheila, on Easter Sunday 1942, by a mutual friend, a young Oxford man, Richard Rumbold. The Colmans had been married for three years and lived at Old Monk's Farm, Lancing, near Hove.

thing. Hoole versified correctly in the manner of Dryden; but he never wrote a line of poetry in his life. Bunyan, with an ear almost better than Shakespeare's, and his unfailing rhythm and melody and soul energy, never wrote anything else. I call myself technically a playwright, but aesthetically I call myself a dramatic poet, and am called so as a matter of course in the German theatre.

T. S. Eliot made a fool of himself in his reaction against formalism, as all young reactionaries do; but his *Murder in the Cathedral* is dramatic poetry good enough to make it ridiculous to dismiss him as a sham poet of no account. Yeats could neither spell nor count; but his *Celtic Twilight* was not a black-out for all that.

All this you know as well as I do; but only extreme intellectual laziness and self-satisfaction could have made you leave yourself open to getting it on your jaw as a cross-counter. However, that is your way; and probably none of the twaddlers will be adroit enough to see the opening and take it.

Quaritch's executors could not legally have left a part of his estate worth two thousand pounds unrealized: it would be a breach of trust. You took your chance of that when you let him have the letters without his giving testamentary direction about them.[1] You mustn't quarrel with them about it.

I must stop. I sent the last of my book [*Everybody's Political What's What?*] to the printers today: a great relief; but it has left me no time over for letter writing (or rather lecturing); so good night!   G. B. S.

---

[1] On 23 May 1913 Douglas had sold twelve of his letters from Wilde to the bookseller Bernard Quaritch for a hundred pounds. A week later he offered thirteen more, 'the last I have left'. (The year before he had burned some hundred and fifty; see *Without Apology*, p. 77.) Quaritch sent another check for a hundred pounds on 2 June. Verbal permission was given by the bookshop for Douglas to make extracts within the next month or two if the letters were not sold by then. At the end of July, while a purchaser was considering the letters, Douglas asked permission to make copies for his book, *Oscar Wilde and Myself*. The bookshop hesitated, Douglas insisted, and the shop sought legal counsel. No determination was made by 27 August 1913, when Bernard Quaritch died. Thereafter the letters were declared to be the property not of his estate but of the company. Douglas's request was denied.

The twenty-five Wilde letters were sold by the Quaritch Company to A. S. W. Rosenbach and by him to John B. Stetson, Jr, and after his auction sale in 1920 they passed to William Andrews Clark, Jr. They are now in the Clark Memorial Library.

3 December 1943   1 St Ann's Court, Hove

My dear St Christopher, If you would read my lecture more carefully you would see that I have carefully emphasized the difference between poetry and verse. I said that the point about Pound, Eliot, Auden and Company was 'not so much that they were bad poets as that they were not poets at all and were therefore incapable of writing even bad verse'. All your argument about Hoole and Bunyan and the authorized version et cet. et cet. et cet. is based on the fallacy that good prose is poetry. Shakespeare wrote incomparable prose but his prose is not poetry, and the authorized version is not poetry nor is Walt Whitman nor Bunyan. You yourself write great prose but you don't write poetry, though, as I said in *Without Apology*, no doubt you could have done it if you had tried. Eliot on the other hand could not write twelve consecutive lines of poetry to save his life. I don't agree with you that *Murder in the Cathedral* is 'good dramatic poetry'. It is feeble stuff and not anything like poetry. Yeats, as I pointed out in my lecture, *was* a poet and could at times write good stuff, but he also had a defective ear for rhythm and constantly wrote lines that don't scan. I wish you would read my stuff before criticizing it! You did exactly the same in the case of my book on the sonnets. You wrote me a long letter containing a lot of praise and appreciation (which pleased me very much) but you also criticized several passages in the book without noticing that *in every case* these passages were quotations from Wilde, and that while I quoted them as being interesting and even brilliant, I expressly said that I did not agree with them, e.g., about Marlowe as the rival poet. I hope the people whom you describe as 'twaddlers' will come on. I shall have no difficulty whatever in dealing with them.

As regards Quaritch's, you tell me not to 'quarrel' with them. But my dear blessed St Christopher, the incident about the sale of Wilde's letters was in *1913*. I have never said a word about it since, and I only mentioned it to you *en passant* as a piece of interesting ancient history. There is no quarrel! Your devoted   CHILDE

1 January 1944   4 Whitehall Court, London

Childe, Childe, If you will not use your reason you must learn your catechism. Here it is.

Q. What is poetry?

A. It is the communication of feeling between living persons by language in scripture or vocally.

Q. Name an authentic example of poetry.

A. Alfred Douglas's sonnets—mostly.

Q. Name an example of scripture that is not poetry.

A. Any entry in the telephone directory.

Q. What then do you call the entries in the telephone directory?

A. Unimpassioned information.

Q. Is rhyme and scannable measure the diagnostic of poetry?

A. No.

Q. Why? The Douglas sonnets are all rhyme and scannable.

A. So is 'Thirty days hath September, April, June and eke November: February hath twenty-eight alone; and all the rest have thirty-one'. This is pure unimpassioned information, like the telephone directory. Therefore the verse form is not the diagnostic.

Q. Can you name a poem that has no rhymes nor scannable verses?

A. Yes. The Book of Job in the authorized English translation.

Q. Lord Alfred Douglas, an authentic poet, denies that Job is a poem and does so on the ground that it neither rhymes nor scans. Account for this.

A. Douglas, being a born poet, has never had to reason about poetry any more than a lightning calculator has to reason about mathematics. What he says is only the first thing that comes into his head.

Q. What then is a true diagnostic? Why is Job a poem though it neither rhymes nor scans?

A. Because it communicates feeling by a musical arrangement of language.

Q. Are all such arrangements poems?

A. No. The feeling must be noble. An obscene limerick communicates a feeling of amusement; but such amusement is not noble enough to be called poetic. A poem is a poem but a limerick is only a limerick.

Q. At what point does feeling become noble enough to make its communication poetic?

A. The point varies with the capacity of the individual.

Q. Which capacity? The intellectual or the artistic?

A. Both. Take two lines of precisely the same musical value: 'The streamlet ripples down the hill' and 'The streamlet ripples up the hill'. A child whose intellect is not yet developed will be equally pleased with both. Sir Isaac Newton would have accepted the first version as pastoral poetry; but the second [would] only make him laugh. Gilbert made many people laugh by a ballad about a Scot trying to play an air on the bagpipes. Of this air he wrote that 'It wandered about into several keys'. I could not laugh at this as Gilbert intended me to, as the bagpipes, with their persistent drone, cannot possibly wander about into several keys. Poetry must satisfy the brain as well as the ear. Intellect is a passion: a scripture addressed to it, like Dante's *Paradiso*, may take high rank as a poem.

Q. The *Paradiso* is in *terza rima*. Does not that show that poetry at its highest demands rhyme and scannable rhythm?

A. No. Shaw writes blank verse as easily as Shakespeare; but in his sublime passages he neither rhymes nor uses established measure. Douglas could not paraphrase any of these passages in blank verse without spoiling them.

If you doubt me, try. But don't deny that the passages are not poetry or shall I call you a sonneteer.

No time for more.   G. B. S.

P.S. Read Tolstoy's *What is Art?* He knew.

4 January 1944   1 St Ann's Court, Hove

My dear St Christopher, You are at your old tricks of 'answering' what I never said or wrote. What I did write was, that *writing which neither rhymes nor scans nor has metrical measure cannot be poetry*. You choose, with complete contempt for logic and intellectual integrity, to assume from this that I maintain that *therefore* anything which rhymes and scans *is* poetry. I never said anything so foolish and preposterous, as you must know if you have read my lecture (which I very much doubt). It is mere impertinence for you to tell me that 'limericks' and 'Thirty days hath September' are not poetry although they rhyme and scan. *À qui le dites-vous?* Don't I know it at least as well as you do? Everything you say on

163

this point is implicit in my lecture. Don't teach your grandmother to suck eggs. And what is the point or relevance of your tedious lecture about Gilbert's Scotsman who 'wandered about into several keys' on the bagpipes? What makes you suppose that I don't know just as well as you do that one cannot wander into different keys on the pipes? And anyhow what have Gilbert's mistakes to do with me? Why must you be forever lecturing and 'giving information' to people on subjects on which they are just as well informed as you are? My dear St Christopher, the Book of Job is lovely prose, but it is no more poetry than your *Saint Joan* is. You have no more right to be offended at my saying, as I do emphatically, that you are not a poet, than I would have if you told me that I am not a dramatist. As for your pathetic delusion that you can write blank verse as well as Shakespeare, it is impossible to answer it politely. So I refrain. Your devoted   CHILDE ALFRED

11 January 1944   4 Whitehall Court, London

Dear Childe Alfred, It is no use telling me what you said or didn't say, or what you know or don't know, or what nice things Quiller-Couch and Company have said and not said.[1] If your article does not mean that the diagnostic of poetry is rhyme and regular metre it means nothing. And on this point Eliot can knock you into a cocked hat. The technical distinction between prose and verse has nothing to do with the difference between poetry and 'Thirty days hath September'.

I read your lecture as carefully and critically as I read my own stuff before passing it for press, and of course at once found out its weak spots. This you never do. You pick up the nearest brick and shy it at somebody you disagree with. Wyndham Lewis and all who agree with you are delighted and amused; for you do it very readably; but the bricks don't make a building. Now it is no use my arguing with you; for as, however much you know, you never take the trouble to ratiocinate what you know—fit your bricks into structures—you cannot argue,

[1] Quiller-Couch 'purred' over his lecture, and many at Cambridge were 'sickened of the T. S. Eliot game' (Douglas to Marie Stopes, December 1943, British Library Add. Mss. 58495).

and feel hurt when I arrange the bricks for you. So just adopt my definitions if the controversy goes any farther; and thank your stars that you have me to do all that patient drudgery for you.

A limerick can be poetry just as any other quatrain can if it is written by a poet on the poetic plane. I said 'an obscene limerick'.

I did not say that I could write blank verse as *well* as Shakespeare could: I said 'as easily'. And that is a simple fact. I could have written Caesar's first speech in *Caesar and Cleopatra*, or Lilith's last in *Back To Methuselah*, *more* easily in blank verse than in prose. Why did I not? Because blank verse was not poetic enough. Why did Ibsen, who in *Peer Gynt* proved his command of all verse forms, abandon rhyme and regular metre, and write all his later plays in prose? For the same reason. Fielding's *Tom Thumb* proves that he, like me, could write blank verse as easily as Shakespeare. Why didn't he write *Tom Jones* in blank verse? Well, paraphrase our purple passages in blank verse, you who are a poet, and you will find out.

Don't be too disrespectful to Eliot. His cathedral play not only took him out of the mob of would-be moderns whose stuff is neither prose nor verse but just twaddle: it shows that he is a bit of a virtuoso in versification when he needs it to express himself. Anyhow do not treat him as a moral delinquent. That is a bit too Victorian and pre-Shavian. In haste—very busy   G. B. S.

13 January 1944   1 St Ann's Court, Hove

My dear St Christopher, Is it softening of the brain or are you merely trying to pull my leg? You say you could have written your *Methuselah* (one of your least successful efforts by the way) in blank verse but that you preferred to write it in prose. You truly admit the distinction between prose and verse and completely give away your own crazy case which appears to be that when you write prose you are really writing poetry!! *Voyons mon pauvre monsieur*, what is the object of writing that sort of drivel? Do drop it. You are in danger of becoming as monumental a bore as your precious Ibsen, who in my opinion was little more than half-witted. (I have never been able to sit through one of his idiotic plays.)

D. B. Wyndham Lewis (not to be confused with Percy Wyndham Lewis) said in the article which I sent you that 'no addict of the moderns' could answer any of the judgements in my lecture 'without rejecting human reason and looking like a fool', which is exactly what you are doing. Why go out of your way to make a b—— fool of yourself? Your devoted but exasperated   CHILDE

1 February 1944 [postcard]   Ayot St Lawrence

Dear Childe, I am sorry I cannot make the case intelligible to you; but it cannot be helped; and I shall not try again. Simple as it seems to me, it is evidently beyond your powers.

Besides, the mischief (if any) is done, and may as well be done *with*.

Meanwhile, if you must relieve your feelings by furious letters they had better come to me than to less magnanimous victims. And so, let us drop it.   G. B. S.

6 February 1944   Ayot St Lawrence

Dear Childe, You HAVE got it wrong this time. I did not disagree with your lecture. I entirely agree with you and with St Thomas Aquinas, whom you quote (and contradict) as happens to suit your mood at the moment. What I did was to criticize the way you did the job, which is a quite different matter. You cannot bear criticism: I dare not tell you that I doubt whether you can play the violin as well as Menuhin or Heifetz: you would immediately shriek that you understood Beethoven and Brahms far better than either of them, and that I am a malicious liar sneering at you.

Nevertheless, Alfred, you cannot play the violin as well as Menuhin. You have not the technique. The only technique you have is that of the Petrarchan sonnet, in which Heifetz is far inferior to you. Now skill in Petrarchan sonneteering is a high accomplishment, difficult of attainment in English because it is essentially un-English, and its rhyme arrangement is the ugliest art form in existence, making it very difficult to achieve a result fulfilling Dante's perfect definition of a sonnet as 'rhetoric made musical'. I once, being madly in love, wrote a sonnet or two; but my ear is like the ear of Shakespeare; and I wrote them in the English form with its more natural sequence of rhymes, and its wonderful coda-couplet at the end of the stanza. But I know that writing a good Petrarchan sonnet in English is a much more difficult feat, and that your command of it ranks you as a master technician. I am in comparison a duffer.

So far, you will heartily agree. But when it comes to criticism, I am the master technician and you are the duffer. (Now don't start screaming and writing frantic letters.) You have not been through the mill. I supported myself for ten years by criticism of the arts: literature, painting, music, the theatre. I began, of course, as an amateur, and made all the mistakes that you make. I read and watched and listened for the diagnostic of the greatness of the great artists I had to criticize. I praised them eloquently for some feat of execution, and next week found some third-rater doing it better. I was fascinated by the magic of Edgar Allan Poe, and then found myself up against the fact that Whitman, who had no magic at all, was yet a poet, and, for an American, a great one. In hunting down the diagnostic I had fall after fall. But at last I learnt my job, and gained what I was really after, the power to criticize myself. When I write a chapter I get it down as it comes just as you do; but I then read it over critically once, twice, three times before I let it go to press. If anybody else reads it—wife, secretary, proof-reader, or my cook—and spots a slip in it, I am really grateful to them. Strangers, some of them not too literate, have written to me to point out perhaps thirty blunders in a single first edition; and they all get a picture postcard and an autograph in return. You would rush to your solicitors and instruct them to take an action for defamation and blasphemy. Thirty actions in fact.

Even if you had to go through the mill I doubt if you would ever be a really fool-proof critic. I have a special faculty of analysis which is indispensable in diagnostic hunting. Without it a critic is like a foxhound without a nose. You seem to me to lack it. You mistake your association of ideas—your 'conditioned reflexes' as Pavlov called them —for logic. You do not know what a diagnostic means. You quote with approval the definition of Aquinas and in the next line set up some mug's definition and make it the basis of your attack on somebody you dislike. When the mug's definition is exposed you shriek that you have not been read—that you gave the Thomist definition in a previous paragraph and that there is no justice in the world. You cannot disentangle. I can.

There is another queer difference between us. I have never liked myself much. Your self-love (a very valuable quality, as I know by my experience of the lack of it) is extraordinary. Whatever you do you are delighted with. As to reading it over to get it right as I do, the least suggestion that there could be anything wrong with your masterpiece makes you as wrathful as a god whose omniscience has been questioned. Luckily for you the stuff is always good enough to enthuse a retinue of flatterers, whose compliments give you the keenest pleasure. But poor me, the critic! I am accused of sneering and rebuked for being 'impertinent'. If you can recognize anything of yourself in this, and can humble yourself by communing with your saint instead of writing to the papers, you will be able to produce a marvellous sonnet cycle called 'Narcissus'. I suppose this is what I am trying to evoke from you.

Do not meddle in politics: you do not know your A.B.C. in them. When Henry George[1] shifted me on to economics sixty years ago I read Karl Marx and thought him infallible and became a Socialist fourteen years before Lenin.[2] It took me four years to master economics in the abstract and understand Capitalism from its own and not from the Marxian point of view. Your point of view is that of a second lieutenant in the Guards under Queen Victoria.

Chuck it, Alfred. G. B. S.

9 February 1944 1 St Ann's Court, Hove

My dear St Christopher, Your letter is stupendous. Everything you say in your analysis of my character and methods of writing and arguing is

[1] A lecture by the American economist at Memorial Hall, Farringdon Street, 5 September 1882, led Shaw to George's *Progress and Poverty*.

[2] During the winter of 1882–1883 Shaw began his thorough study of Karl Marx at the British Museum.

exactly applicable to yourself. You are the most conceited man who ever lived (whereas I am fundamentally humble) and you are a hopeless case because you are cut off from the fountain of wisdom (God and the Catholic church) as I was myself before my conversion. If what you say about me and my art, such as it is, were really true, it would probably annoy me to read what you have written, whereas it merely makes me laugh. Your fantastic picture of my dashing off stuff and then refusing to alter or correct it, is the exact opposite of what really happens. I write poetry very slowly, with great effort and 'sweat and blood and tears', as explained in my preface to my *Collected Poems* written twenty-five years ago.[1] When I have written a sonnet or any other form of poetry (you seem to forget that I don't write only sonnets) I always 'sit on it' for several days, and very often almost turn it inside out before it satisfies me.

When I was in prison I wrote *In Excelsis* (seventeen sonnets) in a Borstal-boy school copy-book, kindly supplied by the authorities. In this book is exactly shown the way I write poetry. On the left is the working out of the sonnet with lines and words and phrases scratched out and rewritten, a regular mess, almost unreadable; written out on the right is the fair, final version. (This only applies to poetry. I *do* dash off prose very quickly.) The abominable Home Office have still got this book and refuse to give it back.[2] I have tried to get it back over and over again, but they flatly refuse to part with it. Only a year ago the Conservative M.P.'s Chips Channon and his brother-in-law, Alan Lennox-Boyd (now in the Government as an under-minister), told me that they thought it monstrous that I should be deprived of this manuscript and undertook to get it for me.[3] But they completely failed and only got an

---

[1] Douglas is quoting himself: '[All good poetry] is forged slowly and painfully, link by link with sweat and blood and tears'; *The Collected Poems of Lord Alfred Douglas*, p. 121.

[2] The Home Office still has this manuscript.

[3] Henry Channon (1897–1958, knighted 1957) and Alan Lennox-Boyd (created Viscount Boyd of Merton, 1960) had called on Douglas in October 1942, at the suggestion of Lady Diana Cooper. They 'were resolved not to mention Oscar Wilde, prison, Winston, Robbie Ross or Frank Harris, but [they] were soon well embarked on all five subjects, though not at once. . . . [Douglas] was very pathetic . . . alone, poor, almost friendless . . .' *The Diaries of Sir Henry Channon*, ed. Robert Rhodes James (1967), p. 338. After Queensberry withdrew his support, they joined Marie Stopes and Lord Tredegar as the two other covenanters, pledged to pay the rent of the St Ann's Court flat (Douglas to Marie Stopes, March 1943, British Library Add. Mss. 58494).

incredible (and very offensive about me) letter from Osbert Peake, an under-minister at the Home Office, who was backed up by Herbert Morrison, his chief. . . .

You say my political opinions are those of a second lieutenant in the Guards. But all second lieutenants in the Guards don't have the same opinions, and one or other of them might be a saint or a genius. As things are now, thanks to your poisonous propaganda, one or other of them might easily be a Socialist or a Marxist! So that little gibe does not get you very far. You would probably say that my religious opinions are those of a child at its mother's knee. I wouldn't object. I hope they are. You can call my views about religion and politics (they go together in my case) what you like. The point is that they are right, being founded on humility and the love of God, and yours are *hideously* wrong, as you will find out when you come to die. A year ago I sent you a book, *The Song of Bernadette*,[1] which you told me your wife would read, implying that you wouldn't read it yourself. I advise you to read the two chapters about the poet Hyacinthe de Lafitte. They apply, *mutatis mutandis*, in a remarkable way to you with your 'insane, laughable, absurd pride which stood at the very cradle of [your] mind'. I have said a prayer for you to Saint Bernadette twice a day every day of my life since I read the book. Meanwhile you know nothing whatever about me. Your devoted   CHILDE

P.S. By the same post as your letter I received one from Logan Pearsall Smith[2] 'thoroughly agreeing' with all my views in my lecture. This makes up a galaxy of literary stars on my side. You were the only one out of about fifty to whom I sent the lecture who disagreed with it. All the rest were *enthusiastically* in favour of it.

26 February 1944   Ayot St Lawrence

Peace, perturbed spirit. Let dogs delight to bark and bite. . . . There must be something radically antipathetic in me for you. You cannot bear agreeing with me. When I tell you that you are a master technician

[1] By Franz Werfel (1942).
[2] Pearsall Smith, an American essayist (1865–1946) who spent most of his life in Britain.

in virtue of your Petrarchan sonnets, and your putting real master-work into them, touching and retouching until you get them as perfect as possible, you don't touch (or retouch) your hat, and gracefully accept the high compliment. You declare that I have alleged that you cannot write a Drayton-Shakespeare sonnet, nor a ballad, nor an ode, nor an epic, nor a triolet, nor a pantun, nor a limerick, nor even a clerihew. Nobody has ever denied that you can. So can I. So can anybody with half an ear, a rhyming dictionary, a metronome, and a supply of pen and paper. But no competent critic ranks a master by his doing what anybody can do. I spend an hour or two every day in the garden sawing logs and splitting them with an axe: but nobody has yet described me as a master carpenter or woodman. Shakespeare wrote epitaphs, but is not now remembered by them. Cut your Petrarchan sonnets out of your record and you are hardly even a poetaster. Cut my plays out of mine and I am only a retired journalist.

After describing how you work and work over your sonnets to get them right (echoing what I said in my letter) you proceed to confess that you never dream of doing this with your lectures and essays, but stick them down slap-dash just as they come and never think them over. The result is a scamped job, clever and 'brilliant' enough to be very readable and to keep an audience awake, but often inconsecutive and contradictory. And when I say that you contradict yourself you do not say, as Whitman did, 'Well: if I contradict myself I contradict myself'. Shakespeare, who 'never blotted a line' and mixed up his time plots absurdly (I did it myself in *Fanny's First Play*) is not reported to have screamed with rage when the blunders were pointed out to him, and accused his critics of bad faith and of having declared that he could not write plays. Why, in short, do you behave like a minor poet instead of a major one?

Your letters and lecture are mighty smart; but why don't you take the same trouble you take with your much more difficult job as a sonnet-wright? If you had got your definition right, which you might have done in half an hour of revision, you would not have been driven into such monstrous gaffes as denying all poetic quality to the Book of Job, to Shakespeare's unversified dialogue and to all the unversified master-pieces of literature in the world. Poets Laureate have written oceans of

Shaw sawing and splitting logs

doggerel without achieving as much poetry as Doughty put into every page of *Arabia Deserta*, which is not in verse.[1]

However, I am tired of kicking you. It is unkind; and it is useless, because it does no good. So write me half a dozen more abusive letters and get your spleen off your chest.

I have had to do three days' work in the last two, and must go to bed. Why did I ever let you seduce me into corresponding with you?

G. B. S.

28 February 1944   1 St Ann's Court, Hove

Dear Idiot, I *knew* you would pitch on that one footnote in my letter in which I told you that I write prose very rapidly. I thought of it after I had posted the letter and was on the point of writing another letter by the next post to explain that while I write prose very quickly (a habit I acquired when I was editing the *Academy* and *Plain English* and in both cases writing an enormous lot of stuff every week) I always revise most carefully anything except current journalism, which I often had to write with a boy waiting for 'copy' for the printer. I took nearly three months, on and off, to write my lecture after dashing off the first draft, and there is not a word in it I would now change. I first had that draft typed and then added about two thousand words, or rather I did not *add* them, I put them in front of what I had already written. The lecture originally began with the reflections on Plato. All the first nine pages before that were written later, and I also altered and rewrote and interpolated numerous other passages. I had it typed three times and sweated over it before I got it right. So please don't write more rot about what you know nothing about, namely my methods of doing my stuff.

Your remarks about Job and Shakespeare merely illustrate your own wooden-headed density. While you have spent a great part of your life making a fool of yourself by running down Shakespeare, I have always worshipped him; and I consider that not only is he the greatest poet who

[1] This record of a two-year journey with a pilgrim caravan by the geologist and poet Charles Doughty (1843–1926) was in a prose influenced by Chaucer, Spenser and Arabian tales. The book had recently been loaned to Shaw by Sir Sydney Cockerell.

ever lived but also the greatest writer of prose. But that doesn't mean that I share your incredible and owl-like inability to distinguish between his poetry and his prose. Are you so stupid that you can't understand that a great poet may sometimes prefer to express himself in prose?

A. D.

P.S. I think you might have thought of sending me a word of sympathy about poor little Olive's death.[1] Although she treated me very badly at times I was devoted to her and I feel very desolate now she is gone.

29 February 1944   Ayot St Lawrence

Are we both widowers, within six months? I never look at the first page of *The Times*: your letter was a surprise. Olive wrote to me sometimes: her name is in my address book.

Marriage is a mystery, even when, like mine, it is effected by a registrar (we neither of us could stand the Church of England service). I suppose every marriage is different: some are failures and never consummate themselves except physically, which means that they are not human marriages at all. I don't know why you did not live with Olive; her treating you very badly (as I do) has nothing to do with it: all couples who live together treat each other badly occasionally, and treat third parties very well. But the relationship is unique and mysterious. I have known women with whom I could get on with less friction than with Charlotte; but their deaths have not affected me in the same way. Her ashes are preserved at Golders Green, and my instructions are that mine are to be inseparably mixed with them, after which they may be scattered to the winds or immured in Westminster Abbey for all I care. When I come across something intimate of her belongings I have a welling of emotion and quite automatically say something endearing to her. But I am not in the least desolate; on the contrary I am enjoying my solitude and have improved markedly in health since her death set me

[1] Olive had died on 13 February at her flat in Hove, of a cerebral hæmorrhage. She was sixty-seven. As a lapsed Catholic her funeral service (18 February) was not held in a church but in the Brighton Crematorium. According to her written directions, her ashes were to be scattered in the sea, but no instruction for this was given until 1950.

free. But you, who lived alone, feel desolate. There is no logic in it: it is a mystery.

As I got about eighty letters a day for a fortnight after Charlotte's death was announced, I might very well have refrained from writing out of the friendliest consideration for you; but here I am writing away without mercy. I could not write so to many people; so there must be something sympathetic between us after all.

By the way, I was once with Charlotte in the Stratford Theatre at a performance of *Lear*. At the first long interval she rose to go; and I asked her was she going back to the hotel for tea, and was she sure she could get back in time. She stared at me amazedly, said, "Haven't you had enough of this drivel?" and marched out. I stayed. It was certainly not a thrilling performance; but drivel!!!!! That was how it affected her.

The reception of Irving's infamous mutilation of *Lear* was typical of the provocation under which I attacked Shakespeare in the nineties. The critics—even Walkley[1]—betrayed in every line that they had never read the play, and were puzzled by the unintelligible intrusions of Edgar and Gloucester, whom Irving had carefully made mincemeat of. But none the less they raved about the Bard like the bishops who knelt down and kissed the manuscript of Ireland's forged *Vortigern*.[2] I was so disgusted, being full of Shakespeare myself, that I resolved to make him human and real; and to do this I had to begin by kicking him off his throne, or rather his altar. Besides, I was enthroning Ibsen, who had taken the theatre into another world. If you want to praise Shakespeare you must forget *The Master Builder*. Enough for tonight. Were you with her?

G. B. S.

---

[1] Arthur Bingham Walkley (1855–1926), drama critic for the *Star* from 1888 to 1900.

[2] William Henry Ireland (1777–1835) at seventeen forged Shakespeare documents, including scenes from *Hamlet*, a full manuscript of *Lear* and a 'hitherto unknown play by Shakespeare', *Vortigern and Rowena*. An exhibition of the documents was held at the house of the antiquarian Samuel Ireland, William's father, and many spectators were filled with wonder. No bishops knelt down and kissed the manuscript of *Vortigern* but James Boswell honoured the manuscript of *Lear* in this way and both Drury Lane and Covent Garden vied for the right to produce *Vortigern*.

Dear St Christopher, Thanks for your letter. I took it for granted that you would have seen the announcement of Olive's death which was prominently announced in *The Times* (not on the first page, but with a headline in the middle of the paper) and many other papers. I was devoted to her and she to me (as far as she was capable of devotion to anyone) but she wasn't very kind to me. You know how frightfully worried I have been all these last ten years about money. I was within an ace of losing this flat and having to go and live in a cheap lodging, yet she never helped me though she was very well off. When I had money when we first married I lavished it on her. She had over six thousand pounds a year when her father died in about 1925 and she then gave me five hundred pounds a year (not exactly lavish but I was quite content with it), but she kept on reducing it till it came down to three hundred pounds, and I would have lost my flat if Tredegar and three others [Marie Stopes, Channon and Lennox-Boyd] hadn't subscribed to pay the rent, which they now do, a hundred and thirty pounds a year, by a legal covenant.

Of course Olive was impoverished by the war like everyone else, but I can't help feeling that she might have been kinder (especially as she always professed almost extravagant devotion to me!). Her money all goes to my son, Raymond, but this, to do her justice, is not her fault. She would have left it to me with reversion to him if she had had the power. It was fixed that way by her father, who hated me and always did all he could to injure me and to smash our marriage. It's not possible to avoid feeling rather bitter about the way she left me for so many years on the brink of destitution. How different was the case of your wife.

I rather think that Raymond, my son, will increase my income as soon as (or if) he gets control of his money. (He will have about two thousand pounds a year after taxation.) Of course the death duties make him much poorer than his mother was. He is very fond of me, and the first thing he said when he saw me the day of the funeral was that "of course" he would make up my income to a decent figure. I am left with an annuity of five hundred pounds reduced by taxation to three hundred and forty. Unfortunately poor little Raymond[1] is in a mental home, where he has been for fifteen years. But I'm told he is now practically cured and will shortly be de-certified. If this comes off it will make things easier. My wife left me her personal property, which includes a few hundreds in the bank, but I've just heard that any money I get will be sent to the Official Receiver, as I am a bankrupt![2] I don't have much luck, do I? Your devoted   CHILDE A.

2 March 1944   1 St Ann's Court, Hove

My dear St Christopher, I've been reading your last letter again and it occurs to me that my reply posted earlier in the day was rather egoistical (all about my own troubles) and unsympathetic to you. So I am writing again, to say that your letter greatly touched me in what you say about your wife, and also to thank you for sending me her photograph. As you say, marriage is a mysterious thing and it creates bonds in the case of people who have souls which appear to be unbreakable.

You say you don't know why I didn't live with Olive. The simple explanation is that she left me in 1913 just when I was in the worst trouble of my life and when, in addition to a mass of other troubles, I was involved in a fight with her father which I had taken on entirely to protect her and in her interest. She cleared out of the house (taking more than half the furniture et cet.) while I was away staying with my mother and keeping up a most affectionate correspondence with her. When I got back I found to my utter amazement that she had gone, leaving a note for me in the classic fashion. She didn't go off with another man, but there were more than one with whom she *might* as well have done so! After that we were completely estranged for many years,

[1] For the story of Raymond, see Appendix IV.

[2] At any time during the past thirty years Douglas could have sought a discharge but he stubbornly refused to do so. After he died, his devoted friend, Edward Colman, attempted to clear his name and persevered in this effort for thirty-six years. On 17 August 1981, at a private hearing in London, the stigma of bankruptcy was finally removed from Douglas's name. It took the court only two minutes to accept Colman's contention that Douglas's debts, a little over two thousand pounds, had been paid by royalties from republished writings and biographies.

MRS BERNARD SHAW
1857 – 1943

Photograph taken by Shaw, made into a memorial postcard

but we had a reconciliation and thereafter for twenty years or more always remained on the best of terms though we didn't live together. My really *tremendous* love for her was killed at that time (when she left me), and it never could come back. It was replaced in time by strong affection and sentimental friendship, but there never was any question of setting up a ménage again, especially as by this time she was rich and I was poor. Can you imagine your wife leaving you to live on three hundred pounds a year? I trow not, but then of course in your case things were quite different, as you had a large income of your own, earned by your own brilliant brain. Whereas poets, as a general rule, don't manage to make money unless they are also dramatists. Your devoted   CHILDE A.

28 March 1944   1 St Ann's Court, Hove

My dear St Christopher, I must honestly say that I have a good deal of sympathy with what you tell me your wife said about *King Lear*. I have *always* thought that it is the least good of Shakespeare's plays, and really if anyone else except Shakespeare had written it, most people would agree that the plot *is perfectly drivelling and imbecile*! It is full of great lines and fine stuff, but everyone in the play is a congenital idiot, beginning with Lear himself and Cordelia (a complete nincompoop!). The sheer imbecility of Gloucester in swallowing all Edmund's obvious and grotesque lies about Edgar, without the slightest proof or shadow of probability, is unsurpassed in any play or book I ever read. Supposing the play had been by Greene or Nash or someone else, would *not* the critics have used it as an example of their inferiority to Shakespeare? I read the play all through last night and found myself saying, "Well, by Jove, Mrs Shaw was quite right, it *is drivelling*!" I hadn't read it for several years as I never liked it much and always felt it was not up to Shakespeare's standard. I wish someone would now discover a contemporary document proving that he never wrote it. In any other of his plays, even the worst (or least good) there is *something* terrific to make up for the obvious weaknesses. *The Taming of the Shrew*, for instance, is pretty poor stuff (though full of delightful prose) but the Christopher

Sly part is so good that it makes up for everything else and one writhes with joy as one reads it.

Your intensely interesting and revealing letter does give me an explanation which I have always wanted to have of your supposed anti-Shakespearean attitude. I expressed something of the same feeling in one of my early sonnets . . .

> For now thy praises have become too loud
> On vulgar lips, and every yelping cur
> Yaps thee a paean. . . .

You will, I dare say, be glad to hear that I now have good hopes that the little bit of money and furniture et cet. I inherited from Olive will not after all be filched from me.[1] I went through several weeks of agony about it, but it looks now as if, after all, I shall get at any rate the greater part of it, and the nightmare of perpetual grim poverty recedes to a great extent.

As you ask me if I was with Olive when she died, I may tell you that I spent several hours holding her hand on the afternoon and evening before she died, though I don't think she was conscious at the time. I had to go back by the seven o'clock train to Lancing, where I was staying,[2] and I heard of her death from her maid on the telephone at nine-thirty the next morning. Your devoted   CHILDE

P.S. There is a long article by 'Menander' (Charles Morgan) about my lecture[3] in the current *Times Literary Supplement*. I don't think much of it, but it gives me a good 'boost' generally speaking.

6 June 1944   9 Viceroy Lodge, Hove

My dear St Christopher, I have been constrained by financial needs to start drawing again on that hundred-pound overdraft at my bank which

[1] Olive had left Douglas her opal necklace and all movable chattels and effects not otherwise bequeathed, also an annual sum not exceeding five hundred pounds, without deduction except for duty and income tax. She also left him the residue of her estate (will of Olive Eleanor Douglas, dated 4 August 1943).

[2] At Old Monk's Farm with the Colmans. Only her maid was with Olive when she died in the early morning hours of Sunday, 13 February.

[3] 'Form in Literature' (25 March 1944).

you kindly guaranteed. I hope you won't mind. I am left very badly off and there will be *months* to wait before I get the first instalment of the very small annuity left me by my wife. . . . She has left me her 'personal property' (the rest all goes to my son) which, besides furniture et cet., should include a few hundreds in her bank. But it will be at least nine months before I get this, and the annuity (almost *halved* by taxation) does not begin till August 15th, so I wrote to my bank and asked for an overdraft. In reply the manager told me that the overdraft guaranteed by you, which I paid off two or three years ago, is still extant and that I only had to draw on it. When I get my wife's legacy of her 'personal property' I will at once pay it off again.

I was so distracted and upset at having no money and few friends that I got into a panic and cleared out of my flat at St Ann's Court when my housekeeper was taken ill and carried off to the hospital and I was left with no servant and an *utter impossibility* of getting one even at double her wages. . . . Without a servant I couldn't live [in the flat] and had to go to hotels at ruinous expense. So I am selling everything and shall probably go to London. Meanwhile I am staying here at my wife's flat which is being kept on, pending probate by the trustees of her father's estate. Her maid remains temporarily (paid by the trustees) and she is cooking and 'doing for' me.[1] But I shall not be here more than two or three weeks. I will let you know where I go as soon as I know myself. At present I am in a miserable state of health caused by worry and anxiety (and also by *old age!*) and inability to sleep.

Please don't write me an unkind letter as I would not be able to bear it. Your devoted   CHILDE

P.S. I have given three months' notice that I am quitting my St Ann's Court flat, which means that I have got it and have to go on paying the rent till September 29th. All the furniture has been removed, mostly for sale by auction and some for storing till (if ever) I get another flat or

---

[1] Eileen Adrian, huge, jovial, red-faced and with sparse black hair, always referred to by Lord Tredegar as the 'Irish Giantess'. Eileen was an incongruous figure in Olive's flat, with its delicate background of blue and white, exquisite porcelains and bookcases filled with a collection of poetry (her book-plate had been designed long before by Aubrey Beardsley). Despite her appearance, however, powerful Eileen managed well, and Olive had been devoted to her.

lodging. . . . My nephew Queensberry doesn't care what becomes of me though he remains 'friendly' enough. The same applies to most of my friends. My son, Raymond, is very fond of me and promises to increase my income as soon as he gets control of his own money. He will ultimately have about sixteen hundred pounds a year [when he leaves the] mental home at Northampton. He is now declared to be cured and will be de-certified almost at once. . . .

P.P.S. My hand appears to be partially paralysed and I can't write properly.

9 June 1944   Ayot St Lawrence

Dear Childe Alfred, What horrid luck! I did not know that my guarantee is still in force; but so much the better: draw on it by all means.

The St Ann's people ought to be able to let your flat profitably for the September quarter now that the battle has shifted to the other side of the Channel.

I am myself overwhelmed with widower's troubles and have been unable for months to write any letters except urgent business ones; but at least I have not been uprooted: a dreadful calamity at our ages. This is only a hasty scrawl of sympathy. Keep me advised of your whereabouts.   G. B. S.

[During the summer Shaw continued to be 'overwhelmed with widower's troubles'. He was alone at Ayot, suffering the pains of staff upheaval; the faithful couple, Clara and Harry Higgs, cook-housekeeper and gardener, had left. The Higgses were in their seventies and had long wanted to retire but out of loyalty had stayed through Charlotte's last illness. Now there was another cook-housekeeper, Alice Laden, who proved very satisfactory in time, but Shaw at the moment was irritated by the whole breaking-in process. He refused, however, to leave Ayot, and went to London only for literary work or business involving Charlotte's estate. Death duties and war-time taxation were harassments and, facing the prospect of his own death, he was trying to arrange a gift of his property in Ireland to that country. Most businessmen, he complained, retired long before eighty but, approaching ninety, he was forced to do more than he ever had before. And it was hard going. He was deaf, unsteady on his legs and often felt giddy. But he carried on and satisfied himself that he gave the stage effect of being exceptionally able-bodied and able-minded for his age.

He did not feel called upon to write a second letter, and Douglas did not answer Shaw's request to advise him of his whereabouts; Douglas hardly knew himself what was happening after he gave up the flat in St Ann's Court. He auctioned virtually all his possessions, holding back only a little silver, some family pictures and a few books. The entire sale fetched only two hundred and ninety-eight pounds.

Some days before the auction he threw out waste-paper baskets full of letters and documents. 'The only things I have kept', he wrote to Adrian Earle (24 May), 'are Bernard Shaw's letters and the manuscripts of my poems and books. I am in a state of dull and dazed despair. . . .'. When Edward Colman heard about the papers, he tried to retrieve the 'rubbish' from the refuse dump, but it was too late: the 'rubbish' had been pulped. Colman helped Douglas sort out and preserve the papers that remained.

After leaving St Ann's Court Douglas stayed first at the Bedford Hotel, then at the Dudley, but the charges at both were too much for him. In June, when he was in Olive's flat, plans were made by Lord Tredegar to have him move to London. Douglas's friend, the ballet agent Poppoea Vanda, had offered board and lodging in her Hampstead house (6 Tanza Road) for a hundred and fifty pounds a year. Mr Oppenheimer, Lord Tredegar's solicitor, was to oversee the new arrangement.

Poppoea Vanda, long an admirer of Douglas's poetry, had met him in 1942 when, failing to find a copy of his *Lyrics* and *Sonnets* at Hatchard's, she had written directly to the author. They had become good friends during the past two years; he had seen her often in London and she had come often to Hove.

Douglas's clothes were actually taken to Miss Vanda's house, but in the end he decided not to go. A young friend, a schoolmaster and collector of his manuscripts, W. A. Gordon, found a satisfactory lodging for him in Hove, with a Mrs Turle at 16 Silverdale Avenue, very close to St Ann's Court. Douglas was settled at Mrs Turle's by mid-July, her only lodger. He paid four guineas a week for his sitting-room, bedroom and bath (all meals included). She was a forceful and protective landlady and Douglas managed fairly well during the summer. But early in September he received a letter from Mr Calvert, the Custance family solicitor in Norwich, which so shocked and distressed him that it brought on a heart attack.]

17 October 1944   23 The Drive, Hove

My dear St Christopher, I have been very bad with a 'leaky valve' to my heart for some time. As I got steadily worse the doctor told me I should try a 'rest cure'. So here I am in bed in this nursing home. Have been here for a fortnight and expect to stay another fortnight. I am a little better. My 'heart' was brought on by worry and general affliction, and by being suddenly informed by the lawyer who is administering my wife's will that my annuity of five hundred pounds is reduced by iniquitous taxation and exorbitant death duties to a hundred and sixty-three pounds. Imagine the cruelty of *not* making it tax free. I have been shockingly treated by everyone (including Olive) but that has been a chronic state of affairs all my life. Fortunately my son, Raymond,[1] has undertaken to help me out and make a decent income for me. He inherits the property of which my wife was the life tenant. So after all I shall manage to exist when (in about six months) affairs are settled. I just lie in bed in a semi-comatose condition all day. If I had known that Raymond would do what he promises, I would not have been [*The rest of this letter is missing.*]

20 November 1944   16 Silverdale Avenue, Hove

Dear St Christopher, I have recently emerged from four weeks in the nursing home. It did me good, but as soon as I came out I was worse

---

[1] Raymond was de-certified from St Andrew's Hospital on 9 June and allowed to take over his mother's flat in Viceroy Lodge. Douglas, greatly heartened, envisioned this as a sort of haven. It was not long, however, before Raymond suffered a brain-storm, and major tragedy was only prevented by Eileen, who was able to overpower him. Raymond was taken back to St Andrew's Hospital.

than ever. I suppose I am going to die. I don't mind that too much (thanks to my religion) but I do object to being suffocated, which is apparently what is going to happen to me. Reading your last book,[1] the part about doctors, I find myself agreeing with you. I've always so far avoided doctors, but feeling so bad I felt I must call one in. He is a dear old man, but he does me *no good at all* and his medicines do not produce the slightest effect.

I have just finished your book. My dear St Christopher, what fearful balderdash you do talk about religion (all the rest of the book is very good)! You seem *incredibly* ignorant about it. Have you ever studied it at all? Do you really suppose that the Church of England or the numerous idiotic Protestant sects in this country have any bearing on Christianity? Catholicism is the only Christianity that counts, or is otherwise than self-evidently ridiculous. I was brought up a Protestant and only became a Catholic at forty. You don't seem to know the first thing about it. What you say is just as idiotic as what I might say about mathematics if I were foolish enough to talk about that. . . . Your arguments are just on the level of the Hyde Park 'atheist' stump orator. I remember telling Frank Harris the same thing apropos of his childlike assumption that Tolstoyism represented Christianity and that Tolstoy was a 'saint'!! However what does it matter? In spite of your density and blindness on that point, I feel a great affection for you. But it hurts me to see you (brilliant as you are) making such an exhibition of yourself. Your devoted   CHILDE

P.S. Catholicism stands or falls on the authenticity of miracles. If there are no miracles then the whole thing is a fraud.

21 November 1944   Ayot St Lawrence

Dear Childe Alfred, Having reached the age of retirement from business I find myself so overwhelmed by it that I have no time to write about anything else. And if I employ an agent I have to undo his work and do it myself after he has messed it up. Doctors cannot cure erring hearts,

[1] *Everybody's Political What's What?* had finally been published in September.

and are very dangerous when they are young and innocent enough to try. They either dose you with digitalis, which upsets the unfortunate organ worse, or else forbid you to walk up or down stairs, and immobilize you and stimulate it with whisky until your liver enlarges and you die. Thank your stars that you have a harmless veteran to talk to you.

My wife was doomed to die of suffocation; but just as her breath was getting shorter she suddenly became young and beautiful and died happy after thirty hours of ecstasy, babbling of green fields. A man of whom I knew had been told when he was twenty that if he ever hurried up steps or exerted himself in any way he would drop dead. He was eighty when I made the acquaintance of his son, and had always, being naturally impetuous, run upstairs two steps at a time. Another elderly gentleman was sitting at the fire with his wife when he said, "My heart has stopped. Goodbye," and perished without a pang.[1] There is nothing to be done: just don't bother about it.

Ask your doctor whether he has heard anything professionally about A.C.S., the treatment discovered by the Russian Bogomolets[2] which has produced such amazing results in the field hospitals of the Red Army. They say it mends bone injuries, formerly incurable, in a week. It evidently does something to the glands, and may act on the heart.

If miracles are your test of religion, then you are no more really religious than the Italian peasants for whom the blood of St Januarius has to be liquefied every year. You are certainly not a Christian; for when some soldiers, who had heard of Jesus from John the Baptist, came to Jesus and asked him to prove himself the Messiah by performing a few miracles for them, he lost his temper and said, "An evil and adulterous generation seeketh a sign". In short, he told them to go to hell; and Mahomet did the same when he too was pestered by people whose notion of God was an almighty conjuror.

You know you don't really believe all that, and will not leave the

---

[1] Shaw used this incident in the first chapter of *Cashel Byron's Profession*; the death of Lydia Carew's father.

[2] Aleksander Bogomolets (1881–1946) produced the anti-reticular cytotoxic serum in 1925, from animals immunized with cell elements of the spleen and spine; given in small doses, the serum stimulated the function of connective tissue. It does not seem likely that the serum would have been beneficial for the heart.

church because your patron saint (I forget which he is) has not waved a wand and cured your heart. Death, in whose shadow I daily walk, does not trouble me any more than it troubles you: *la morte e nulla*! To a true believer the world is full of miracles; but they do not occur for our amusement, nor [to] be begged or purchased. There is no such opposition between your religion and mine as that between All Right and All Wrong. Stalin, they say, is likely to have a chat with the Pope. Why shouldn't he? Is there any greater Catholicism than 'Proletarians of all lands: unite'?

Queensberry invites me to visit his Service Club[1] on the strength of my regard for Uncle Alfred.

Excuse all these blots and blunders: I am old.   G. B. S.

23 November 1944   16 Silverdale Avenue, Hove

My dear St Christopher, Thanks for your letter. I have just had a visit from Dr Hall,[2] the leading heart specialist here, who tells me he met you at Glyndebourne and sat next to you at dinner when you ate a hearty meal of (amongst other things) ROAST MUTTON! I was delighted to hear this though personally, for the time being at least, I subsist chiefly on milk and baked potatoes in their skins with butter, which I find delicious and much nicer than meat. You are quite right, they do give me digitalis and tell me not to go up and down stairs, which, however, I am bound to do as in my present lodging my bedroom is on the first floor, whereas in my old flat in St Ann's Court I was entirely on the ground floor. As far as I can make out my heart can't possibly recover and the doctor says it dates from when I had rheumatic fever at the age of twenty-five, although I completely recovered from it and for years after that I used to (e.g.) shoot snipe in winter in the Orkney Islands

---

[1] The club premises were in Old Compton Street for men and women in all military services; providing dancing, table-tennis, billiards, chess and occasionally variety shows and boxing matches. Queensberry worked as a club receptionist and waiter and often exercised his exceptional talent for reciting lengthy passages of poetry.

[2] Donald Hall (1876–1949), a resident of Hove, associated with the Royal Sussex County Hospital. The cardiograph of Douglas taken that day 'looked like a map of the Himalayas', Douglas commented to another correspondent.

and get wet through every day without ever getting rheumatism, and ride gallops at Chantilly and Newmarket, and walk twenty or thirty miles without the slightest inconvenience. In fact the farther I went the better I felt. But anyhow I realize I am finished, and I don't really mind now I know the truth about it. My brain remains as active as ever and that is the main thing.

You are perfectly right in saying that I am no more religious than an Italian peasant (or an Irish or any other Catholic peasant). Why should I be? You have no humility yourself (it is the one weak spot in your armour) and you cannot understand it in others. I have the simple faith of the peasant or the child and I am delighted to know that it is so. The point which you completely miss is that the blood of St Januarius *does* liquefy, and the miracles of Lourdes, and a thousand others, *do* go on happening all the time. I have had miracles in my own life; at least one of them is recorded in my *Autobiography*.[1] Have you ever read *Revelations of Divine Love* by St Juliana of Norwich, fourteenth century? I have a copy which is so thumbed that it is almost falling to pieces. I am always reading it and I *know* it is true, and it consoles me for all the ills of life.

What you tell me about your wife's death I find most touching and beautiful.

You are quite wrong about darling Jesus. He resented people who came and asked for miracles just to gratify their curiosity and wanted to treat him as a sort of conjuror, but he constantly and continually did all sorts of miracles, and he expressly said that his apostles and disciples through the ages would do *even greater miracles* than he had ever done himself. And so they have done all through the ages—right down to the present day. To doubt the miracles of the saints (St Philip Nain, for example) is to doubt the good faith and sanity of a host of the best people who ever lived who actually saw them happen. The evidence is quite overwhelming, and it is only idiots who say "even if I saw a miracle I would not believe it" as I have actually heard one very 'clever' man say. When my mother was buried at the Franciscan Monastery at Crawley, the Franciscan monk[2] who performed the rites said to me after it was over, "We have just buried a little saint". How did he know? He

[1] See Douglas's *Autobiography* (pp. 286–288).
[2] Father Walstan of the Franciscan community in Oxford.

had never seen or spoken to my mother. He just *knew*, and his saying that lifted me out of the frightful black misery I was in into complete happiness.

I am amused to hear Queensberry has asked you to go to his club. You ought to go and see it. He has made a marvellous success of it and I believe he has got over two hundred thousand members. As you are an authority on boxing you would be interested. Queensberry himself used not to be the least interested in boxing, but old Lonsdale[1] persuaded him that (on account of his name) it was his *duty* to take up the leading position in the business! He has made hundreds of thousands for the Red Cross by it. Your devoted   CHILDE

P.S. Have you seen Marie Stopes's poems for which [I] wrote a preface?[2] I gather they are out from a letter I've just received from the editor of *Truth*.

25 November 1944   Ayot St Lawrence

Dear Childe Alfred, One flight is just right. Go down and up for every meal, one step at a time, but smartly enough to give your heart the necessary exercise in elasticity. Throw the digitalis down the sink. Remember that if your heart goes wrong your whole life force, depending on it, will sail in to cure it, if you let it alone. But if you keep kicking it and prodding it with drugs in allopathic doses the *vis medicatrix naturae* will sulk and stop, and you will get worse. Nature is both sulky and lazy, doing nothing that anything outside is pretending to do for it, and resenting the attempt. That is why, if you wash a cat, it will never wash itself again.

Tell your heart specialist, not that he is a damned liar, but politely that if he sat next a diner at Glyndebourne who fed on roast mutton, that cannibal was not G. B. S. I have a double in America who is not a vegetarian; and he may have taken a holiday here. If anyone tells you that I have eaten fish, flesh or fowl during the last sixty years, you may contradict him flatly, even if he alleges that he has seen me do it. This

[1] The fifth Earl of Lonsdale, Hugh Cecil Lowther (1857–1944).
[2] *Wartime Harvest* (1944) had not only a preface by Douglas but also a note by Shaw.

does not mean that I live on green vegetables; I eat no more of them than you do. I eat butter, honey, cheese and eggs (which I dislike) when I can get nothing else; and I would drink cod-liver oil if I needed it, which I don't.

It is reported that St Januarius has not liquefied his blood this year, presumably on political grounds. If this occurs too often the priests will have to liquefy it lest their flocks should cease to respect religion and become ungovernable. Miracles, contrived and uncontrived, occur every day; but they prove nothing but the fact of their occurrence. They have no more to do with the tenets of the creeds than the Lisbon earthquake with the virtue of Beecham's pills. George Fox raised a planter who had died of a broken neck from the dead, and rode off with him after setting his neck straight; but that will not make a Quaker of you. Mrs Eddy's miracles rival those of the Blessed Virgin at Lourdes and Knock: but you have not therefore joined the Church of Christ Scientist. So there is nothing for us twain to disagree about.

I am too old to do a bit of clowning for Queensberry. Besides, I never do anything that is being done well enough without me. It is greatly to Queensberry's credit that he has taken on this big job; and he is entitled to the centre of the stage and the focus of the spotlight without any intrusion of my publicity.

Your son's recovery is very encouraging. I have not the least notion of what his particular disablement was; but his case is evidently an extraordinary one. I am called away to dinner.   G. B. S.

28 November 1944   16 Silverdale Avenue, Hove

My dear St Christopher, The day before yesterday (Sunday) I was given Extreme Unction, which, as I dare say you know, consists in being anointed by a priest on the eyes, nose, ears, lips, hands and feet. It is given to Catholics when they are so ill as to be in danger of death. The whole ceremony only lasts about five minutes. The priest had promised to come on Monday (yesterday) afternoon about four-thirty, but for some reason, of his own accord, he came a day sooner and rang up to say he was coming at four-thirty on Sunday. By the time he came I was so bad I could hardly speak and the dreadful feeling of suffocation which I have had on and off for weeks had become almost unbearable. I was panting like a dog that has been running. I was much overcome by emotion while the ceremony was going on and the tears (quite involuntary) ran down my cheeks. To my amazement when the anointing was over I found that the feeling of suffocation was *gone*, and I was breathing quite normally. I thought to myself, 'I suppose it will come back worse than ever in a few minutes'. So I said nothing about it to the priest and simply thanked him, and he went away and left me alone, promising to bring me Holy Communion next morning. But the suffocation *did not come back*. I felt almost perfectly well except for the general extreme weakness, which today is much relieved. To cut a long story short, I had a boiled egg for supper and went to bed at nine and slept without a drug for six hours for the first time for weeks. The priest came at nine next day (yesterday) to give me Holy Communion, which should have been my Viaticum, and I still felt perfectly well, and when he had gone, had a good breakfast. I had often been told that dying people sometimes recovered in an amazing way after Extreme Unction, but to tell you the truth when it happened in my case I simply didn't believe it or realize it and kept on thinking the suffocation feeling would come on again. I can hardly believe now that it really happened as it did. Please if you can refrain don't write and give me a scientific explanation.

My farmer friend Colman wants to carry me off to Lancing and if I feel strong enough to make the journey in a car I shall go and get all sorts of good food! But I don't expect to move till Friday. Meanwhile my sister, Edith Fox-Pitt,[1] and my nephew Queensberry were both coming to assist at my death-bed, and I am writing to put them off! Of course I may get bad again but I don't feel somehow as if I would. *Nous verrons*. I was quite resigned to death and not at all frightened. Your devoted   CHILDE

---

[1] His sister (1874–1963) was always a loyal supporter of Douglas. In 1899 Edith had married St George Fox-Pitt (born 1856), second son of Lieutenant General Fox-Pitt-Rivers. They had no children and she had been a widow since 1932.

30 November 1944   Ayot St Lawrence

My dear Childe Alfred, I am unspeakably delighted by your news. The benighted doctors killing you painfully; and St James's treatment calling the attention of the Holy Ghost and curing you painlessly in a turn of the hand! Do not let the defeated heathen get away by blaming science for their disgrace. The church did not repudiate Aristotle: it annexed him. St James's science is genuine, and that of the digitalis-mongers stupid quackery. Very, very interesting; and a triumph for the church and the Peculiar People, who also know that health is fundamentally spiritual.[1]

The last time Extreme Unction was described to me it inspired a great play of mine. Lena Ashwell[2] was telling me all about her father, a sea-captain who was also a preacher and a captain of souls. Like you he was condemned to death by the medicos, and Lena had to break their sentence to him and asked him whether he desired Communion. He consented; but when it was administered he absolutely refused to eat the consecrated bread without cheese.

I interrupted Lena with roars of laughter; but in that moment Captain Shotover of *Heartbreak House* was born. All truly sacred truths are rich in comedy.

Do not be afraid of the stairs. Immobilization is more dangerous than digitalis. You are more likely to underdo them than to overdo.

What a subject for a sonnet sequence! If you don't write it I will put Marie Stopes on to it.

Glory hallelujah!   G. B. S.

6 December 1944   Old Monk's Farm, Lancing

My dear St Christopher, You don't distinguish between Holy Communion (which in the Catholic church is the reception on the tongue of a

[1] The Plumstead Peculiars, a small sect of faith-healers, founded in London in 1838. They based their power on the Epistle of St. James 5:14, believing they could cure illness by prayer and anointing with oil.

[2] Lena Ashwell (1872–1957) was a favourite actress of Shaw's and one of Charlotte's closest friends. Not only did Commander Pocock, Lena's father, inspire the character of Captain Shotover, but also his ship-shaped habitation suggested the setting for the first two acts of *Heartbreak House*.

consecrated wafer) and Extreme Unction which is something quite different, namely the anointing by a priest of the eyes, lips, ear, nose, hands and feet of anyone who is deemed to be in danger of death. Your rather revolting story about the sea-captain who required cheese with the piece of bread which he fondly imagined to be Holy Communion, does not shock me because, as neither the Anglican church nor any other of the thousand and one heretical Protestant bodies possesses real priests with valid orders (the apostolic succession having been deliberately broken at the Reformation), the piece of bread which the sea-captain took would just remain a piece of bread. The 'ministers' of Protestant churches have no power to consecrate bread and wine and can no more do so than you or I could do it by picking up a piece of bread and saying, "This is the body of the Lord". Our saying so wouldn't make it so, whereas if a real priest in valid orders did, it would actually become the body of our Lord hidden under the 'accident' of bread. The Greek Orthodox priests, though schismatic, *do* have valid orders and can give valid absolution to a Catholic *in articulo mortis*.

My miraculous cure on being anointed has, I'm sorry to say, not persisted and I'm almost as bad as I was before I had Extreme Unction. In fact it looks as if my number is definitely up. I am staying at Lancing with my farmer friend and his girl wife, so at least I get good pre-war food, which farmers alone now have. Also they are exceedingly kind to me and do their best to coddle me. I don't mind dying but I would rather it were not such a long-drawn-out and painful business. As for you, I really believe you are good for twenty years yet! You are marvellous. Good luck to you. Your devoted   CHILDE

P.S. My special saint, by the way, is St Jude[1] not, as you say, St James. I enclose a picture of him which is issued by the Carmelites at Faversham.

7 December 1944   Ayot St Lawrence

Dear Childe, Have you been overhauled by an osteopath? It is possible that it is not your heart that is the root cause of your trouble.

[1] The saint of impossible situations; Douglas's chosen protector because of the closeness of St Jude's birthday (28 October) to his own (22 October).

St James is the saint of the Peculiars. I knew he was not the help of the hopeless.

What a charming novena! First-rate medicine.

I know all about the various forms of sacramental magic. They are all alike to me in respect of having the same kernel of scientific validity. But I reject the cannibal theory of transubstantiation, being not a medieval Aztec but a modern vegetarian. So do you, too, subconsciously; so it doesn't matter. Probably you have never gone into its history. In great haste—only a scrawl   G. B. S.

9 December 1944   Old Monk's Farm, Lancing

My dear St Christopher, I became a Catholic in 1911, thirty-three years ago. I completely and radically changed my whole life thereafter, became and remained absolutely chaste as I have remained ever since and I went to Holy Communion at eight *every day of my life for at least twenty-five years of those thirty-three years.* It is only in the last few years that I have dropped daily Communion, and that simply because my health began to break up and I no longer felt able to get up early every day, but I have always continued it weekly (and generally at least twice a week). So it's rather idiotic to suggest that I don't believe in transubstantiation!!! Any Catholic child of six knows about transubstantiation and it is the fundamental basis of the Catholic religion. It's all in the 'penny catechism'. So please don't irritate my poor heart with indignant bumps by writing such nonsense.

I'm too ill to write more. I had an awful night last night and the priest came to give me Holy Communion this morning early. I have not been outside the house now for many weeks. I can't stand staying in bed, but I just lie in a chair and drowse and occasionally read a little. My miraculous recovery after Extreme Unction was, I fear, only a dying flicker, as I'm worse than ever now. Thanks for the pamphlet. I don't require converting to nature cure and osteopathy because I have always believed in them. I also have great faith in homœopathy but there doesn't seem to be a homœopath in Brighton. I am trying to hear of one in Worthing.

I used to know one, Byres Moir,[1] the head of the Great Ormond Street Homœpathic Hospital for Children, a sheer magician. But he, alas, died ten years ago. I'm afraid I am too far gone for care now, and I don't expect to recover. I'm not afraid of death and have many consolations, but the long *process* of dying is painful and miserable. I wish it were over. Your devoted   CHILDE

12 December 1944   Ayot St Lawrence

Dear Childe Alfred, In jumping to a conclusion be careful not to jump too far. The Unction cured you. Only for a day; but it did cure you for that day, proving that you are not incurable. The problem is to cure you for many days and not too many years, but enough.

I have nothing to contribute but my strong wish that the problem will be solved, which is my form of prayer, and as good, I hope, as anybody's.

I enclose another pamphlet,[2] which may amuse you if you don't know all about it already. I know Perkins and have been through the whole business with him, but only got a trace of staphylococcus reaction, not worth bothering about. Send him a scrap of white blotting paper with a spot on it reddened by your blood; and he will tell you whether you have any undiscovered reactions.

From your letters I should say you have a lot of life left in you yet.

There are many degrees of belief. The child of eight believes; so does the vieillard of eighty-eight, but not in the same light. Though I discard the Aztec touch, I have more faith in the consecrated wafer than in digitalis, and agree with Mephistopheles that blood is *ganz besonderes saft*.[3] Good night.   G. B. S.

[1] Byres Moir (M.D. Edinburgh, 1891) had been the house surgeon at the London Homœopathic Hospital, not the Children's Hospital.

[2] *New Concepts in Medical Diagnosis and Treatment*, by Eric McLeod Perkins (1943).

[3] 'Quite a special juice'.

POSTSCRIPT

Thus ended the correspondence between poet and playwright. They had seen each other only once, at the Café Royal in March 1895.

After December 1944 Douglas no longer had the strength to parry words with Shaw nor to write many words to anyone. He was too tired and ill.

The month before, when the Colmans realized he could no longer care for himself in the lodging house, they had brought him to live with them at Old Monk's Farm. They gave him a cheerful room with bath, supplied him with books and daily papers and saw to it that he was closely watched by a kind Irish doctor, their friend Brendan Betty. They comforted him with their presence and welcomed visitors who came to see him: his sister, Edith Fox-Pitt, his nephews Francis and Cecil, Marie Stopes, Lord Tredegar and a number of young admirers. Adrian Earle was no longer among these; he was a friend who had failed on every count.

On 4 December Douglas wrote a new will, and in this he bequeathed any money in both or either of his two banks to his sister, Edith (beyond a specified fifty pounds to his former housekeeper, Mrs. Humphry, and twenty-five pounds to Olive's maid, Eileen). To Poppoea Vanda he left Olive's opal necklace; and his books, manuscripts and copyrights to Edward Colman, whom he named his literary executor.

When the time came that nurses were needed, they were provided, and the Colmans themselves stayed within call. Douglas had long talks with them, read a little, continued to see a few callers and every day looked forward to the visit of Father Corley, who brought him Communion. In February, with great effort, Douglas wrote a detailed letter to Hesketh Pearson, commenting on several typescript chapters of Pearson's biography of Wilde which had been sent him to read. Douglas's last scrap of writing was a pencilled note on an envelope, directions to Sheila Colman for placing a bet on a horse.

Douglas's last picture with Sheila Colman, Old Monk's Farm, 1944

For many months Douglas had known that he could not recover and he waited for the end with childlike faith. He died in the early morning of Wednesday, 20 March 1945, at seventy-four, the age Shaw had been when this correspondence began. Ironically, since Douglas died a bankrupt, his money bequests could not be made, and the opal necklace could not be found.

On Friday 23 March about thirty persons attended a Requiem Mass for Douglas at the Franciscan friary in Crawley. He was buried in the cemetery there, beside his mother. One gravestone covers them both.

At the time of Douglas's death Shaw was eighty-eight, much slowed down but still managing well. He had given up the Whitehall Court flat after Charlotte's death, auctioning most of its contents. Although he took a small service flat in the same building, this was used mainly as an office for Miss Patch. He himself remained at Ayot St Lawrence, where Alice Laden, his now-expert housekeeper, took excellent care of him; and Miss Patch came out from London to work whenever needed. Shaw remained very active despite the fact that he was increasingly unsteady on his legs, deafer and more forgetful.

He continued to write: "As long as I live I must write. If I stopped writing I should die". Though comparatively unimportant, his last pieces are entertaining: *Buoyant Billions*; *Farfetched Fables*; *Sixteen Self-Sketches*; the puppet playlet *Shakes vs. Shav* (he had written almost twice as many plays as Shakespeare); and a rhyming guide for Ayot St Lawrence, illustrated by photographs he had taken. His last, unfinished, work was a play, *Why Should She Not*, in which the final words written were 'The world will fall to pieces about your ears'.

In June 1950 Shaw made his final will. It was a contrast in every way to Douglas's. After a number of liberal personal bequests, he gave his huge residual estate to a project for reforming the English Language. If this project was not undertaken (which it was not) his residual estate was to be given in equal thirds to those institutions from which he had most benefited: the National Gallery of Ireland, the British Museum and the Royal Academy of Dramatic Art. Shaw's will is one of the most public-spirited legal instruments ever drawn.

He was ninety-four in 1950, and the summer went along as easily as so many others had before it. He hoarded time for writing, kept a rigid diet and a strict routine; this included vigorous exertion, for he had a strong belief in the necessity of exercise. One day in September, while he was pruning trees in his orchard, he fell and fractured his thigh. He was alone when the accident occurred and it was some time before he was found. He was rushed to hospital in nearby Luton, and at first the doctors were hopeful he would recover. But kidney trouble developed, and the specialists soon knew, and Shaw knew, that there was no cure. He asked to be brought home and was taken to Ayot on 4 October. He died on 2 November.

The whole world paid tribute. There were leading articles in the press, the Indian Government adjourned a cabinet meeting, Broadway dimmed its lights. The British Empire showed its admiration and affection in many ways but one honour, which was mentioned in these letters, it could not offer—burial in Westminster Abbey—for in his writings and in his will itself Shaw denied belief in any established church or religion. His only belief, he maintained to the end, was in Creative Evolution.

Shaw's body was cremated at Golders Green while his friend Sir Sydney Cockerell read the passage Shaw had long admired in *Pilgrim's Progress*, the description of the death of Mr Valiant-for-Truth. Shaw's ashes and those of Charlotte were mingled and were scattered in their garden at Ayot St Lawrence.

With the death of Shaw the copyrights of all his literary properties, including his letters, passed into his estate, and all requests for publication were handled by the Society of Authors. After Douglas's death, the copyrights of his literary property, because of his bankruptcy, became vested in the Official Receiver. Mr Colman, however, by an assignment of purchase, was able to take possession of his papers and his copyrights. The star piece in the archive was the Shaw-Douglas correspondence, which for the time being Mr Colman had no desire to see published.

A large portion of the Shaw correspondence Douglas had interleaved with sheets of pale green paper, on which he made his own comments (when pertinent, they have been noted in this book). Douglas's comments indicate either that he was doing preliminary work on an edition of Shaw's letters or that he was writing descriptions that would be useful if he disposed of the letters. The second supposition is more probable, for Shaw's postcard of 20 June 1939, 'Yes, of course: why leave them there doing no good to anybody?' provoked Douglas's final comment on the last pale green sheet, 'This refers to a private matter not at present discussable'.

The 'private matter' was the possible disposal of the letters, and now that Shaw had said he was for it, Douglas began to make inquiries. When Rupert Croft-Cooke came to Hove just before the outbreak of the war, Douglas showed him a thick packet of Shaw's letters and told him that a bookseller had made a standing offer for every letter Shaw had written or would write. No such sale took place, however, and it was 1942 before Douglas parted with a single item. Then, he tested the market by presenting a Shaw postcard (28 May 1938) to the benefit Red Cross sale which Sotheby's held on 13–15 October. The postcard, lot 676, was purchased by 'McCallum' for one guinea, the same price that a Shaw postcard of no importance had sold for at Hatchard's.

Douglas parted with no more of the correspondence even though Shaw gave him ample encouragement in November of 1943 when, going through papers after Charlotte's death, he found a great number of Douglas's letters and returned them. He told Douglas that they were recklessly outspoken and he thought he had destroyed them years ago but now, finding them, he saw nothing for it but to send them back. This was dramatizing a generous gesture; Shaw knew that Douglas was very hard up and that having both sides of the correspondence added to its value. Shaw had done the same kind thing before, sending G. K. Chesterton's letters back to his wife and Frank Harris's back to Nellie because he had realized that both widows were in straitened circumstances. Shaw's gift delighted Douglas, who was well aware of the fact that he now had a property of increased worth. In November 1944, when he went to live with the Colmans, he brought the joint correspondence with him and it was in his possession when he died at Old Monk's Farm in March of 1945.

Not long thereafter Mr Colman, as Douglas's literary executor, received requests to see the correspondence, requests to study and to publish it. An early applicant, and one who was hard to refuse, was Francis Queensberry, who wished to write a book about his uncle and wanted to include the Shaw-Douglas letters. Queensberry had found out about this surprising correspondence only on his visit of 1 December, when Douglas showed him some of the letters and allowed him to take away the note Shaw had written the day before. Queensberry's application was not accepted by Mr Colman, who said that, in Douglas's interest, he wished no publication of letters or manuscripts at this time. When the Marquess approached Shaw, he immediately received the last letters from Douglas still at hand (the five written in late 1944); but, though Shaw was glad to dispose of the physical property, he cautioned Queensberry that permission to publish any letter must come from its writer or his literary executor. When Queensberry's book, *Oscar Wilde and the Black Douglas*, written in collaboration with Percy Colson, appeared in 1949, it contained no Douglas letter nor manuscript. It did reproduce, with permission, Shaw's letter of 30 November 1944 (the one in Queensberry's possession) and part of Shaw's letter of 16 April 1930, which had been published twice in books by Douglas.

As the years passed, Mr Colman received many requests to use the Shaw-Douglas letters, but he continued to withhold permission. It was in the late 1960s that I heard about the letters and met Mr Colman. He had by this time decided to dispose of the entire Douglas archive, and a number of persons were interested. In 1969, after several visits and conferences, I was successful in acquiring the archive, and a few years later when I considered editing the Shaw-Douglas letters, I found that Mr Colman no longer had objections. More than a quarter of a century had passed since Douglas's death and he felt that the poet was no longer a controversial figure. So I began to study the correspondence.

By fortunate chance, the letters Shaw had given to Queensberry were already in the Four Oaks Farm library, as were two from Douglas which Shaw had sent to Constable's. Besides these letters, I was able to locate a few more in various places: Douglas's letters of 1 July 1933 in the Humanities Research Center at the University of Texas in Austin; Douglas's telegram of 21 July 1938, in the Bernard F. Burgunder Collection at Cornell University, Ithaca, New York; Shaw's letter of early November 1943, at Colby College, Waterville, Maine; and twenty-four Douglas letters (found among Shaw's papers after his death) in the British Library; also Douglas's letters of 3 January and 11 May 1936 and 22 July 1941 at Ayot St Lawrence. All are included in this book.

Very little of the correspondence has been published. Shaw's letter of 16 April 1931, a line from his letter of 29 May and Douglas's reply of 30 May 1931 were printed in the second edition of Douglas's *Autobiography* (1931). A brief quotation from Shaw's letter of 16 April 1931 was reproduced in Douglas's *Without Apology* (1938) and almost all of Shaw's letter of 9 August 1939 in Douglas's *Oscar Wilde, A Summing-Up* (1940). Marie Stopes quoted six lines (with a significant omission) from Shaw's letter of 1 January 1944 in her *Lord Alfred Douglas, His Poetry and His Personality* (1949).

I have many acknowledgments to make: to the Society of Authors, as agents for the Shaw estate, I give my thanks for permission to publish his letters; and to Edward Colman, holder of Douglas's copyright, my thanks for permission to publish his.

To Edward and also to Sheila Colman I owe additional thanks for assistance and hospitality. I have come many times to Steepdown, their present farm, not far from Old Monk's Farm, where Douglas stayed, and it is easy to imagine the warmth with which he was received. The Colmans have taken great pains to answer my queries. They have let me examine their Douglas correspondence files and have helped in many ways. I am extremely grateful.

I also deeply appreciate the assistance of Sir Rupert Hart-Davis, through whom I met the Colmans. He has fostered my project from the start and has given invaluable assistance. So, too, has Professor Dan H. Laurence, literary adviser to the Shaw estate and editor of Shaw's *Collected Letters*. Despite many commitments of his own, Professor Laurence has answered questions with patience and miraculous speed, and I have benefited from his encyclopædic knowledge of Shaw and his general good judgement. My very warm thanks go as well to H. Montgomery Hyde, for throughout he has been extremely helpful and understanding.

Another association which has added to my pleasure in the undertaking has been with Sidney Ives. His readiness to pursue even the most elusive clues has helped to bring many interesting facts to light. He has also read proof, as have Mrs Douglas Bryant and Gabriel Austin. This is a time-consuming, vital task for which an editor can never give suffi-cient thanks. A final acknowledgment of great importance must go to Felix Kelly, who has worked with me from the beginning with extraor-dinary sympathy and generosity.

In both the United States and in England I am beholden to those who have assisted me: Gerald Eades Bentley, Charles Berst, John Bidwell, Herbert Cahoon, Peter Coats, Dennis Cole, J. C. Comer, P. J. Conk-wright, Baroness Leo d'Erlanger, J. B. Dobkin, Sir Anton Dolin, the late Lord Cecil Douglas, Colonel and Mrs Gerald Draper, Ellen S. Dun-lap, Dr John Edgcumbe, Richard Ellmann, Arthur Freeman, John Flem-ing, G. Fraser Gallie, A. G. Heritage, A. R. A. Hobson, Felix Hope-Nicholson, the late Sir Douglas Hubble, Dr Ernst Jokl, the Reverend Canon Darwin Kirby, Kenneth Lohf, William Matheson, the late Sir George Pickering, Gordon Ray, Peter Sanderson, Sir Sacheverell Sit-well, Christopher Sykes, Roy Whiting, Mrs Roma Woodnutt and Thomas Wright.

I am grateful for kindnesses extended by a number of libraries, insti-tutions and businesses: in England, the British Library, General Register House, Hanningtons Limited (Brighton), Bernard Quaritch Limited, the Royal College of Physicians, the Royal Society of Literature and St Andrew's Hospital (Northampton); in the United States, the Wil-liam Andrews Clark Memorial Library at the University of California, Los Angeles, the Columbia University Library, the Library of Congress in Washington, D.C., the Houghton and Widener Libraries at Harvard University, the Humanities Research Center at the University of Texas in Austin, the Berg Collection and the Reference Department at the New York Public Library and the Princeton University Library.

Finally, I offer my abiding thanks to Rose McTernan, who has aided in research both at home and abroad and has cheerfully typed and re-typed copies of transcripts, notes, revisions and letters of inquiry. She has helped as well with the long-drawn-out tasks of sorting, checking and rechecking. Shaw and Douglas have filled the hours of her days as completely as they have mine.

APPENDICES

APPENDIX I

The Earlier Exchange of Letters

(These letters were published in the *Academy*, 30 May and 6 June 1908.)

'For Shame, Mr Shaw!' was the title of the *Academy* review of Shaw's *Getting Married*. 'Not a play at all', the reviewer said, 'but a conversation': two ladies, a waiter and a general talking about marriage. The play should never have been passed by the censor. Mr Shaw, the vegetarian, teetotaler, non-smoker and someone who 'does not possess a masculine intellect', has no right to give instruction in sociology and morality. Mr Shaw 'is beginning to make serious inroads on the British home'. People should cleave to their heritage and the wisdom of the ages; 'the sooner Mr Shaw learns that he is not in a position to preach the better it will be for him'.

Shaw sent the editor of the *Academy* the following letter by special messenger:

25 May 1908

Dear Lord Alfred Douglas, Who on earth have you been handing over your dramatic criticism to? Your man, who must have been frightfully drunk, has achieved the following startling libel:

> The waiter, disguised as a butler, told us, among other things, that his mother was very fond of men and was in the habit of bringing them home at night.

For that statement, which I need hardly say is pure invention, you will have Vedrenne and Barker [producers], Frederick Harrison [manager of the Haymarket] and Holman Clark (the actor concerned) demanding damages from the *Academy* at the rate of about twenty-five hundred pounds apiece.

Can you not manage to volunteer in your next issue a withdrawal of the article? As a rule, I do not like asking an editor to throw his contributor over; but when the contributor throws over the editor so outrageously as in this case, I do not see what is to be done.

I feel rather in a difficulty about it, because I do not know who the writer is; and am afraid that he may turn out to be some unfortunate friend of mine. Anyhow, since ——— let ——— in for £—— damages and endless costs by a wild attack on ———, there has been nothing quite so reckless as this article.

You will see that the writer gives himself away hopelessly at the beginning by saying that he left the house at the end of twenty-five minutes. Later on he describes a scene which he did not wait for, and contrives to get both a libel and a flat mis-statement of fact into his reference. However, it is really this howler about the man's mother which makes the article entirely indefensible. As you may not have seen the play, I should explain that what actually does happen is that the greengrocer who is in charge of the wedding breakfast describes certain escapades of his sister-in-law, who ran away from home several times. He adds that the men 'brought her home the same night, and no harm done'. It is conceivable that a critic, if very drunk, might possibly have muddled this honestly in the way your man has done; but that does not make it any more defensible; and you can see how the gross coarseness of the blunder would affect a jury if the case came into court.

I suggest that the best and friendliest thing to do is to state in your next issue that since the sentence above quoted is a misdescription, you feel bound to withdraw the whole article unreservedly. If you think well of this, or some equivalent course, you might let me have a line so that I may try and smooth matters. Yours faithfully

G. BERNARD SHAW

Douglas replied on the instant.

25 May 1908

Dear Mr Bernard Shaw, I received your letter this morning with the greatest surprise. I strongly resent the accusation of being drunk which you bring against the writer of the article. It seems to me that it is characteristic of the feminine quality of your intellect, to which reference was made in the article, to make such an outrageous suggestion. As a matter of fact I wrote the article myself. If I misheard any particular sentence in the dialogue the error was, on your own showing, a very trifling one, and it is ludicrous to suggest that it is libellous. That part of the play which I heard simply teems with indecencies, and I should be delighted to go into the witness-box in any court and say so. You must be perfectly aware that I am not actuated by any malice towards you. You have had nothing but praise from the *Academy* during the whole time that I have edited it, and now on the first occasion when I find it compatible with my duty as a critic to find fault with you, you resort to the rather mean expedient of asking me to throw over a supposed contributor. I confess that I am surprised that a man of your intellectual attainments should exhibit such pettiness. You are at perfect liberty to take what action you choose in the matter. My solicitors are Messrs Arthur Newton and Company, 23 Great Marlborough Street. Yours faithfully ALFRED DOUGLAS

Shaw sent a second letter, again by special messenger.

27 May 1908

Dear Lord Alfred Douglas, Thank goodness it was you, and not some poor devil whom it would have been your duty to sack. You MUST have been drunk—frightfully drunk—or in some equivalent condition; no normal man behaves like that. Now go right off to your solicitors, and show them my letter, and ask them whether they think the error a trifling one from the point of view of a British jury. Show them the article also. They need not consider me: I do not propose to take any action in the matter, and have only intervened to get you out of a scrape, leaving you to settle with yourself what you ought to do as regards your own honour. But the libel affects both the Haymarket Theatre (Harrison) and Vedrenne and Barker; and they are neither of them in any way disposed to take that dangerous sentence amiably. I feel pretty sure that your solicitors will advise you to admit the blunder and withdraw it. If they don't, change them. Yours faithfully

G. BERNARD SHAW

Douglas replied:

29 May 1908

Dear Mr Bernard Shaw, Your letter is a piece of childish impertinence, but as it was evidently written in a fit of hysterical bad temper,
I shall not count it against you. I am immensely amused by your professed desire to 'get me out of a scrape'. I do not consider that I am in
any scrape at all, and I think you will find that I am a person who is
very well able to look after himself without any assistance from you.
Yours faithfully   ALFRED DOUGLAS

Shaw's last word was:

31 May 1908

Dear Lord Alfred Douglas, I asked you for a friendly reparation: you
have given me a savage revenge. However, perhaps it was the best way
out. As you have owned up, we are satisfied; and the public will forgive
you for the sake of your blazing boyishness.

There is always the question—Who is to edit the editor? Fortunately,
in this case there are two Douglases—A. D. the poet and—shall I say?—
the hereditary Douglas. Make A. D. the editor. It needs extraordinary
conscientiousness, delicacy and Catholicism to criticise unscrupulously,
brutally, and free-thinkingly, as the *Academy* is trying to do, and, indeed,
derives all its interest and value from doing. That hereditary Douglas,
when he gets loose from A. D., is capable of wrecking a paper—even
of wrecking himself. Most people are—hence the need for editors. Excuse my preaching; I am a born improver of occasions. *Sans rancune*
                                                        G. BERNARD SHAW

APPENDIX II

The Publication of *De Profundis*

The story of the publication of selections, suppressed portions and finally the full text of *De Profundis* is complicated. This, in brief, is what happened.

Wilde was not permitted to send his long letter of accusation to Douglas from prison, but the authorities handed him the manuscript (eighty closely written pages) when he left prison on 18 May 1897. Next day, in Dieppe, Wilde gave the manuscript to Ross, whom he had already designated as his literary executor. He directed Ross to send the original to Douglas and to have complete typed copies made, one for Ross and one for himself. Wilde also asked that copies be made of specific passages, 'good and nice in intention', showing 'what is happening to my soul', for 'two sweet women' who had helped him (Adela Schuster and Frankie Forbes-Robertson; Wilde to Ross, 1 April 1897).

Ross had two typed copies of the *De Profundis* letter made but in the next step, after discussion with Wilde, he departed from the original direction, retaining the manuscript himself and sending one of the typed copies to Alfred Douglas on 9 August 1897. This Ross firmly maintained. Douglas, as long as he lived, denied ever having received a copy of the *De Profundis* letter.

In 1905 Ross published the selections specified for the two women and Douglas actually reviewed this publication, favourably. In 1908 Ross again published selections, with additional material, still giving no indication of the intended recipient, nor indeed that the piece was a letter. In 1909, after Douglas and Ross fell out, the latter deposited the manuscript of *De Profundis* in the British Museum, to remain under seal until 1960. There, the full text would have slumbered for fifty years if Douglas had not sued for libel when the book *Oscar Wilde, a Critical*

Study was published in 1912. The young author, Arthur Ransome, son of a Leeds University professor, had worked under the guidance of Ross. The volume, dedicated to Ross, was restrained in style, academic in tone. The author thanked 'Mr Robert Ross, Wilde's literary executor, who has helped me in every possible way, allowed me to read many of the letters that Wilde addressed to him, and given much time out of a very busy life to the verification, from documents in his possession, of the biographical facts included in my book'. Douglas's name, as Ross had requested, was never mentioned in the book, but it was clear to readers who was meant in several passages. On page 157 Ransome said that *De Profundis* 'was not addressed to Mr Ross but to a man to whom Wilde felt that he owed some, at least, of the circumstances of his public disgrace'. On page 182 Ransome further said that Wilde, after leaving prison, hoped to work and to live a life of comparative simplicity but that suddenly 'he flung aside his plans and resolutions' because of the 'iterated entreaty of a man whose friendship had already cost him more than it was worth'. On page 196, commenting on the time that Wilde spent in the villa in Naples, Ransome said that his 'friend, as soon as there was no money, left him'. These were the statements on which Douglas sued Ransome for libel.

In the trial, Ransome's counsel pleaded justification and the manuscript of *De Profundis* was subpoenaed from the British Museum as evidence. Passages were read in court on 17 and 18 April 1913 and quotation followed in the London press. Ransome won his case on justification of the charge that Douglas was the cause of Wilde's downfall. (In subsequent editions of the book Ransome omitted the offending paragraphs out of consideration for Douglas's feelings, though under no obligation to do so.)

Douglas, wishing to retrieve the letter addressed to him, considered proceedings against the British Museum for illegal possession of what he claimed was his property, but he had no money to fight the case, and the fact that the original manuscript had not been posted and routinely delivered was a technicality against him. As an alternative he considered publishing *De Profundis* from the copy provided him by the court, answering Wilde's charges point by point in notes. Ross quickly protected his American rights against this threat by having *The Suppressed Portion* published in New York by Paul R. Reynolds (22 September 1913) in an edition of fifteen copies, a sufficient number for copyright. In his letter to Douglas, 16 April 1931, Shaw referred to one of the copies of Reynolds's edition belonging to Carlos Blacker.

The text of *De Profundis*, still with several hundred mistakes and the omission of a thousand words, was published in 1949 by Methuen from the Ross typescript, with an introduction by Wilde's son, Vyvyan Holland. It was not until 1960, when the British Museum allowed the manuscript to be inspected, that Rupert Hart-Davis was able to publish the complete and accurate text in his *Letters of Oscar Wilde* (pp. 423–511).

APPENDIX III

Douglas's Copy of a Letter to Frank Harris

16 September 1925   16 Draycott Place, London

Dear Harris, I have been thinking over your last letter with its black-mailing threat about the letter I gave you concerning my relations with Wilde during the three years before his conviction. I wrote that letter, as you know, as an act of the very highest moral courage to serve as a basis for you as the more or less official biographer of Wilde, so that you privately might know the exact truth (bad enough I admit but a great deal less bad than you in your black malice and vindictive spite had made it out to be). To write such a letter and give it to a man of your character was, of course, from a worldly point of view, the height of folly on my part. Nevertheless as my actions are not, and never have been, dictated by considerations of worldly wisdom, I don't regret it. I would rather put myself right by telling the truth, even to a heartless enemy, than pose as the possessor of virtue I did not pretend to have all those years ago. The immorality I was guilty of took place more than thirty years ago. I have long since bitterly repented it and have openly confessed it and expressed my sorrow for it in the witness-box, which is the most public confessional in the world.

The difference between me and you is that whereas I did wrong in my youth and bitterly repented it, you have gone on living like a hog all your life and glorying in it and making money by it. You talk about the effect my letter to you about my relations with Wilde would produce before a jury. Well, I know a great deal more about juries than you do, and I can tell you that if you produced my letter in a law court and put it to me in cross-examination, I would turn it into a two-edged sword for my own justification and your utter damnation. It would just about add six months to your sentence.

And what about the effect of reading a few passages from your filthy book *My Life and Loves*? What would a jury think of that? Also how would you like it if I were to start and do [to] you what you have done to me, namely write and publish all I know about your private life, while strictly confining myself, as you have *not* done, to the truth? I know, for example, the details of some of the things you did at Éze (I am not referring to your getting two thousand pounds out of me in my youth in exchange for 'dud' shares in your restaurant and casino with an alleged, but really non-existent, gambling concession attached to it). I am referring to other things.

When you have the infernal impudence to write to me as you do and complain about the expense you have been put to in making the corrections of your self-admitted lies from material supplied by me at your own urgent request, you ignore the fact that you have already made thousands of pounds by selling your disgusting book with its filthy and deliberate lies about me.

Go to, Frank Harris; you are a clumsy fool as well as a rogue. I wash my hands of you. I tried the effect of generosity and kindness on you, but it was simply 'casting pearl[s] to hogs'. I shall take care to let my friends at Nice know the line you have taken up and the way you turned on me with blackmailing menace directly you found you were not going to have things all your own way. Meanwhile you can do what you please about your preface. I have the original with your own autograph corrections and signature and I also have your letter admitting that practically everything about me in your book is false and humbly apologizing. I want nothing more. Yours et cet.

ALFRED DOUGLAS

P.S. I am keeping a copy of this letter.

APPENDIX IV

The Story of Raymond Douglas

Raymond Wilfrid Sholto Douglas was born on 17 November 1902. He was a beautiful infant and became an attractive, affectionate child, healthy but highly strung. His early life was unsettled and full of tension, reflecting the difficulties and insecurity felt by his parents. By the time Raymond was six, the dominant force in his life was his grandfather, Frederic Custance, a retired colonel in his sixties, now a widower, a respected and important man in his community. Custance took a possessive interest in his grandson. He wanted Raymond with him as much as possible at Weston Hall, the big and lonely house near Norwich. Deaf, demanding, fond but stern, Custance kept the boy at Weston for long periods, confident that Raymond was better off there and that he was more qualified to watch over the boy's health and progress than his parents were.

These long visits, matters of discipline and decisions for education caused friction between Raymond's father and grandfather, and soon there was open hostility. The conflict grew bitter in 1911 when Douglas was converted to Roman Catholicism, and even more bitter when, soon after, Raymond was converted.

Colonel Custance sued for the custody of his grandson in 1913 and was awarded three-fifths of his holiday time. The boy's affections were now even more severely torn between his grandfather and father.

In the autumn Douglas prevailed in sending Raymond to Ampleforth, a fine Roman Catholic school. The next year, however, Custance attempted (without success) to send Raymond to another school. Douglas tried to reopen the custody suit and persuaded Olive to make a joint plea in Chancery for full control of Raymond. If they had the boy, Douglas told the judge, they would re-establish a household. Their petition was denied.

This decision so enraged Douglas that he took Raymond to Scotland, beyond the jurisdiction of the English court, and placed him in the Benedictine monastery school at Fort Augustus, headed by his friend (and Wilde's) Abbot Sir David Hunter-Blair. The Colonel fought back by kidnapping the boy, whereupon Douglas applied for a warrant for Custance's arrest. Before the process was served, however, Douglas discovered that Raymond had known of and consented to the kidnapping plot. Douglas dropped the charge and did not see his son for eight years.

Raymond remained at Ampleforth until 1920, during which time he pleased his grandfather by becoming a cadet in the Officers' Training Corps. Custance hoped that Raymond would have a military career, but his brief service as a second lieutenant in the Scots Guards, which began in December 1921, ended by his being placed on probation in March 1922.

In April 1925, shortly before Colonel Custance's death, Raymond wrote an affectionate letter to his father: 'I hope we shall be good friends again but it must be understood that I retain a strictly neutral attitude with regard to the differences between my grandfather and yourself'. Raymond once more implored his father 'to forgive and forget. . . '.

In 1926 Raymond wanted to marry a young woman of twenty-three, Gladys Lacey, whose deceased father had kept a grocer's shop in Oswestry; her mother, left almost penniless, was now manager, but not owner, of a small pub in the same town. Raymond had met the girl in Nice when he was there with his father in January of that year. Douglas and Olive violently opposed the inappropriate marriage, as did the Marchioness of Queensberry, and in the end Raymond did not marry Gladys Lacey.

He entered St Andrew's Hospital, a mental institution in Northampton, certified as a schizo-affective patient, on 26 August 1927. During the periods of affliction he was given medication, electro-convulsive therapy and narcosis. When well, he had full freedom within the extensive grounds of St Andrew's and freedom to go about the town of Northampton, also to make train journeys alone to London, where he paid visits to members of his family. He was also allowed to make other journeys alone; many of these were to race meetings, a sport about which he knew a great deal and enjoyed as much as his father did. Ray-

Raymond Wilfrid Sholto Douglas

mond was liked by everyone at St Andrews. He was friendly and 'full of jokes', as his father and others said. Raymond was a well-known figure in Northampton.

By 1932 Raymond's condition seemed so much improved that he was de-certified in April, but he soon suffered a breakdown and had to return to St Andrew's in June. Twelve years later (9 June 1944) it was finally thought that Raymond could manage a normal life and he was again de-certified. Raymond, now over forty, was kept as a 'voluntary boarder' in Northampton until October and then allowed to take over his mother's flat (he had attended her funeral in February). The faithful maid, Eileen Adrian, was to keep house for him at Viceroy Lodge. Soon after he came to Hove, however, his 'conduct deteriorated' and he was taken back to St Andrew's on 13 November 1944. He did not leave the control of the hospital for the rest of his life. Raymond died at St Andrew's Hospital on 10 October 1964.

INDEX

INDEX

Academy, The: Douglas editor of, xxix; controversial stands of, xxxi; Douglas owner of, xxxii; sells, xxxiii; Shaw's comment on, 4; *Getting Married* review in, 12–13; Douglas's rapid composition working on, 173

Adelphi Terrace: Shaws at, xxxi

Adey, More, xxi, xxiii, xxvii, 34

Adrian, Eileen (Olive Douglas's maid): at her deathbed, 180; works for Douglas, 181; for Raymond, 184; Douglas bequest to, 197, 199

Agate, James: wires Douglas, 40; reviews *Without Apology*, 53; signs Douglas petition, 114 n.2

Albemarle Club: Queensberry's card left at, xi, xiii

Alexander, George: Wilde outlines *Daventry* scenario to, xxiv

'Alfred's Animal Book' (or 'Bosie's Fables' or 'Bosie's Bestiary'): Shaw's suggested titles for, 131

Allan, Maud, xxxv

America: Douglas goes to, xxvii; poor sales of Douglas's *Autobiography* in, 7–8; no new edition of Harris's *Wilde* in, 87; no interest in Wilde in, 89; Douglas's plans for lecture tour in, 103; Shaw has double in, 189

Androcles and the Lion, xxxvi

Aristotle, 37, 192

Armada: and Shakespeare sonnets, 17

Arms and the Man: produced in Germany, xxix; Douglas rereads, 87

Arnold, Edward: published Douglas's *Tails with a Twist*, 132

Arnold, Ralph (of Constable's): visits Douglas, 78

Arts Club: production of the Stokeses' *Oscar Wilde* at, 95; Douglas sees play at, 101

Ashwell, Lena, 192

Asquith, H. H. (first Earl of Oxford and Asquith): *Academy* attacks, xxxi; signs Ross testimonial, 4 n.4; bust of, 99 n.1

Asquith, Margot (Countess of Oxford and Asquith), xxix

Astor, Lady, 156 n.1

Auden, W. H.: Douglas attacks poetry of, 39, 155 n.2, 161

Australia: Ross going to, xxxv

Autobiography of Lord Alfred Douglas, The: visit to America in, xxviii; publication of, xli; Shaw has read, 3; Douglas reports poor sales of, 6–7; begs Shaw preface for new edition of, 6–7; Shaw refuses but letter may be printed in, 8; no sales increase of, 10 n.2; galley of Shaw's letter for, 11–12; *Daventry* story in, 34; offensive review of, 54 n.2; American edition of, 64; true account of Chantilly interview in, 65, 75, 78, 79; early refusal by publishers of, 119; Douglas miracle in, 188

Avenue Kléber: Douglas at, xxiii

Avory, Horace, xvii

Ayot St Lawrence: Shaws lease house in, xxxi; buy house in, 25 n.2, 138; break-up of staff at, 155; Shaw alone at, 182; Shaw's rhyming guide for, 199

Back to Methuselah: New York and Birmingham productions of, xxxvi; Shaw preferred prose for, 165

Bacon, Francis, xxvii

Ballad of Reading Gaol, The: Wilde begins, xxii; publishes, xxiii; no writing after, 60; Douglas's opinion of, 65, 67, 74

Bankruptcy Court: Wilde declared bankrupt, xx; Douglas declared bankrupt, xxxiii, 177

Beamish, Rear-Admiral T. P. H., 136

Beardsley, Aubrey, 181 n.1

Beerbohm, Max, 34

Belgium, xxxvi

Bell, Thomas: article on *Mr and Mrs Daventry* by, 14

Bergner, Elisabeth: as St Joan, 91

Bernard, Jacques, 14

Bernard Shaw: Harris biography completed by Shaw, 13; Douglas's opinion of, 14, 15; Shaw as editor of, 24–25; Harris's attempt pitiable in, 33, 151

Bernard Shaw, Frank Harris and Oscar Wilde: Sherard's defence of Wilde in, 22; preface by Douglas in, 22 n.1; Shaw's opinion of, 27; Douglas's criticism of, 90

Bernhardt, Sarah, 73

Betty, Brendan, 197

Bevin, Anthony, 137 n.2

Bewick, Thomas, 131

Bickerstaffe-Drew, Monsignor, 64

Billing, Pemberton, xxxv

Blacker, Carlos: loans Shaw suppressed part of *De Profundis*, 3

Blunden, Edmund: willing to sign Douglas petition, 110, 111 n.1; signs, 114 n.2

Bogomolets, Aleksander, 186

Border Standard, The: review of *Without Apology* in, 57; Douglas's Churchill sonnet in, 144

Boston: Douglas visits, xxviii

Bowden, Father Sebastian, 20

Bow Street Police Station, xvi

Brasol, Boris, 70

Bright, John, 131

Brighton: Constable representatives come to, 78; Olive Douglas's flat in, 81; gives up flat in, 94

British Museum: accepts *De Profundis*, xxxiii; MS subpoenaed from, xxxiv; Shaw studied Marx in; 168 n.2; Shaw's bequest to, 199

Brown, Ivor, 45

Brown, W. Sorley, 57 n.2

Bunyan, John: poetry of, 160; prose of, 161; passage for Shaw's funeral from, 200

Buoyant Billions, 199

Butler, Samuel ('Erewhon'): book on Shakespeare's sonnets, 15; on Mr W. H., 15–16, 18; Shaw's article on, 21; *Luck and Cunning* by, 135

Byron, Lord: admired by Olive Custance, xxvii; established 'Childe' (Harold), 54; revolutionist, 143–44

Cadogan Hotel, xvi

Caesar and Cleopatra, xxix, 165

Café Royal, London: Harris, Shaw and Douglas confer at, xi, xiii, xiv; Douglas at time of meeting at, 4 n.3; Harris hurt by Douglas's rudeness at, 32; only meeting of Shaw and Douglas at, 197

Calais: Douglas goes to, xvii

Calvert, Edwin, 184

Campbell, Mrs Patrick: in *Mr and Mrs Daventry*, xxv; a Joan play for, xxxvi

Candida, xxix

Candid Friend, The: Harris editor of, 32

Canterbury, Dean of, 52, 53

Carfax Gallery, London, xxvii

Carpenter, Edward, 120

Carr, Comyns, 38

Carson, Edward, xv

Casement, Sir Roger, xxxvi

Cashel Byron's Profession: Douglas meant *The Admirable Bashville*, 40; death of Carew in, 186

Catalani, Giuseppi, 132

Catholic Poetry Society, 49–50

Chamberlain, Neville: Douglas petition submitted to, 107; friendly letter from, 111; petition presented to, 114 n.2; refused by, 115 n.3; refused again by, 137 n.2, 140

Chance, Wade, 77

Chancery: Wilde's boys controlled by, xxi; Raymond Douglas controlled by, xxxiv

Channon, Sir Henry ('Chips'): undertakes release of *In Excelsis*, 169; joins Douglas rent syndicate, 169 n.3, 176

Chantilly: Douglas's racing stable at, xxiv; Douglas-Harris interview at, 65, 68, 74–76, 78–79, 81 n.2, 82

Chapman, George: Shakespeare's rival poet, 16, 19

Charles, Mr Justice (judge at second Wilde trial), xvii

Chartres: Shaw and Ross in, 6

Chelsea: the Douglases' house in, xxviii; Shaw-Wilde meeting in, 37

Chesterton, G. K.; *Weekly Review*, 64; his letters returned to widow, 201

Cheyne Walk: Francis Queensberry's house in, 63; gives up house in, 109

'Childe Alfred': name chosen for Shaw to address Douglas, 48; Shaw begins to do so, 59–60; protection of, 82; inscriptions

'Childe Alfred' (*cont'd*)
requested by, 86; troublesome actions
of, 121
China: Stalin helps, 147
Churchill, Winston: sues Douglas for libel,
xxxix, 108; Douglas comments on war
and, 107, 130; Shaw comments on
Irish ports and, 134–36; attitude toward
Douglas, 137 n.2, 138; Douglas's sonnet
on, 142; Shaw requests copy of, 143;
praises sonnet on, 145
Clarke, Sir Edward: counsel to Wilde in libel
suit, xiii, xiv; refuses Douglas testimony,
xv; Douglas thanks, later blames, xvi;
Wilde counsel second and third trials,
xvi, xvii; letter in *New Statesman*
explaining prosecution withdrawal,
89; Douglas's comment on, 90
Clifford, Lady (Mrs Henry de La Pasture)
and Sir Hugh, 154
Clonmore, Rev. Lord: signs Douglas petition,
114 n.2
Cockerell, Sir Sydney: sends Shaw a St Joan
book, xxxvii; reads at Shaw's funeral,
200
Collected Poems of Lord Alfred Douglas: sonnet
to Wilde in, xxvi; Douglas's method of
writing poetry described in, 169
Collins, Lottie, 89
Collins, Michael, 134
Collins, Mr Justice (judge in Wilde libel suit),
xiv, xv
Colman, Edward: Douglas has met, 159;
discharges Douglas's bankruptcy, 177
n.2; tries to retrieve Douglas's papers,
183; taking Douglas to farm, 191;
Douglas with Colmans, 193; literary
executor of Douglas, 197; controls
Shaw-Douglas correspondence, 201–2
Colman, Sheila (Mrs Edwards): Douglas has
met, 159 n.1; kindness to Douglas of, 197
Colson, Percy, 202
Common Sense About the War: Shaw attacks
British policy in, xxxvi
Complete Poems, The: of Douglas, xli
Congreve, William, 128
Constable's: Shaw begins association with,
xxix; to publish Harris's *Wilde*, 24 n.1;
Shaw sends edited copy to, 25; worry
about Douglas's claims for libel, 56 n.2;

send him amiable letter, 57; simultaneous
Dodd, Mead publication with, 63;
Douglas threatens, 69; relents toward,
76; negotiations with, 78, 82
Cooper, Alfred Duff (first Viscount Norwich):
threat of, 107; Coopers meet Douglas,
137 n.2
Cooper, Lady Diana (Viscountess Norwich):
suggests alternative to Douglas's pension,
137–39; Shaw and Douglas comment
on, 140–43
Corley, Father: gives Extreme Unction to
Douglas, 190–91; visits Douglas, 194,
197
Covici Friede edition of Harris's *Wilde*: 10 n.3;
Douglas letter in, 22; Douglas wishes to
see, 23; two Douglas letters in, 24, 72–73,
82–83; Constable's buying out, 63; Shaw
sending Douglas copy of, 74–75;
bankruptcy of, 87–89
Cowan, Ashley (of Rich and Cowan), 41
Crawley: Douglas's service and burial at, 199
Cripps, A. R., 56
Crosland, T. W. H.: *Academy*'s assistant editor,
xxxi; collaborates on *Oscar Wilde and
Myself*, xxxiv, 80; assistant editor of *Plain
English*, xxxix; Shaw comments on, 4;
pictures of, 27
Custance, Colonel Frederic: father of Olive,
xxvii; enraged by her marriage to
Douglas, xxviii; entertains Douglases at
Weston, xxviii; sues Douglas for libel,
xxxiii; Chancery decision regarding,
xxxiv; death of, xl; hatred of Douglas,
176–77; *see also* Appendix IV
Custance, Eleanor (Mrs Frederic): wife of
Colonel Custance, xxvii
Custance, Olive (daughter of Frederic and
Eleanor): meets Douglas, xxvii; marries
Douglas, xxviii; *see also* Douglas, Olive
Cymbeline: Shaw's new Act V for, 34

Daily Express, The, 40
Daily Herald, The, 76
Daily Mail, The: Shaw's interview about
German take-over of Czechoslovakia in,
106; Douglas's Churchill sonnet in, 142
Daily Telegraph, The: review of *Without
Apology* in, 43; review of Harris's
Wilde in, 76

Dante, 163, 167

D'Arcy, Father, 95

Dark Lady of the Sonnets, The, 16

Darling, Mr Justice (judge in Ransome libel trial), 98

Davies, Gwendoline and Margaret, 127 n.1

de la Mare, Walter, 111

Denham-Smith, Mrs, 126

De Profundis: Wilde writes in prison and takes from, xxi; Ross gives to British Museum, xxxiii; subpoenaed and publicized, xxxiv; Douglas rages over, xxxv, 79; Shaw comments on suppressed section of, 3; deleted from Constable's *Wilde*, 27 n.3, 65 n.1; Holland owns copyright of, 75; Douglas tries to gain possession of, 108; Douglas's libel threat concerning, 126; *see also* Appendix II

Derby, the, 111

d'Erlanger, Edythe Baker (Baroness): tries to save flat for Douglas, 109

Deutsche Allgemeine Zeitung: Douglas's letter published in, 111

de Valera, Eamon: difficult position of, 134–36; misjudged Shaw, 138

Devil's Disciple, The, xxix

Dickens, Charles: characters in, 11, 32; dependence upon alcohol, 121; Shaw borrowings from, 125; burned old letters, 152

Dictionary of National Biography, The: Shaw's model for Wilde history, 120

Dieppe: Wilde arrives at, xxi

Disraeli, 131

Doctor's Dilemma, The, 61 n.1

Dodd, Mead: simultaneous publication of Harris's *Wilde*, 63; American edition has collapsed, 89

Dogberry, 11 n.2

Dolin, Sir Anton: Douglas ballet scenario considered by, 152 n.1

D'Orsay, Count, 11

Doughty, Charles, 173

Douglas, Lord Cecil (Douglas's nephew): suggests American tour, 103 n.3; visits Douglas, 197

Douglas, Olive (Lady Alfred): publishes poems, xxix; attempts reconciliation between Douglas and Ross, xxxii; returns to father, xxxiv; leads separate life, xli, 177; at Bembridge, Isle of Wight, 44; appreciates Shaw's kindness, 46; Douglas visits, 49; upset by Harris's *Wilde*, 77, 81; has Brighton flat, 78; sends birthday telegram to Shaw, 81; Shaw writes to, 82 n.2, 84; Shaw sends photograph to, 89; moves to London, 94, 98; sees play (*Oscar Wilde*), 101; doctors advise hospital treatment for, 130; her death, 174, 180; Douglas inherits from, 177, 180, 181; *see also* Custance, Olive

Douglas, Raymond: birth of, xxviii; becomes Roman Catholic, xxxiii; Chancery decision concerning, xxxiv; Douglas seeks reconciliation with, xli; mother's money goes to, 176; in mental home, 177; to be de-certified, 182; de-certified but recommitted, 184 n.1; Shaw's comment on, 190; *see also* Appendix IV

Dowson, Ernest: corrected proof sheets of *Opals*, xxvii

Doyle, Sir Arthur Conan, 125

Drake, Sir Francis, 17

Dryden, John, 160

Duckworth: publisher requests book on Wilde, 115; Douglas worried about book, 116, 118; has sent MS to, 118, 121–22

Duke Street, London, xxvi

Dunn, Lady: Douglas to visit, 50, 55; *see also* Queensberry, (Irene) Marchioness of, first wife of Francis

Dunn, Sir James, 51

Durand's Restaurant, Paris: Harris's *Daventry* deal at, 33–34

Earle, Adrian: new close friend of Douglas, 157 n.1; Douglas writes concerning Shaw letters to, 183; fails Douglas utterly, 197

Eden, Sir Anthony (first Earl of Avon): threat of, 107

Edward VII, King: friend of Custances, xxviii

Einstein, Albert: Shaw gives Douglas *Evolution of Physics* by, 33; not a joke, 37; ghastly book Douglas says, 39; scorpion, 40; refuses to read, 99

Eliot, T. S.: Douglas attacks poetry of, 21, 39, 155 n.2; Douglas's friends agree concerning, 159; Shaw's praise of, 160,

Eliot, T. S. (*cont'd*)
164–65; Douglas's criticism of, 161
Ellis, Havelock, 120, 122, 126
England: Douglas agrees to leave, xvi; Ross
returns to, xix; Wilde leaves forever,
xxi; Shaw on Germany and, xxxvi;
poets in, 39; Germany and Italy heap
abuse on, 106; and the Irish ports,
134–36
Ervine, St John: signs Douglas petition,
114 n.2
Evans, Geoffrey, 59 n.1
Evans, M., 137
Evening News, The: falsely reported Douglas's
death, 38 n.1
Evening Standard, The: review of Thomson on
Shakespeare's sonnets in, 42; Douglas's
'Blimp' sonnet in, 144, 145
Everybody's Political What's What?: Shaw
writing, 147 n.1, 151 n.2; to printers,
160; Douglas reading, 185 n.1
Éze: Harris almost lynched near, 59 n.2;
see also Appendix III

Fanny's First Play, 171
Farfetched Fables, 199
Fausset, Hugh l'Anson, 93 n.2
Fielding, Henry, 165
Fitton, Mary, 16 n.1, 17, 19
Fitzrandolph, Sigismund, 119
Flaubert, Gustave, 110
Fortnightly Review, The: Kingsmill slates
Oscar Wilde in, 67 n.2; Kingsmill
article in, 91–92
Fortune Press: publishes Harris's *New Preface*,
72, 73: Shaw remembers, 74
Fourth Avenue, Hove: house of Douglas's
mother on, 6
Fox-Pitt, Lady Edith (Douglas's sister): at
wedding, xxviii; becomes Roman Cath-
olic, xxxiii; visiting Douglas, 191, 197
France: Wilde and his family pressed to go to,
xiii, xvi; Douglas in, xix; if attacked by
Germany, xxxvi
Franco, Francisco, 147
Frankau, Julia ('Frank Danby'): thought
Harris 'sensitive', 151
Freud, Sigmund, 120, 122, 126

Geneva: Shaw's play at Malvern, 84 n.1;

praises dictators, 86; thesis of, 106 n.1
Genoa: Constance Wilde travels from to
Reading, xx
George, Henry: influence on Shaw, 168
Germany: Shaw on England and, xxxvi;
Douglas's views on, 111 n.3, 119
Getting Married: Douglas slates Shaw's play,
xxxi; Shaw refers to review of, 12;
Douglas hated, 12–13; *see also* Appendix I
Gide, André: Douglas speaks kindly of in
Without Apology, 43 n.1
Gielgud, Sir John: signs Douglas petition,
114 n.2
Gilbert, Sir William, 163–64
Gilbert Samuel and Co (Queensberry's
solicitors), 41, 43
Gill, Charles (counsel for the Crown), xvii
Gladstone, W. E., 131
Glyndebourne: Shaws had tickets for, 63;
false Shaw report from, 187, 189
Golders Green: Charlotte Shaw's funeral
service at, 156; her ashes at, 174;
Shaw's funeral service at, 200
Goldsmith, Oliver, 129
Gordon, W. A., 183
Gosse, Edmund: signs Ross testimonial, 4 n.4
Grain, J. P. (counsel for Taylor), xvii
Graves, Charles, 106 n.1
Graves, Henry: portrait of Douglas at eight
by, 84
Gray, John: corrected proof sheets of
Opals, xxvii
Gregynog Press: publishes Shaw *Miscellany*,
127
Grey, Sir Edward: policies opposed by
Shaw, xxxvi

Hailsham, Viscount: friendly toward
Douglas, 108, 110
Halifax, Edward (first Earl of): friendly
letter to Douglas from, 111
Hall, Donald, 187
Hamish Hamilton: Douglas's charges against,
139–40
Hampshire, H.M.S.: sinking of, xxxix
Hampstead: Douglases move to, xxix
Handel, George Frederick: borrowings of,
124; favourite composer of Charlotte
Shaw, 156
Harris, Frank: with Wilde, Shaw and Douglas,

Harris, Frank (*cont'd*)
xi–xiii; predicts outcome of libel trial, xv;
Wilde visits on Riviera, xxiv; confronts
Douglas at Chantilly, xxiv, 65, 68, 74–76,
78–79, 81 n.2, 82; buys *Daventry*
scenario, xxv; writes play, xxv; praises
Douglas's sonnets, xxxvii, 32; Douglas
cooperates on English edition of Harris's
Wilde biography, xl; Harris's biography
of Shaw, 3 n.4, 24–25, 151; past advice
to Wilde, 11; swindled Wilde, 14–15,
33–34; *Life and Loves*, 15; Mary Fitton,
16, 19; his death, 21 n.1; a past letter to
Douglas from, 22; Shaw compares
George Washington and, 30; Douglas
disliked by, 32; *Saturday Review* and, 32,
33, 59; Douglas kind about, 43 n.1;
excesses of, 58–59; Douglas's letters to,
83; comic person Shaw claims, 148;
letter to Douglas from, 149; really 'a
daisy', 150 n.1; thought Tolstoy a saint,
185; Shaw returns letters to widow, 201;
Douglas's letter to, 215–16
Harris, Nellie (Mrs Frank): Shaw helps her
with publications, 13 n.1, 21–22; seeks
Douglas's consent for English edition of
Harris's *Wilde*, 23; Shaw completes
editing English edition for, 25; Wilde's
son told the plight of, 27 n.3; Douglas
always liked, 67; Shaw has done his best
for, 68; Douglas recalls visit from, 72;
hospitable to Douglas in Nice, 77; sends
S.O.S. to Shaw, 148; collects damages
from Stokeses' Wilde play, 153; her death,
153 n.1
Harrods': Douglas receives damages from, 61
Hart, d'Arcy: handling Rich and Cowan suit
for Douglas, 43, 45; concerned with
Douglas's flat, 109
Hassall, Christopher: signs Douglas petition,
114 n.2
Hatchard's: Douglas receives damages from,
61; sells Shaw postcard, 152, 201; Douglas
Lyrics and *Sonnets* out of stock at, 183
Headlam, Stewart: goes bail for Wilde, xvii;
meets him on release from prison, xxi
Heartbreak Hóuse: Shaw's war disillusionment
in, xxxvi; character of Captain Shotover
in, 192
Henley, W. E., 22
Henry VI, King, 17

Herbert William: Mr W. H. and, 16;
Shakespeare's sonnets not addressed
to, 19
Higgs, Harry and Clara (Shaw's gardener
and cook-housekeeper): retire, 182
Hinsley, Cardinal: dealing firmly with Noyes,
93 n.1; criticizes the press, 110
Hitler, Adolf: Douglas's opinion of, 94; take-
over of Czechoslovakia, 106 n.1; recent
speech of, 110; has Russian supplies, 125;
race nonsense of, 129; Douglas pamphlet
on, 133–35; confronts Russia, 143 n.1,
146; Douglas meditating sonnet on, 145
Hogg, Douglas: counsel for *Evening News*,
38; counsel for Churchill 108; *see also*
Hailsham, Viscount
Holland, Vyvyan: letters from Ross to, xxiv,
xxxv; Constable's terms with, 27 n.3;
Chantilly section deleted for sake of, 78
n.1, 149; parentage of, 117, 119, 121;
Shaw has not met, 126
Holloway Prison: Wilde imprisoned in, xvi;
Douglas visits, xvi
Hoole, John, 160–61
Hope, Adrian, xxi
Hôtel de la Plage, Berneval, xxii
Hôtel de Nice, Paris, xxiii
Hove: Shaws planned week in, 63; Reeveses
leave, 97, 113
Humphreys, C. O. (solicitor for Wilde),
xiii, xvi
Humphry, Mrs (Douglas's housekeeper): is
ill, 181; Douglas's bequest to, 197, 199
Hunter-Blair, Abbot Sir David: failed to
deliver lecture on Wilde, 49–50; pub-
lished later in *Victorian Days and Other
Papers*, 49 n.1; would sign Douglas
pension petition, 110

Ibsen, Henrik: reduced Shakespeare to flapdoodle, 128; preferred prose, 165;
Shaw enthrones, 175
Ideal Husband, An, xi
Importance of Being Earnest, The: Shaw de-
nounces, xi, 37; successful revival of,
105, 128
In Excelsis: Douglas writes sonnets in prison,
xl; MS retained there, xl; method of
composition, 169; attempts retrieval
of, 169
In Good King Charles's Golden Days: Shaw's

In Good King Charles's Golden Days (cont'd)
new play at Malvern, 118
Inn of Dreams, The: Olive Douglas's verse,
xxix
Ireland: attempts to 'free', xxxvi; understanding of, 117; an Englishman
changed by residence in, 129; Shaw
castigates Douglas pamphlet on, 133–37;
stamps an Englishman for life, 146;
Shaw arranging gift to, 182–83
Ireland, William Henry, 175
Ireland and the War Against Hitler: Douglas
pamphlet, 133–37
Irving, Sir Henry: mutilated *Lear*, 175
Isle of Wight: Olive Douglas living in, xli, 44
Italy: Douglas invites Wilde to, xxii; Turner
living in, 30 n.2, 34

Jackson, Barry (producer), xxxvi
James, Mrs L. W.: Clarke letter submitted
89 n.3
Japan: non-aggression pact, 146
Jepson, Edgar: comes to Douglas, 35; Harris's
'ghost', 36
Joan la Romée: Harris's Joan of Arc play,
14 n.1, 60
Job, Book of, 162, 164, 171, 173
John Bull's Other Island: successful in London,
xxix; Shaw explains Fathers Keegan and
Dempsey in, 131, 152
Jones, Richard: assists Douglas with lecture,
155 n.2
Jutland, battle of: Douglas's accusations
concerning, xxxix

Kean, Edmund: alcohol addiction of, 121
Keats, John: Shaw's politics those of, 155
Kennard, Coleridge: not at Père Lachaise, 86
Kennet, Lady: her bust of Shaw, 99
King Lear: 'Child Rowland to the dark tower
came', 48 n.4; Douglas thought it was
'childe', 51; Charlotte Shaw dislikes,
175; Douglas dislikes, 179
Kingsmill, Hugh: slates *Oscar Wilde* in *Fort-
nightly*, 67 n.2; asserts Douglas W. H.
'redivivus', 92 n.1
Kitchener, Lord: death of, xxxix
Krafft-Ebing, Baron Richard von, 126
Kyllmann, Otto (of Constable's): uneasy
about Harris's *Wilde*, 56 n.2, 72 n.1;
visits Douglas, 78; Douglas requests

second copy Harris's *Wilde* from, 81
n.2, 84; notifies Shaw of Stokeses'
play damage suit, 153

Labouchere, Henry, xviii
Laden, Alice: Shaw's new cook-housekeeper,
182; now expert, 199
Lake Farm, near Salisbury: leased by
Douglases, xxix
Lane, Allen: discusses Harris biography with
Douglas, 23
Lane, John: published Olive Custance's *Opals*,
xxvii
Laurie, Werner: reports Harris's *Wilde* easily
obtainable in England, 61; a publisher of
Sherard, 61; of Crosland, 62 n.1
Lawson, Frank: embarrassed host, xxxii
Lemonnier, Léon: treats Douglas sympatheti-
cally, 70
Lenin, Nikolai, 168
Lennox-Boyd, Alan (Viscount Boyd of
Merton): undertakes release of *In
Excelsis*, 169; joins Douglas rent
syndicate, 169 n.3, 176
Leslie, Sir Shane: poetry meeting at house
of, 51
Leverson, Ada (Mrs Ernest): Douglas writes
to, xx
Leverson, Ernest: Wilde stays with Leversons
during bail, xvii
Lewis, D. B. Wyndham: article on *Without
Apology*, 64; admires Douglas's lecture,
164, 166
Lewis, Sir George: advises Ross, xxxiii; solici-
tor for both Ross and Custance, 98 n.3
Lincoln's Inn Fields: *Academy* office in, xxix
Lloyd George, David: *Academy* attacks, xxxi;
Plain English attacks, xxxix
Lockwood, Sir Frank (counsel for Crown,
third Wilde trial), xvii
London: Douglas remains in, xvi; Wilde
leaves, xxi; postponement of Shaw-
Douglas meeting in, 53; Olive Douglas's
flat in, 81, 94; Shaw too old for, 155;
Douglas plans move to, 181, 183
Londonderry House: Shaw collapses at, 103
London Mercury, The: Shaw's Act V for
Cymbeline in, 34; Douglas's letter
in, 93
Lonsdale, fifth Earl of, 189
Looten, Camille, 20

Low, Sir David (the cartoonist): Douglas's bête noire, 145

Lucy, Sir Thomas: deer-poaching jingle adapted, 12, 48; Douglas dislikes jingle, 49; discovers source, 102

Luther, Martin, 37

Luxembourg: charcoal people in, 133

Lyrics: Douglas sends Shaw his, 20; Poppoea Vanda seeks, 183

Macaulay, Rose: drafts petition for Douglas, 111 n.2

MacCarthy, Desmond: Constable's should withdraw *Oscar Wilde*, 68 n.1, 70; Shaw's answer to, 75; Douglas's comment on, 80

McCarthy, Lillah (Barker-Keeble): declaims sonnets to Shaw, 147–48

Machen, Arthur: false obituary of Douglas by, 38 n.1

McLachlan, Dame Laurentia (Abbess of Stanbrook): friend of Shaw, 155 n.1

Maclean, Grant, 116

MacStinger's, Mrs, baby: Shaw likens Douglas's howls to, 11; Agate quotes, 53; Douglas's 'infantile complex' resembles, 93 n.2; low-spirited noises of, 94, 123, 126

Man and Superman, xxix

Manchester: Ancoats Brotherhood in, 114 n.1

Manchester Guardian: Shaw's article on Butler in, 21

Marjoribanks, Edward, 108

Marlowe, Christopher: not Shakespeare's rival poet, 16, 19, 161; Canterbury connexion of, 53

Marx, Karl: Goldsmith anticipated, 129; Shaw's politics those of, 155; Shaw's study of, 168

Maynooth: Roman Catholic seminary, 152

Melanchthon, Philip, 37

Melbourne Art Gallery: position offered Ross by, xxxv

Mellor, Harold: Wilde meets, xxiv

Mercure de France, Le: Douglas's proposed article for, xix

Methuen: edition of Wilde's *Works*, xxxii

Metropolitan Club, Washington, D.C.: Douglas insulted in, xxviii

Middleton, George: Harris's borrowings from *Pantomime Man* of, 19–20

Minto, William: identifies Shakespeare's rival poet, 16

Misalliance: Shaw changes 'Saumarez' to 'Summerhays' in, 95

Moir, Byres, 195

Montagu, George: heir to Earl of Sandwich, xxvi; Winchester friend of Douglas, xxvii; Olive Custance engaged to, xxviii

Monte Carlo: Douglas visits Harris in, 68

Morris, William: singer of an empty day, 25 n.1; Shaw's politics those of, 155

Morrison, Herbert: releases Mosley from prison, 158 n.1; backs up Peake, 170

Mortimer, Raymond: review of Harris's *Wilde*, 84 n.2

Mosley, Sir Oswald: Shaw interviewed on release of, 158

Mr and Mrs Daventry: Wilde sold scenario of to many, xxv; Harris wrote play of and sold, xxv; Wilde's distress over, 14–15; Shaw's opinion of, 30; Douglas's account of, 33–34

Mrs Warren's Profession, xxix

Muggeridge, H. T., 54 n.1

Muggeridge, Malcolm: reviews *Without Apology*, 54 n.2

Murray, John: turns down *Man and Superman*, xxix

Mussolini, Benito: occupies Albania, 106

My Life and Loves: Harris's privately printed autobiography, 15, 59–60; *see also* Appendix III

'My Memories of Oscar Wilde' (by Shaw): Douglas complains of, 3 n.1, 4 n.1, 6

Naples: Wilde and Douglas in, xxii; Posillipo near, xxiii; the Wilde-Douglas break-up in, 45; Douglas's letters to his mother from, 46 n.1

Napoleon: Viereck idolizes, 87 n.1; mother's expression concerning, 143; attacks Russia, 146

National Bank of Scotland, London (Douglas's bank): concerning Shaw's guarantee, 44, 46, 48

National Gallery of Ireland: Shaw's bequest to, 199

Nervi: Constance waiting for Wilde in, xxii

Newhaven: Wilde takes night boat from, xxi

New Statesman, The: Shaw attacks Foreign
Minister in, xxxvi; Shaw's comment on,
33; Douglas rarely reads, 34; Raymond
Mortimer reviews Harris's *Wilde* in, 84
n.2; misprints in Douglas's reply in, 86;
Clarke's letter and Douglas's reply in,
89–90
Newton, Sir Isaac, 163
New York: Douglas visits, xxviii; profits of
Stock Exchange in, xxxix
New York Herald, The: reports insult to
Douglas, xxviii
Nice: Wilde visits Harris in, xxiv; Douglas
with Harris in, xl, 14, 77–78; failure of
Wilde English edition project, xl, 72, 216;
Nellie Harris plans tea-shop in, 24;
Harris's letters to Douglas from, 65;
Nellie Harris's S.O.S. to Shaw from,
148; she dies in, 153 n.1
Nicolson, Harold: reviews *Without Apology*,
43; reviews Harris's *Wilde*, 76; signs
Douglas's petition, 114 n.2; lobbies
for it, 142
Northcliffe Press: Douglas recieves damages
from, 70
Norway: produces in extremes, 133
Nowell-Smith, Simon: apologizes to
Douglas, 56 n.1
Noyes, Alfred: did not prevent Hunter-Blair
from lecturing, 49–50; controversy
stirred by *Voltaire*, 93 n.1

Observer, The: review of Harris's *Wilde* in,.
67 n.2
Old Bailey: the three Wilde trials at, xiii–xvii,
xx; Ross libel trial against Douglas at,
xxxv; Churchill libel trial against
Douglas at, 108
Old Monk's Farm: the Colmans' farm, 159
n.1; Douglas visiting, 180; coming to
stay at, 191; living at, 193, 197; his
death at, 199; had brought Douglas
correspondence to, 201
Opals: Olive Custance's first volume of
verse, xxvii
Oppenheimer, Albert (Tredegar's solicitor):
arranges Douglas syndicate payments,
140 n.1; arranging Vanda payments, 183
Orléans, xxxvi
Orme, Dr, 57

Osborn, Peter: 'Douglas' in play at Arts
Club, 101
Oscar Wilde: play by Leslie and Sewell Stokes,
95; other productions and publication of,
96 n.1; Douglas suggests Shaw collaborate
on a Wilde play, 97; Shaw declines, 98;
Douglas sees Stokeses' play, 101; Olive
sees, 102; Shaw sees, 103
Oscar Wilde, a Critical Study Arthur Ransome
biography, xxxiii; Douglas claims libel-
lous, xxxiii; Shaw says respectable and
judicial, 24
Oscar Wilde, A Summing-Up: Shaw will read
Douglas's MS, 117; Douglas sends, 118;
'report' from Shaw on, 119; argument
ensues over, 121–226; Shaw's scenario
for, 123–26; Shaw finds readable, 127
Oscar Wilde and Myself: by Douglas and
Crosland, xxxiv; bitter truth in, 80;
Douglas needs Wilde letters for, 160 n.1
Oscar Wilde and the Black Douglas: by Francis
Queensberry and Percy Colson, 202
Oscar Wilde and the Yellow Nineties (by Frances
Winwar): Douglas's libel settlement
concerning, 139; Douglas's preface for
future editions of, 140; Shaw appraises
Douglas's MS, 148–49
Oscar Wilde: His Life and Confessions (published
in America, 1916, 1918): Harris's biography, xl; Douglas's marginal notes in,
xl, 27 n.1, 149; Shaw's 'Memories' of
Wilde in, 3 n.1, 4 n.1, 6; best Wilde life,
4, 24, 68, 120; large sale of, 7; libellous to
Douglas, 8, 10, 28; Shaw presses English
edition of, 21 n.1, 24; will make inoffensive to Douglas, 22; Douglas's conditions
to Nellie Harris, 23; copies easily available
in England, 61; no new American edition
of, 87, 89, 91
Harris's *New Preface to 'The Life and Confessions of Oscar Wilde'* (1925): Shaw had
read, 3 n.3; Harris admits lies in, 6, 12,
13, 65, 68, 77; Shaw denies reading, 70;
republication condition for English
edition of Wilde biography, 72; Douglas
sends Shaw *New Preface* (1927), 73, 78;
Shaw remembers earlier reading, 74;
Douglas 'Note' in 1927 edition, 75–76;
Douglas denies Harris wrote under
'duress', 76–77; discrepancies in, 79; Shaw

Harris's *New Preface* (cont'd)
quotes from, 84 n.2; press ignores, 86;
Secker wants to republish, 93; *see also*
Appendix III
Oscar Wilde (English edition, 1938): Douglas receives copy of, 65; libels remain,
68–72; slated by reviewers, 67, 84, n.2;
upsets Olive Douglas, 77, 81; Douglas's
Autobiography corrects, 79; 'ordurous'
book, 80, 122; Sherard's charge against,
115
Shaw's preface to English edition: Shaw
writing, 21 n.1, 22; Nellie Harris approves
proof, 35 n.1; Douglas approves proof,
44 n.2; Douglas anticipates publication,
46; requests revise, 50; anxiously awaiting,
56; Constable's sends revise of, 58;
Douglas's praise of, 65, 67, 122; Shaw
not first to deny Douglas deserted Wilde,
69; Douglas burns book except for, 81;
Dodd, Mead offers separate publication
of, 89, 92, 94; Douglas quotes from,
115–16; libels answered by, 140
O'Sullivan, Vincent: sympathetic treatment
of Douglas, 70
Oxford: Douglas fails to get degree at, xi;
with Franciscans at Greyfriars in, 41;
unhappy return of Douglas to, 96–97
Oxford Book of English Verse, xxxvii

Pannell, E., 84, 87, 113
Pannett, Professor Charles, 61–63
Pantomime Man, The: Douglas's introduction
for Middleton's, 20 n.1
Paris: Douglas in, xviii; Sherard lives in, xix;
Douglas returns to, xxiii; Wilde in,
xxiii; Wilde's death in, xxv; Turner at
deathbed in, 30 n.2
Parker, Agnes Miller, 131
Pascal, Gabriel, 151 n.2
Patch, Blanche: ill, 129; poor typing of, 132;
at Charlotte Shaw's funeral, 156 n.1;
with Shaw, 199
Patriot, The, 33, 34
Pavlov, Ivan, 167
Payne-Townshend, Charlotte: marries Shaw,
xxx; *see also* Shaw, Charlotte
Peake, Osbert, 170
Pearson, Hesketh: slates Harris's *Wilde*, 67 n.2;
his Wilde biography, 153; Douglas

sends letter to, 197
Pearson's Magazine: Harris editor of, 33
Pentonville Prison: Wilde imprisoned
in, xviii
Père Lachaise, 86
Petrarch, 166, 170–71
'Phrases and Philosophies for the Use of the
Young', xv
Piazza, Mr, 116 n.1
Picture of Dorian Gray, The: defence of, xi,
xiii; quoted in Wilde's libel trial, xv
Plain English: Douglas editor of, xxxix;
dropped as editor of, xxxix; has
not lived down, 133; forced to
write quickly on, 173
Plain Speech: Douglas launches, xxxix
Poe, Edgar Allan: Harris recites *The Raven*,
149; Shaw fascinated by, 167
Porteus, Dr Arthur, 61–62
Posillipo, xxiii
Pound, Ezra, 155 n.2, 161
Principles of Poetry, The: Douglas's Tredegar
lecture, 155 n.2, 173; Secker publishes,
157; Douglas requests Shaw's comment
on, 159, 161; doubts Shaw has read, 163;
other friends praise, 164, 166, 170; Shaw
comments on, 171
Procès d'Oscar Wilde: Rostand's play, 101
Pygmalion, xxxvi, 48 n.1, 125

Quaritch, Bernard: Douglas sells remaining
Wilde letters to, 160 n.1, 161
Queensberry, (Cathleen) Marchioness of,
second wife of Francis: 51 n.1, 63
Queensberry, (Francis) eleventh Marquess of:
Shaw writes to, xiii; installs Douglas
and his mother at St Ann's Court, 20
n.4; no help with Rich and Cowan, 39,
41–43; on verge of ruin, 52; arranges
for Douglas's operation, 57–58; important
in hospital world, 62 n.2; cannot pay
Douglas's rent, 106–7; Shaw advises
Douglas to 'whitemail', 108, 126, 138;
joins Douglas syndicate, 139–40, 143;
friendly with Churchill, 142; withdraws
from syndicate, 169 n.3, 182; invites
Shaw to Service Club, 187, 189–90;
visiting Douglas, 191, 197; wishes to
publish Shaw-Douglas correspondence,
201; book by, 202

Queensberry, (Irene) Marchioness of, first
wife of Francis, 50–51
Queensberry, (John Sholto) ninth Marquess
of: Wilde's libel suit against, xi, xiii–xv;
second Wilde trial, xvii; precipitates
Wilde's bankruptcy, xix; his death,
xxiv; Douglas's irresistible description of,
24; in *Without Apology* generous amends
to, 43 n.1; dissipated his inheritance, 52;
Douglas cleared from innuendo of, 67;
mis-statements of, corrected, 70; free-
thinking of, 117
Queensberry, (Percy) tenth Marquess of: as
Lord Hawick gave bail for Wilde, xvii;
death of, 39 n.1; had dissipated his
inheritance, 52, 108–9
Queensberry, (Sybil) Marchioness of, divorced
wife of ninth Marquess, mother of
Douglas: distressed by reunion of Douglas
and Wilde, xxiii; not at Douglas's
wedding, xxviii; helps him buy *Academy*,
xxxii; becomes Roman Catholic, xxxiii;
Douglas living at house of, 6 n.1; moves
to St Ann's Court, 20 n.4; her death, 20
n.4; Douglas's letters from Naples to, 45–
46; 'a little saint', 188–89; Douglas buried
beside, 199
Quickly, Mrs, 40
Quiller-Couch, Sir Arthur: admirer of Douglas's sonnets, xxxvii; will sign Douglas's
pension petition, 110, 111 n.1; signs,
114 n.2; praises lecture, 164

Rainbows: Olive Douglas's verse, xxix
Ralli, Augustus: Douglas visits, 94
Ransome, Arthur: Douglas's libel suit against,
xviii, xxxiii, 98; his biography of
Wilde, 24
Reading Gaol: Wilde imprisoned in, xx
Reeves, Norma: Douglas's affection for child
neighbour, 93; Douglas's presents to, 94;
the Reeves move to Birmingham, 97;
Shaw's stamps for, 99; Douglas depressed
by departure of, 101; stamps forwarded
to, 113
Registry Office, Henrietta Street, London:
Shaw and Charlotte married at, xxx
Renier, Gustav, 70 n.1
Revelations of Divine Love, 188
Review of Reviews, The, xviii

Revue Blanche, La: Douglas's article in, xx
Rich, Charles, 41, 92
Rich and Cowan: publishers of Douglas's
Lyrics and *Sonnets*, 20; difficulties over
publication of *Without Apology*, 28; book
published by Secker, 28 n.1; suit against
Douglas by, 36–39, 41–43; Shaw gives
Douglas guarantee, 44–45, 139 n.1; no
further trouble, 46 n.2; Douglas grateful
to Shaw, 69, 77; business-like firm, 87;
request new book, 92
Richards, Grant, xxix
Richards Press, 133
Richmond, Sir Bruce, 52
Ringsend: waterside people of, 133
Robson, Thomas: alcohol addiction of, 121
Roe, Humphrey Verdon, 106
Romeo and Juliet, 18
Ross, Robert: takes Wilde to solicitor, xiii, at
first Wilde trial, xvi; goes to Rouen,
xvi; returns to England, xix; informs
Douglas of Wilde's hostility, xx; meets
Wilde at Dieppe, xxi; literary executor
of, xxi; incensed by Wilde's return to
Douglas, xxii; offers Douglas half of
Wilde royalties, xxiv; at Wilde's death-
bed, xxv; discusses Wilde's papers with
Douglas, xxvi; runs Carfax Gallery,
xxvii; observes Douglas's marriage,
xxviii; suggests Douglas edit *Academy*,
xxix; differs on *Academy* stands, xxxii;
falls out with Douglas, xxxiii; gives *De
Profundis* to British Museum, xxxiii;
backs Ransome at trial, xxxiv, 98; sues
Douglas for libel, xxxiv; plans trip to
Australia, xxxv; his death, xxxv; testi-
monial for, 4; Wilde had 'lived' on, 30,
34; More Adey shares house with, 34;
source of information for Harris, 69;
Shaw treats kindly, 76 n.2; Mortimer
defends, 84 n.2; forgotten, 121; attempted
silence on, 169 n.3
Ross, William, 130
Rostand, Maurice, 101
Rouen: Ross goes to, xvi; Wilde meets
Douglas in, xxii
Rowley, Mrs Charles, 114 n.1
Royal Academy of Dramatic Art: Shaw's
bequest to, 199
Royal Society of Literature: Douglas's lecture

Royal Society of Literature (*cont'd*)
for, 155–57; Shaw's advice concerning,
158
Royalty Theatre, London, xxv
Rubinstein, H. F.: warns Constable's that
Douglas has cause for libel, 56 n.2
Rumbold, Richard: introduces Colmans to
Douglas, 159 n.1
Ruskin, John: Shaw's politics those of, 155
Russell, Earl (Bertrand), 105
Russia: *Devil's Disciple* produced in, xxix;
Kitchener's mission to, xxxix; Hitler
supplies from, 125; Shaw writes *Times*
about, 126; Douglas's broadsheet on,
130; Shaw has visited, 131–32; Shaw's
prose sonnet to, 143, 145; has problem
with Japan, 146

St Andrew's Hospital: Raymond Douglas in,
177, 184 n.1; *see also* Appendix IV
St Ann's Court, Hove: Douglas and his mother
have flats at, 20 n.4; Douglas cannot
afford flat, 125; lease expiring, 126 n.2;
syndicate to renew lease, 140, 142, 169 n.3,
176; Douglas clears out of, 181; auction
of flat contents, 183
St Anthony of Padua: Douglas lights candle
for Shaw to, 54–55, 83, 152 n.2
St Bernadette: Douglas offers Shaw prayer to,
170
St Christopher: Douglas's name for Shaw, 46;
candle to, 54; statuette not in Hove, 55;
in Westminster Cathedral, 56; Douglas
requests prayer from, 60; finds Childe
heavy midstream, 68; Douglas's nasty
remark about, 76; Douglas's sonnet on,
81, 92–94; has landed Childe safely, 82;
'epitaph' of, 99–101; must not desert
Childe, 113; Christopher ring, 127
St George's, Hanover Square, London:
Douglas's marriage at, xxviii
St James: a day too soon, 130; saint of
Plumstead Peculiars, 192–94
St Januarius: blood liquefying, 186, 188; not
liquefying, 190
Saint Joan: play long in Shaw's mind, xxxvi;
first productions of, xxxvii; published
and selling well, 89; Shaw sees at Malvern,
91; Douglas now likes, 93; prose of, 164
St John of the Cross, 101

St Jude: rescues Douglas, 126; Douglas
blames, 135; Douglas thanks, 142;
invokes, 144–45; Douglas's special
saint, 193
St Mary's Hospital, London: Douglas in,
60, 61
St Pancras: Shaw council member of
borough, xxx
St Thomas Aquinas, 37, 166, 168
Salomé: Maud Allan's production of, xxxv;
Sarah Bernhardt and, 73
Saturday Review, The: Harris's successful
editorship of, 32; finished Harris as
writer, 33, 59; three exceptions, 60
Savoy Hotel, London, xv, 91
School for Scandal, The, 128
Scotland: Ross cables Douglas in, xxv;
Douglas meets Strabolgi in, 41; loss of
Queensberry property in, 52; produces
in extremes, 133
Scott, Sir Walter, 25, 48
Secker, Martin: publishes Douglas's *In Excelsis*,
xl; his *Complete Poems* and *Autobiography*,
xli; new edition of, 6; wants Shaw
preface, 7; Douglas's request of, 20;
publishes *Without Apology*, 28 n.1, 38;
book going well, 40; miraculous appearance of, 41; Douglas considers request to,
50; not business-like, 86–87, 92; wishes to
publish Harris *New Preface* with new
Douglas 'Note', 93; interested in publishing *Summing-Up*, 122–23; publishes
Douglas's poetry lecture, 157
Shackleton, Sir Ernest, 91
Shakespeare: jingle absurdly ascribed to, 12,
48–49, 102–3; the rival poet of, 16;
Shakespeare a Roman Catholic, 18;
borrowings from Montaigne, 124; Shaw
compares to Ibsen, 128; a conservative,
144; admired by Lillah McCarthy, 147–
48; Shaw-Douglas argument on prose
and poetry, 161, 163–65, 167; mixed
time plots, 171; Shaw makes human,
175, 180; Shaw wrote twice as many
plays as, 199
Shakespeare's sonnets: Douglas's sonnets
compared to, xxxvii; infantile complex
in, 13; Douglas on, 15, 19; another
imbecile book about, 42; more nonsense
about 52, 56; one split infinitive in, 87

Shakes vs. Shav, 199

Shaw, Charlotte (Mrs Bernard): good manager and uncompetitive, xxx; enthusiastic about St Joan, xxxvii; Shaw dictates libel release letter to, 56 n.2; Douglas disappointed not seeing Shaws, 63; the Shaws' favourite children's books, 91; Charlotte's illness diagnosed as lumbago, 125; Shaws sleep through air raids, 131; osteitis deformans the illness of, 155 n.3; death and funeral service of, 156, 186; Shaw tidying up after death of, 158; remembers her dislike of *Lear*, 175, 179; sends Douglas her photograph, 177

Shaw, Mrs G. C. (Shaw's mother), xxx

Shaw Gives Himself Away, 127 n.1

Shelley, Percy Bysshe: admired by Olive Custance, xxvii; Douglas's sonnets compared to, xxxvii, 97; Shaw mentions, 22; doggerel in, 25; a revolutionist, 143–44; Shaw's politics those of, 155

Shelleys, The, in Lewes: Douglas spends night at hotel, 61; once house of Timothy Shelley, 63

Sherard, R. H.: visits Wilde in prison, xix; warns Douglas will dedicate *Poems*, xx; defends Wilde against Harris and Shaw, 22 n.1; Shaw's opinion of, 23–25, 120, 148; underestimates Harris, 32; Shaw's preface to Harris's *Wilde* treats, 44–45; letter to Douglas from, 61; exposes Harris's statements, 67 n.2; attacks Renier, 70; letter from, 73; disproves Harris's lies, 79; cautions Douglas, 80; annoys Douglas, 90; Douglas can answer, 115

Sheridan, R. B.: Drury Lane shares compared to *Daventry*, 30; Wilde's superiority to, 128

Sinn Fein, xxxix, 133–35

Sixteen Self-Sketches, 199

Smith, Freddie (Ross's secretary), xxxii

Smith, Logan Pearsall, 170

Smithers, Leonard, xxiii

Song of Bernadette, 170

Sonnets (by Douglas): Douglas sends to Shaw, 20; rhyme and scan, 162; Poppoea Vanda seeks, 183

Sorrento: Douglas in, xx

Sotheby's: auctions an uninteresting Shaw postcard, 115; auctions Shaw-Douglas postcard, 152, 201

Southampton, Earl of, 19, 52 n.1

Spain, 147

Sphinx, The: Wilde's poem, 119

Spirit Lamp, The: Douglas's article in, 87

Squire, Sir John: signs Douglas petition, 114 n.2

Stalin, Joseph: has shot the right people, 146; may see the Pope, 187

Stead, W. T., xviii

Stokes, Leslie and Sewell: authors of the play *Oscar Wilde*, 95; arrangements with Douglas, 96

Stopes, Dr Marie (Mrs Humphrey Verdon Roe): writes to Douglas, 105; Shaw pension petition (1939), 110–11, 113; signs, 114 n.2; Chamberlain's answer to, 115 n.3; presents second petition (1940), 137 n.2; time for third (1941), 137 n.2; new plan, 140; member of Douglas syndicate, 143, 176; verse volume published, 189; visits Douglas, 197

Story of Anne Whateley and William Shaxpere, The: Shakespeare a woman, 130

Strabolgi, Baron: a director of Rich and Cowan, 36; Douglas dislikes, 41; on Russia, 147

Stratford-upon-Avon: Shaw's Act V of *Cymbeline*, 34 n.3; Douglas visits new theatre in, 96; Shaws see *Lear* at, 175

Sullivan, Francis: 'Wilde' in play, 101; Sullivans take Douglas to *The Importance of Being Earnest*, 105

Sunday Graphic, The: Shaw interview in, 136

Sunday Pictorial, The: Douglas interview in, 119

Sunday Times, The, 40 n.1, 75, 78, 80

Sweden, 133

Swift, Jonathan, 146

Switzerland, xxiv, 133

Sykes, Lady Jessica, 32

Symons, A. J. A.: Wilde biographer, 23; opposes English edition of Harris's *Wilde*, 27; Douglas loans Shaw letter to, 73; Douglas visits, 116; advises Douglas, 119; Shaw criticizes, 121

Tails with a Twist: by Douglas, 132 n.1

Talbot, Lord Edmund (Viscount Fitzalan): prevents lecture, 49

Taming of the Shrew, The, 179–80

Taylor, Alfred, xv, xvii

Tennant, Edward: buys *Academy* for Douglas, xxix; withdraws support, xxxii

Tennant, Pamela Wyndham, xxix

Thomas à Kempis, xxxix

Thomson, Walter, 42, 45

Time and Tide: review, 54 n.2

Times, The: Wilde urged to write letter to, xiii; rejects Douglas letter, 111; Shaw article on Russia in, 126; Douglas claims paper 'pink', 130 n.3; Olive Douglas's death reported in, 174, 176

Times Literary Supplement, The: review of *Without Apology* in, 40; Douglas sends letter to, 51–52, 54; answer from, 56; Douglas writes again to, 57; review of *Summing-Up* in, 127; on Douglas's lecture, 180

Tite Street, Chelsea, xvii

Tolstoy, Count: his *What Is Art?*, 163; a saint to Harris, 185

Tredegar, Viscount (Evan Morgan): joins Douglas rent syndicate, 140, 176; Douglas to give Tredegar lecture, 155 n.2; Douglas's fee, 157; plans Douglas's move, 183; visits Douglas, 197

Trinity College, Dublin, xv, 146

True History of Shakespeare's Sonnets, The (by Douglas): author sends copy to Shaw, 15 n.2; Shaw praises, 19–21; Shaw criticizes, 161

Truth, xviii, 189

'Truth about Shakespeare, The': Shaw's review of Tyler's, 19

Turle, Mrs (Douglas's landlady), 183–84

Turner, Reginald: advice to Wilde from, xvi; meets Wilde at Dieppe, xxi; Shaw's query about, 30; friend of Beerbohm, 34

Tyler, Thomas: on Shakespeare's sonnets, 15; identifies rival poet, 16

Upcher, Peter, 102

Vanda, Poppoea: suggests Douglas write ballet scenario, 152 n.1; Douglas to lodge with, 183; opal necklace bequest to, 197; necklace not found, 199

Vanity Fair: Harris editor of, 32

Victoria, Queen: Douglas's Wilde petition to, xviii; in time of, 168

Victoria Station, London, xxviii

Viereck, G. S., 87

Walkley, Arthur, 175

Wallas, Graham, 105

Walpole, Sir Hugh: signs Douglas petition, 114 n.2

Walstan, Father, 188 n.2

Wandsworth Prison: Wilde imprisoned in, xviii, xx

Wartime Harvest (Marie Stopes's poems): with Douglas preface and Shaw note, 189

Washington, D.C.: Douglas in, xxviii

Watson, Sir William: receives pension, 109

Waugh, Evelyn: signs Douglas petition, 114 n.2

Webb, Sidney and Beatrice, xxx, xxxi, xxxvi

Weekly Review, The, 64, 136 n.1

Weldon, Georgina, 89

Wells, H. G., 4 n.4, 49

Westminster Abbey, 174, 200

Westminster Bank, London (Shaw's bank), 45, 48, 50

Weston Hall, Norwich: property of Colonel Custance, xxvii; Douglases visit, xxviii

W. H., Mr: Shaw feels Douglas understands, 15; Shaw thinks not an actor, 16; Shakespeare's sonnets to, 17–18; Douglas thinks W. H. was an actor, 18 n.1; fresh evidence on Will Hughes, 21, 24–25; a discredited claimant, 42 n.1; news from Canterbury concerning, 52–53; Cripps's suggestion concerning, 56; Douglas, W. H. 'redivivus', 92 n.1

Whistler, James, 36

White, Mrs (cook of Douglas's mother), 83, 84

Whitehall Court, London: the Shaws' flat in, 8; Shaw's smaller flat in, 199

Whitman, Walt, 161, 167, 171

Why Should She Not, 199

Wild, Sir Ernest (Ross counsel), 90

Wilde, Constance (Mrs Oscar): should go to France, xiii; homeless, xvii; tells Oscar of mother's death, xx; made joint guardian of boys, xxi; waiting for

Wilde, Constance (*cont'd*)
Oscar at Nervi, xxii; stops allowance to
him, xxiii; her death, xxiv; Shaw
comments on, 120; Douglas comments
on, 122
Wilde, Lady: death of, xx; was Dublin
grande dame, 117, 122
Wilde, Oscar: Café Royal with Harris, Shaw,
Douglas, xi, xiii; Shaw advice to, xiv;
first trial of, xv; second and third trials
of, xvii–xviii; imprisonment of, xviii;
declared bankrupt, xix; death of mother,
xx; refuses Douglas *Poems* dedication,
xxi; writes *De Profundis*, xxi; begins
Ballad, xxii; rejoins Douglas, xxii; failure
of life together, xxiii; Shaw proposes
Wilde for honour, xxiii; visits Harris,
xxiv; illness and death, xxv; papers of,
xxvi; scandal hurts Douglas, xxvii,
xxviii; bankruptcy discharged, xxxii;
Ransome book about, xxxiii; Ransome
trial and *De Profundis*, xxxiv; Douglas
rages against, xxxv, 79–80; Douglas's
celebrity as friend of, xxxvii; Douglas's
renewed affection for, xl, xli; Shaw on
biographers of, 3; after prison, 8; on
Mr W. H., 16, 18; connexion with
Father Bowden, 20 n.3; and Robert
Sherard, 22–23, 148; playing games, 27;
master liar, 30; collapse as writer, 32–33;
Daventry play, 33–34; Shaw's relationship
to, 36–37, 117; Douglas's loyalty to, 46
n.1; Hunter-Blair's planned lecture on,
49–51; never quite sober, 58; ferocious
will, 58–59; lunatic reactions to, 75 n.1;
Shaw loyal to, 76 n.2; Viereck idolizes, 87
n.1; America not interested in, 89;
Stokeses' play about, 95–96, 98, 101–103;
possible Shaw-Douglas play about, 97–98,
103; court costume of, 117; Douglas
writing life of, 120–26; Shaw on, as
playwright, 128; a first folio of, 129;
letters to Douglas from, 160 n.1, 161;
attempted silence on, 169 n.3
Wilde's sons: should be taken to France, xiii;
homeless, xvii; taken from Wilde, xxi;
surname changed, xxii
Wills, Mr Justice: judge at third Wilde trial,
xvii; sentences Wilde, xviii; scenario
chapter on, 126
Winchester College: Douglas and Montagu
at, xxvii; Adrian Earle at, 157 n.1
Without Apology (by Douglas): to be published
soon, 22–23; problems with Rich and
Cowan, 28; published by Martin Secker,
28 n.1; Shaw enjoys, 30; Douglas omits
Jepson from, 35; Shaw finds nothing
objectionable in, 36; review of, 43; Shaw
plans changes because of, 45–46; offensive
review of, in *Time and Tide*, 54 n.2; not
selling, 86; Douglas discusses split
infinitives in, 87; story of burning
Wilde's letters in, 160 n.1
Wolfe, Humbert: Douglas's pension petition,
111 n.1; signs, 114 n.2
Woman of No Importance, A, 128
Woolf, Leonard, 34
Woolf, Virginia: signs Douglas's petition,
114 n.2
Wormwood Scrubs: Douglas imprisoned in,
xxxix; Douglas overcomes bitterness in,
xl; Wilde never in, 33 n.1
Wright, Sir Almroth: Douglas in ward of, at
St Mary's, 60–63; *see also Doctor's
Dilemma, The*

Yeats, W. B.: Shaw-Douglas criticism of,
160–61
You Never Can Tell, xxix, 45